Praise for *Our Hymns, Our Heritage*

It is my great pleasure to offer hearty, unqualified endorsement of *Our Hymns, Our Heritage*. The Leemans understand as few others the crucial importance of theological and musical education among children, but also for people of all ages. The marriage of great texts and timeless music is beyond calculation for how it informs a thoroughgoing and unshakable Christian worldview, and the Leemans achieve this lofty goal in exquisite ways, which makes their hymnal an unmatched treasure for all times and ages. As a concert pianist, Steinway Artist, and inductee to the Steinway Teacher Hall of Fame, but also deeply committed to transcendent Christian worship, I have enormous admiration for the accompaniments and their recordings available as supplements to this hymnal. They provide training of young pianists and singers as significant tools in the art of listening and accompanying, not to mention technical development. Every piano studio whose instructor values hymn-playing and the training of future accompanists should own this hymnal as both reference and resource for students.

Stephen Nielson | Concert Pianist

Our Hymns, Our Heritage represents the finest hymns ever written, both theologically and lyrically. They are hymns that every Christian should sing, memorize, and teach to their children and grandchildren. The accompanying information on the history of the hymn writers and guidance on key elements to focus on while singing the hymns is inspiring and so helpful. These hymns have stood the test of time because they are life-changing and life-giving and stand in stark contrast to so much of what is being taught and sung today.

Tony Jeffrey | Headmaster, Covenant Christian Academy, Colleyville, TX

I have been a huge fan of David and Barbara Leeman's work since I first bought their student hymnal and piano recordings several years ago while compiling the Charlotte Mason's Alveary curriculum. I love that the hymns are not from a single denomination. I have learned so many songs that I otherwise would never have been exposed to. The biographical and historical information the authors have compiled is so rich and adds much to the study of the hymns, and the Scripture and inspirational thoughts provided help children think deeply about the ideas they contain. When parents write in to ask if they really need another hymnal, our answer is always, "Yes! You need THIS one!"

Jennifer Spencer, EdD | Project Manager, Charlotte Mason's Alveary

The history of Christian music is 2,000 years deep and a whole world wide. This collection of carefully selected songs and hymns connects children and their parents with generations of Christian voices who have fallen silent yet still speak through the musical heritage preserved for us today. *Our Hymns, Our Heritage* is a must-have for family devotionals and a treasure to pass on to the next generation.

Janie B. Cheaney | Senior Writer, WORLD News Group

Psalm 145:4 proclaims, "One generation shall commend your works to another, and shall declare your mighty acts." *Our Hymns, Our Heritage* reminds us that we stand on the spiritual shoulders of those who came before us, but equally challenges us to pass the faith once given on to the next generation. To this end, Barbara and David Leeman have given the church an extraordinary, multi-use resource. At one and the same time a hymnal, hymnal companion, and devotional guide, *Our Hymns, Our Heritage* seeks to foster the love of singing God's praise for generations to come. I heartily commend this hymnal to churches, families, Christian schools, Sunday schools, choirs, and anyone who seeks to love the Lord with all their heart, mind, soul, and strength.

Colin Howland | Director of Music, Tenth Presbyterian Church, Philadelphia, PA

What a stewardship we have received in the church's heritage of hymnody—a gift that we must not fail to pass on to the coming generations. That is why I am delighted that Barbara and David Leeman have edited this hymnal. While their intended audience is elementary children, believers of all ages will find soul-stirring edification in these pages. The Leemans offer us a twofold service. They have curated an excellent collection of many of the finest hymns in the English language, and they have provided brief, illuminating, devotional material to make these songs come alive in our hearts. I commend this excellent resource for families, churches, and schools, praying that the Lord would tune your hearts to sing his praise.

Matt Merker | Director of Training for Getty Music; hymn writer, "He Will Hold Me Fast;" author, *Corporate Worship*

We are always seeking ways to instill in our children the reality of how things are—that God is not a thing among things, but The Thing behind all things. "He is the image of the invisible God, the firstborn of all creation. For by Him all things were created, in heaven and on earth, visible and invisible, whether thrones or dominions or rulers or authorities—all things were created through Him and for Him" (Col. 1:15–16). Singing these truths in praise to God sets the imagination and the affections aflame. The special blessing here is how David and Barbara Leeman have artistically, comprehensively, and beautifully told this Grand Story to deeply engage hearts and minds in responsive praise to our Creator and Redeemer.

J. Marty Cope | Director of Music & Arts, Park Cities Presbyterian Church, Dallas, TX

Hymns are a great treasury of Christian faith and devotion. Previous generations of believers not only sang hymns in church on Sunday mornings, but carried private copies of their hymnals for personal use throughout the week. In *Our Hymns, Our Heritage*, David and Barbara Leeman long to give these riches to you, enabling you to carry the truths of these 120 hymns not just in your hymnal, but in your heart as well. May the Lord use this book in his church to make his praise glorious.

Matthew Westerholm | Associate Professor of Church Music and Worship, The Southern Baptist Theological Seminary; Executive Director, The Institute for Biblical Worship

DAVID & BARBARA LEEMAN

OUR Hymns, OUR Heritage

A HOSANNA HYMNAL

A STUDENT GUIDE TO SONGS OF THE CHURCH

MOODY PUBLISHERS
CHICAGO

Scripture quotations are from the *ESV® Bible (The Holy Bible, English Standard Version®)*, Copyright © 2001 by Crossway, a publishing ministry of Good News Publishers. Used by permission. All rights reserved. Capitalization of deity pronouns was approved by permission of Crossway.

Scripture quotations marked ASV are taken from the American Standard Version (Revised Version, Standard American Edition, 1901).

Scripture quotations marked KJV are taken from the King James Version of the Bible.

Scripture quotations marked NCV are taken from the New Century Version®. Copyright © 2005 by Thomas Nelson. Used by permission. All rights reserved.

"How Great Thou Art" © 1949, 1953 The Stuart Hine Trust CIO. All rights in the USA, its territories and possessions, except print rights, administered by Capitol CMG Publishing. USA, North, and Central American print rights and all Canadian and South American rights administered by Hope Publishing Company. All other North and Central American rights administered by The Stuart Hine Trust CIO. Rest of world rights administered by Integrity Music Europe. All rights reserved. Used by permission.

Edited by Kevin Mungons
Interior design: Erik M. Peterson
Cover design: Faceout Studios
Cover background of gold texture copyright © 2020 by Katsumi Murouchi / Getty Images (1197036787). All rights reserved.
Cover texture copyright © 2020 by Envato Elements. All rights reserved.

Library of Congress Cataloging-in-Publication Data

Names: Leeman, David, author. | Leeman, Barbara, author.
Title: Our hymns, our heritage : a hosanna hymnal : a student guide to
    songs of the church / David & Barbara Leeman.
Description: Chicago : Moody Publishers, 2022. | Includes bibliographical
    references and index. | Summary: "Our Hymns, Our Heritage encourages a
    love and appreciation for the church's hymns-a significant way to pass
    the Christian faith from generation to generation. The book features
    music and lyrics for 121 hymns that every person should know, drawn from
    a cross-section of styles, themes, and historical eras. The hymns are
    divided into sections based on the church year, God's nature and
    attributes, and our responses to Him. Our Hymns, Our Heritage can be
    used by parents and educators alike to instill a lifelong love for the
    richness and beauty of hymns"-- Provided by publisher.
Identifiers: LCCN 2021062293 (print) | LCCN 2021062294 (ebook) | ISBN
    9780802429292 (hardcover) | ISBN 9780802473844 (ebook)
Subjects: LCSH: Hymns--Devotional use. | Hymns, English--History and
    criticism. | Hymns, English. | Choruses, Sacred, Unaccompanied. | BISAC:
    RELIGION / Christian Education / General | LCGFT: Hymns. | Scores. |
    Musical settings.
Classification: LCC ML3086 .L44 2022 (print) | LCC ML3086 (ebook) | DDC
    782.27--dc23
LC record available at https://lccn.loc.gov/2021062293
LC ebook record available at https://lccn.loc.gov/2021062294

Originally delivered by fleets of horse-drawn wagons, the affordable paperbacks from D. L. Moody's publishing house resourced the church and served everyday people. Now, after more than 125 years of publishing and ministry, Moody Publishers' mission remains the same—even if our delivery systems have changed a bit. For more information on other books (and resources) created from a biblical perspective, go to www.moodypublishers.com or write to:

Moody Publishers
820 N. LaSalle Boulevard
Chicago, IL 60610

3 5 7 9 10 8 6 4 2

Printed in China

Our Hymns, Our Heritage
A Student Guide to Songs of the Church

Compiled and written by Barbara and David Leeman
With contributions by Jonathan Leeman
Music Arrangements and Engraving: David Leeman
Editor Music Engraving: Mats Frendahl, Sweden
Additional Resources
Spiral-Bound Piano Accompaniment Book—Arrangements to Enhance Singing
Piano Recordings of All 120 Hymns on USB Flash Drive
Order from www.HosannaHymnnals.com

*This book is dedicated to the children, faculty, and staff of Providence Christian School
of Texas in Dallas, Texas, where Barbara Leeman taught music for twenty-three years.
It was their encouragement and support that inspired its creation.
Hymns are loved at Providence and are sung every week in chapel, and a hymn
of the month is sung each morning in the classrooms.*

Hosanna, loud hosanna,
the little children sang;
Through pillared court and temple
the lovely anthem rang;
To Jesus, who had blessed them
close folded to His breast,
The children sang their praises,
the simplest and the best.

Contents

Foreword

In recent years we have had the privilege in life to become parents. And, though we have not worked as extensively as many in children's music, lately we have spent more time writing and reflecting on the subject since we now have four children of our own.

It is particularly unusual, given the fact that much children's literature today is story-driven, highly involved, complex, mystical, and requiring such intellectual commitment, that in comparison, much current children's theological teaching, songs and even worship to almighty God can be so simplistic and shallow rather than telling the ascendant and beautiful story of Christ. It is refreshing to see a book of hymns selected for children to sing that tell the gospel and teach complex biblical truths in a timeless way.

Our fellow countryman C.S. Lewis said, "No book is really worth reading at the age of ten which is not equally (and often far more) worth reading at the age of fifty." We believe the same is true of songs and singing.

We are so excited about the publication of this hymnbook for children. Our prayer is that our children will be singing theologically rich hymns such as the ones found here long after we are gone and will continue to pass them on from generation to generation.

Keith and Kristyn Getty

Preface

Our Hymns, Our Heritage: A Student Guide to Songs of the Church is written to acquaint students of all ages with a generous collection of our greatest hymns, both ancient and modern. We believe these are among the hymns every child—indeed, every Christian—should know. The target age is students ages nine to twelve; however, we know both younger and older students who use this book—even some senior adults! You should never stop being a student, especially about the truths and glory of God.

In Matthew 19:14 are the unique and powerful words of Jesus, "Let the little children come to me and do not hinder them, for to such belongs the kingdom of heaven." Shortly after He said this, the children followed Him into the temple and cried out, "Hosanna to the Son of David!" The chief priests were indignant, telling Jesus to silence them. But He responded: "Have you never read, 'Out of the mouth of infants and nursing babies you have prepared praise'?" (Matt. 21:16). Jeannette Threlfall retells this story in her hymn "Hosanna, Loud Hosanna," No. 28. Our Hymns, Our Heritage is a collection of "hosannas" for students of every age to learn. This book was first published in 2014 under the title Hosanna, Loud Hosannas.

What is a hymn? We think it is a beautiful word, and you might think of it simply as a song about Him—our great God. We attempted to choose hymns that are some of the best expressions of worship that have ever been written. Since many Christian men and women wrote them over many centuries, this book is like a family picture album with great-great-great-grandparents you have never met, as well as gifted relatives who are still alive. If you never learn or sing these hymns, it is like never seeing these older relatives' pictures. They are the treasured writings of saints through the ages and represent our Christian heritage. Our Christian family. The psalmist said, "Your testimonies are my *heritage* forever, for they are the joy of my heart" (Ps. 119:111, emphasis added). These hymns are the testimonies of people who knew (or know) the Word of God and put them in poetry to be sung.

The word *our* in the title communicates that these belong to the past *and* the present. Not all of them are old. Of 120 songs, twenty-five percent are new enough to still be under copyright laws, meaning they are less than ninety years old.

This is not a typical hymnal you would see at church. It includes biographical stories of each text author and tune composer. Each hymn's story page contains three parts: *Text, Tune,* and *As You Sing This Hymn.*

The *Text* portion describes the author of the words. Many things influence a hymn text, such as when and where the person lived, what school they attended, or life experiences with their family. In many of the stories, God used difficult circumstances to teach people about Himself. Pay attention to the dates as you may discover someone who wrote a hymn who was born on your birthday!

Tune is another word for melody. Often the melody has a history separate from the text. Different tunes can be used for the same text. An example is "Away in a Manger," for which two tunes are commonly sung, and in this book, you will find them both. Tunes are named for a variety of reasons: often for where the composer lived or for an emotion the tune evokes, such as ODE TO JOY. The tune names are always typed in SMALL CAPITAL LETTERS to set them apart from the text or hymn name.

Hymns declare what we believe about God, so it is very important when singing to think about what the words mean for your life. That is why each hymn story includes a section called *As you sing this hymn.* Perhaps a hymn will help you to pray and trust God more. Or maybe you will discover things for which to thank Him. Never sing thoughtlessly, but look for ways to apply each hymn text to your life in God.

As you turn your eyes to the right-hand side and look at the music, pay attention to two things. First, notice the Scripture verse under the title. It describes what Scripture truth the hymn may be based on. It's like a rope between the hymn text and your Bible. Second, notice that the melody line is on top, but sometimes there is a harmony line underneath. If you are singing with others, we encourage you to learn and sing the harmony as well as the melody, because it adds much beauty to the sound, and you will enjoy the hymn even more.

Although sometimes known as verses, we call the multiple paragraphs of the poem stanzas. To make it easier to follow the line of each stanza, every other one is in *italic* font.

Many people love hymns because they can sing them by memory at any time in any place. You don't have to be at church or in a school chapel. You can sing them with your family in the car. You can sing with friends any time. You can sing to your parents and grandparents. You can sing when you are happy or when you are sad. Hymns are friends to take with you anywhere because hymns are to and for God, and He is always everywhere. God bless you as you bring these 120 hymns into your heart and life. Sing them often and sing them as "loud Hosannas"!

To Parents and Grandparents

We love God. We love children and youth. We love hymns. We desire to bring the first two closer together with the help of the third.

Why is it essential that children sing hymns? Is anything wrong with the simple choruses often taught to children at church? We believe it is unfortunate if that is all they sing!

All children love what they know. If we teach our children mediocrity, they will love what is mediocre. If we teach them what is excellent, even if difficult, they will love what is excellent. The goal of this hymnal is to provide children with the best music that has been composed for them to sing praise to God. Zoltán Kodály, the Hungarian composer whose musical educational philosophy transformed music education in the twentieth century, said that "only art of intrinsic value is suitable for children."[1] He adds, "Let us take our children seriously! Everything else follows from this . . . only the best is good enough for a child."[2]

How do you choose essential hymns every child should sing? This may have been the most difficult part of putting this book together. We began with hymns that are common to hymnals of every denomination and age. Hymns like "Holy, Holy, Holy" are sung in churches worldwide. They have stood the test of time. We looked for texts that are particularly appealing to children, such as those with descriptive word pictures. But we did not shy away from hymns that are rich in theology and language. Finally, we looked for hymns that highlight and teach the gospel.

There are many popular hymns from the nineteenth and early twentieth centuries that are known as *gospel hymns* that were not chosen. This is not because they are not wonderful expressions of faith, but because the less formal style of the music does not always support the dignity of the text. These gospel hymns are not universally sung in all denominations or churches. However, we did include a brief collection of the uniquely African American gospel songs because of their important heritage, as well as twenty-five songs written by women authors or composers.

Perhaps the most difficult choices concerned modern hymns since they have not yet stood the test of time and proven essential. We only chose modern hymns that are similar in style to the historical hymns, using multiple stanzas with congregationally singable melodies and rhythms.

With children in mind, we have arranged this hymnal differently than most hymnals. There are four main sections: *The Church Year*, beginning with Advent and Christmas hymns. Children relate to the baby Jesus, a child like them, and the wonderful Christmas story. The second section is simply *God Is*, with hymns that teach who God is—His attributes and the broad categories of what He does for us. *We Respond* offers hymns with which we may respond in praise, thanksgiving, confession, petition, testimony, commitment, and prayer. If you are choosing a hymn for your children, remember to point out the purpose of the hymn as listed at the top of the story page. This will assist them in singing with purpose, rather than simply because they like the song! Of course, the texts often overlap in content and theme, and many hymns could be included in all three sections. This edition from Moody Publishers adds a small selection of *Spirituals* and black gospel songs. They are all first-person expressions of prayer or petition to God and offer songs of lament for times of trouble.

We have taught hymns to children for over forty years and have countless stories to tell of them singing hymns at birthday parties, in the bathtub, in grocery store aisles and church aisles. Those children, in turn, have taught them to their three-year-old siblings and ninety-three-year-old grandparents. In fact, they have sometimes taught their parents to love hymns, too.

Why teach hymns to children? In studying hymns, children glean from a wide spectrum of knowledge. They learn Bible content and doctrine. They observe the hearts of godly men and women. They encounter a little world history. And they imbibe the beauty of melody and harmony, poetry, and literature. A hymn is a treasure chest of learning. Some words, thoughts, and experiences they have not yet encountered, but their truths will serve them throughout life.

These songs will help students memorize the words of Bernard of Clairvaux, St. Francis of Assisi, Martin Luther, St. Augustine, Isaac Watts, the Wesleys, Fanny Crosby, Thomas Ken, and others. In so doing, they create a reference point in the pathways of their minds, construct a framework in the core of their spirits, lay a foundation in the soils of their souls. What is more, they will join their hearts and tongues to the centuries of saints worshipping Father, Son, and Holy Spirit.

Martin Luther said that "next to the Word of God, the noble art of music is the greatest treasure in the world. It controls our thoughts, minds, hearts, and spirits."[3] It is wonderful that you are giving your child the gift of owning his or her own hymnal. Join your child in learning and singing these hymns, and so give your child the gift of placing these truths deep in their hearts. If they love these hymns, hopefully like you, they will pass them on to the next generation.

Barbara and David Leeman

Suggestions for Teaching Hymns

Parents or school leaders will have their own methods for using this book and teaching these hymns. But we have some suggestions to share:

- **Make singing a regular part of family devotions.** Most devotions include a Bible reading, perhaps a thought from a devotional book, and some prayer. But including a song or hymn is a wonderfully unifying participation for the entire family. Dr. Donald Whitney in his most helpful book, *Family Worship,* suggests that there are three elements to family worship: read the Bible, pray, and sing. "Only three syllables to remember—read, pray, sing. . . . You don't need to prepare anything beforehand. Just read, pray, and sing."[4] Obviously, it would be helpful if each family member had access to their own copy of this book. So, quantity discounts are available at www.HosannaHymnals.com.

- **Sing without accompaniment (*a cappella*)** if the hymn is familiar. But if you would feel more comfortable with a piano accompaniment, you may order our recording of all the hymns in this book on a USB flash drive from www.HosannaHymnals.com. These are played as piano accompaniments to all the stanzas.

- **Play the piano accompaniment** if someone in the family or the Christian school plays piano. A book of the accompaniments heard on the USB recording is also available at www.HosannaHymnals.com.

- **Choose a "hymn of the month."** Although you may want to sing a different hymn at each devotional time, in order to truly learn a hymn—perhaps by memory—we suggest using one that is repeated throughout the month. This is also a very important method in a Christian school or homeschool curriculum. The hymn of the month should be sung each week if there is a chapel gathering or sung daily in the classroom where devotions are practiced. Repetition is often the best teacher.

- **Review the hymns at the end of the school year** by singing nine hymns learned from September through May. On HosannaHymnals.com you will find a growing collection of hymn medleys of nine hymns arranged to be sung in succession with appropriate key changes in the accompaniment. The printed music for these is available for purchase at a nominal cost at www.HosannaHymnals.com. It would be important to pick your hymn medley before the beginning of the school year to know which hymns to use in your hymn of the month. Of course, you might arrange your own hymn medley as well.

- **Subscribe online to the *Hosanna Hymnals* blog,** where we provide occasional articles, updates, and content of hymn quizzes that can be used in teaching or reviewing hymn stories.

THE

church
year

ADVENT

CHRISTMAS

EPIPHANY

LENT

EASTER

PENTECOST

Advent O Come, O Come, Emmanuel

TEXT: Latin antiphon, 12th c., Latin hymn, trans. John Mason Neale, 1710

A n *antiphon* is a song sung back and forth between two groups—with a call and a response. When we sing to one another this way, we are singing *antiphonally*. *Anti* means opposite; *phon* means voice or sound. In the church of the Middle Ages, worshippers would sing seven antiphons the week before Christmas, all beginning with "O Come." They were called the "Great O's." Each song would use an Old Testament name for the coming Messiah. Four of these names are:

- Emmanuel (God with us)   Isaiah 7:14
- Rod of Jesse (David's offspring)   Isaiah 11:1,10
- Dayspring (Morning Star)   Numbers 24:17
- Key of David   Isaiah 22:22

By the twelfth century, these antiphons became the "Latin Hymn," sung as one song. Each verse asks the coming Messiah to ransom, save, cheer, guide, and bring peace. After singing each of these "calls," the congregation responds, knowing by faith that God will answer: "Rejoice! Rejoice! Emmanuel shall come to thee, O Israel!"

In addition to this hymn, which he translated, John Mason Neale wrote two other Christmas carols, "Good Christian Men, Rejoice" and "Good King Wenceslas," and the hymn "Of the Father's Love Begotten."

TUNE: Plainsong, 13th c.

T he tune's name, VENI EMMANUEL, is Latin for "Come, Emmanuel." It is based on the Latin plainsongs of the thirteenth century and first appears in *Hymnal Noted, Part II* (London, 1854), arranged by Thomas Helmore. Another word used for plainsong is *chant*.

As you sing this hymn . . . you are waiting for the second coming of Christ, just like Israel waited for Christ's first coming. The word *advent* means "coming," and this song is called an *advent carol* because it anticipates His coming at multiple levels. Stanza 1 addresses Christ as Emmanuel ("God with us") and asks Him to come in the flesh to end Israel's captivity. Stanza 2 addresses Him as the Rod of Jesse (descendant of David) and asks that He come and save us from our sin. Stanza 3 addresses God as Dayspring (Holy Spirit) and asks Him to dwell with us and help us in our daily struggles. Stanza 4 calls Him the Key of David, the One who will unlock the door to our heavenly home. Let your heart rejoice as you sing and pray for God to come. In truth, this prayer has already begun to be answered. Christ came. He comes now through His Spirit. And He will come again!

O Come, O Come, Emmanuel

"Behold, the virgin shall conceive and bear a Son, and they shall call His name Immanuel" (which means, God with us).

MATTHEW 1:23

Ve - ni, ve - ni Em - man - u - el, Cap -
1. O come, O come, Em - man - u - el, and
2. O come, Thou Rod of Jes - se, free Thine
3. O come, Thou Day - spring from_____ on high, and
4. O come, Thou Key of Da - vid, come and

ti - vum sol - ve Is - ra - el, Qui ge - mit in ex -
ran - som cap - tive Is - ra - el, that mourns in lone - ly
own from Sa - tan's tyr - an - ny; from depths of hell Thy
cheer us by Thy draw - ing nigh; dis - perse the gloom - y
o - pen wide our heav'n - ly home; make safe the way that

i - li - o, Pri - va - tus De - i Fi - li - o.
ex - ile here, un - til the Son of God_____ ap - pear.
peo - ple save, and give them vic - t'ry o'er_____ the grave.
clouds___ of night, and death's dark shad - ows put_____ to flight.
leads___ on high, and close the path to mis - er - y.

Gau - de, gau - de! Em - man - u -
Re - joice! Re - joice! Em - man - u -

el na - sce - tur pro - te, Is - ra - el.
el shall come to thee, O Is - ra - el.

TEXT: Latin antiphons, 12th c., trans. John Mason Neale
TUNE: Plainsong, 13th c.

VENI EMMANUEL

TEXT: Charles Wesley	b. December 18, 1707, Epworth, England
	d. March 29, 1788, London, England
	(for more on Wesley, see No. 4, 31, 37, 41, 63, 86, and 103)

This poem was written by Charles Wesley five years after he wrote "Hark! the Herald Angels Sing." He published both in 1744, in a volume called *Hymns for the Nativity of Our Lord*. Of the eighteen carols in this volume, we sing only these two today. Wesley was not content simply to describe the manger scene. His texts are full of prophecy and applications of the gospel. This text is considered an advent carol since it anticipates Christ's coming to earth. The first stanza deals with the first advent. The second stanza speaks of the second advent, the one that we long for yet today when the redemption of God's people will be complete and everlasting.

| TUNE: Rowland Prichard | b. January 14, 1811, Graienyn (near Bala), North Wales |
| | d. January 25, 1887, Holywell, North Wales |

The first tunes used for this text poorly matched it, and therefore the song was not often sung. But it became popular and loved after it was set to the tune HYFRYDOL, written by the twenty-year-old Welshman Rowland Prichard in about 1830. The tune name means "good cheer," which is the message of this text. The same tune is used for "Jesus, What a Friend for Sinners."

As you sing this hymn . . . you are waiting, just like lighting an advent candle or opening a door on an advent calendar signifies waiting. Have you ever used the words, "I wish Christmas would hurry up and get here"? Children who love Christmas can hardly wait for that day to arrive. God's people, Israel, also knew what it was like to long and wait, but they waited centuries for a Savior to free them from slavery. Theirs was no light-hearted hope; it was a deep, painful longing. This carol reminds us that there is something to wait for more than presents. We should wait for Christ's coming. Are you? If you haven't already, ask Jesus to enter your life today by repenting of sin and putting your faith in Him. Then you will join all Christians who wait for His appearing, His coming to earth the second time when we will all be fully set free.

Come, Thou Long-Expected Jesus

And I will shake all nations, so that the treasures of all nations shall come in,
and I will fill this house with glory . . . and in this place I will give peace.

HAGGAI 2:7, 9

1. Come, Thou long - ex - pect - ed Je - sus, born to set Thy
2. Born Thy peo - ple to de - liv - er, born a child and

peo - ple free; from our fears___ and sins re -
yet___ a King, born to reign___ in us for -

lease___ us; let us find our rest___ in Thee.
ev - er, now Thy gra - cious king - dom bring.

Is - rael's strength and con - so - la - tion, hope of all___ the
By Thine own___ e - ter - nal Spir - it rule in all___ our

earth___ Thou art, dear___ De - sire___ of ev - 'ry
hearts___ a - lone; by___ Thine all - suf - fi - cient

na - tion, joy of ev - 'ry long - ing heart.
mer - it, raise us to___ Thy glo - rious throne.

TEXT: Charles Wesley
TUNE: Rowland Prichard

HYFRYDOL

Of the Father's Love Begotten

TEXT: Aurelius Clemens Prudentius
Trans. John Mason Neale, 1854, and Henry W. Baker, 1859

b. 348, Spain
d. 413, Spain

"Of the Father's Love Begotten" is a translation of the Latin poem "*Corde natus.*" It was written in the fourth century by the Roman poet Marcus Aurelius Prudentius, who had been born into an upper-class Christian family in a Roman province in northern Spain. Prudentius studied law and twice served as the governor of his province. He even received a high office in the court of Emperor Theodosius. But later in life he decided that his public work was of little value and retired to write religious poetry.

The translation we sing today comes from John Mason Neale (see "All Glory Laud and Honor") and Henry Baker. Neale helped translate over 400 hymns and is known for his English carol "Good King Wenceslas." He translated Prudentius' text "Of the Father sole begotten."

Henry Baker later edited and extended it to the present version. Baker, an English clergyman, served as the Anglican *Hymns Ancient and Modern* editor-in-chief, an important historic hymnal that has sold more than 150 million copies.

TUNE: 12th c. Plainsong

For centuries the music in the Catholic and Eastern Orthodox churches consisted of plainsong or chant. Plainsong is monophonic (*mono*: "one"; *phonic*: "sound"), which means there is a single, unaccompanied melodic line. And it has a freer rhythm, unlike the metered rhythm of Western music as we know it. Music editor, Thomas Helmore, put the poem with the plainsong named DIVINUM MYSTERIUM—divine mystery.

As you sing this hymn . . . you are telling the divine mystery! Mysteries are intriguing and fun, but the divine mystery is universe-shattering! God loves the world so much that He sent His Son, who existed before creation but who also entered creation, to pay for sins through His death on the cross, so that whoever repents and believes in Him might live forever. John 1 reveals this in one of the most intriguing passages in the Bible: "In the beginning was the Word."

Of the Father's Love Begotten

In the beginning was the Word . . . And the Word became flesh . . .
and we have seen His glory, glory as of the only Son from the Father.

JOHN 1:1, 14

1. Of the Fa-ther's love be - got - ten ere the worlds be - gan__ to be,
2. *O that birth for - ev - er bless - ed, when the Vir - gin, full__ of grace,*
3. O ye heights of heav'n a - dore__ Him, an - gel hosts, His prais - es sing;
4. *Christ, to Thee with God the Fa - ther, and, O Ho - ly Ghost,_ to Thee,*

He is Al - pha and O - me - ga, He the Source, the End - ing He,
by the Ho - ly Ghost con - ceiv - ing, bore the Sav - ior of__ our race;
powers, do -min-ions, bow be - fore__ Him, and ex - tol our God_ and King;
hymn and chant and high thanks-giv - ing, and un - wea - ried prais - es be:

of the things that are, that have_____ been,
and the Babe, the world's Re - deem - - - er,
let no tongue on earth be si - - - lent,
hon - or, glo - ry, and do - min - - - ion,

and that fu - ture years shall see, ev - er-more and ev - er - more!__
first re - vealed His sa - cred face, ev - er - more and ev - er - more!__
ev - ery voice in con -cert ring, ev - er-more and ev - er - more!__
and e - ter - nal vic - to - ry, ev - er - more and ev - er - more!__

TEXT: Aurelius Clemens Prudentius
TUNE: Plainsong, 12th c.

DIVINUM MYSTERIUM

Hark! the Herald Angels Sing

TEXT: Charles Wesley	b. December 18, 1707, Epworth, England
	d. March 29, 1788, London
	(for more on Wesley, see No. 2, 31, 37, 41, 63, 86, and 103)

The first line of Charles Wesley's poem read, "Hark! How all the welkin rings, glory to the King of kings." *Welkin* is the ancient English word meaning the "vault of heaven makes a long noise." A friend of Wesley's, the famous evangelist George Whitefield, took the liberty of publishing the carol and changing the words to "Hark! the herald angels sing glory to the newborn King." Wesley was furious with his friend. He did not mind others copying his poetry, but he did not like them changing the words. Although Wesley himself never would sing the changed words, these are the ones that gained popularity the world over.

This text is rich in theology and Scripture, which is typical for Wesley. Many different Scriptures are woven into this beautiful poem describing Christ's coming to earth: Luke 2:10–14; 2 Cor. 5:19; Rev. 15:4; Heb. 1:6; Matt. 1:21–23; John 1:1; Phil. 2:7; Isa. 9:6; Mal. 4:2; and 1 Peter 1:3.

TUNE: Felix Mendelssohn	b. February 3, 1809, Hamburg, Germany
	d. November 4, 1847, Leipzig, Germany

Felix Mendelssohn was a famous composer of the nineteenth century. He was born into a wealthy Jewish family in Berlin, Germany, but later converted to Christianity. Some of his best-known works include *Midsummer Night's Dream* and *Elijah*. A vital contribution he made to Western culture was to revive the music of Johann Sebastian Bach, which was largely unknown one hundred years after that composer's death. In 1840, Mendelssohn wrote this tune as a tribute to Johann Gutenberg, the printing press inventor. He expected that singers would love its melody, but it would never do for sacred words. However, one of his singers, William H. Cummings, found that the tune perfectly fit Wesley's words, written one hundred years earlier. Neither the hymn writer, Wesley, nor the composer, Mendelssohn, ever knew their creative works were combined in this beloved carol now loved the world over. The tune's name is MENDELSSOHN.

As you sing this hymn . . . you are a herald, announcing the most important event in history: the very God of heaven has come to earth to save us! You may picture long, gleaming herald trumpets, which are twice as long as ordinary trumpets and are used in fanfares. The fanfare here is the refrain, "Hark! [Listen attentively!] the herald angels sing, 'Glory to the newborn King!'" When you sing the stanzas, you become a messenger of that good news. So stand tall and proclaim it!

Hark! the Herald Angels Sing

*And suddenly there was with the angel a multitude of the heavenly host
praising God and saying, "Glory to God in the highest!"*

LUKE 2:13–14

1. Hark! the her - ald an - gels sing,_ "Glo - ry to the new - born King;
2. *Christ, by high - est heav'n a - dored,_ Christ, the ev - er - last - ing Lord!*
3. Hail the heav'n-born Prince of Peace! Hail the Sun of Righ-teous-ness!

peace on earth, and mer - cy mild,_ God and sin - ners rec - on - ciled!"
Late in time be - hold Him come,_ off - spring of the Vir - gin's womb.
Light and life to all He brings, ris'n with heal - ing in His wings.

Joy - ful, all ye na - tions, rise,_ join the tri - umph of the skies;_
Veiled in flesh the God - head see;_ hail th'in - car - nate De - i - ty,_
Mild He lays His glo - ry by,_ born that man no more may die,_

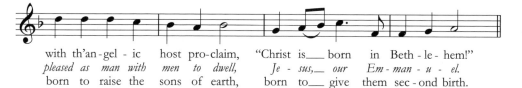

with th'an - gel - ic host pro-claim, "Christ is__ born in Beth - le - hem!"
pleased as man with men to dwell, Je - sus,__ our Em - man - u - el.
born to raise the sons of earth, born to__ give them sec - ond birth.

Hark! the her - ald an - gels sing, "Glo - ry__ to the new-born King!"

TEXT: Charles Wesley

TUNE: Felix Mendelssohn

MENDELSSOHN

TEXT AND TUNE: John Francis Wade | b. ca. 1710, England
d. August 16, 1786, Douay, France

Englishman John Francis Wade was a Catholic layman at a time when persecution drove many Catholics to flee England for France. In order to support himself in his new country, Wade took work as a copyist of music at a French Catholic center in Douay (or Douai). In those days copying music was an art form, and Wade excelled at it. He soon became known for his exquisite copies of plainsongs and sacred music, which were sold to chapels and private homes.

During his years in France, Wade composed the hymn "O Come, All Ye Faithful," originally a Latin poem that began *"Adeste Fidelis, Laeti triumphantes."* Formerly, it was believed that he merely found and translated the carol, but more recently, some musicologists believe that he actually wrote the Latin carol text.

The carol was translated from the Latin into English almost one hundred years later by the Reverend Frederick Oakeley for his congregation at the Margaret Street Chapel in London. Oakeley's first attempt was "Ye Faithful, Approach Ye." Several years later, after he had increased his skill in Latin, he tried again, writing the English words we know and which are now translated into over 150 languages.

Wade also wrote the tune for his carol text and named it ADESTE FIDELES for the first two words. It first appeared in 1751, in his *Cantus Diversi*, music compiled for use in the Roman Catholic Church. Almost one hundred years later, in 1845, Samuel Webbe, organist at the Portuguese embassy in London, arranged it in its present form. It is therefore sometimes called PORTUGUESE HYMN.

As you sing this hymn . . . a verse in Latin is provided for you to sing the first stanza in this carol's original language. The beautiful language not only sings easily, it connects you across the centuries, across the cultures, even across the Christian denominations that have made this carol an important part of Christmas worship.

The hymn calls to worship all the "faithful"—all those who possess faith and are steadfast in their love toward God. The second stanza reflects the Nicene Creed, a profession of faith established by a council of church leaders at Nicaea, Turkey, in AD 325. This stanza lets you declare, "This is what I believe," but also encourages you to join with all the choirs of angels and all the citizens of heaven, who sing, "Glory to God in the highest." Though you do not hear and see these multitudes today, look at the people singing around you, and understand that one day you will see and hear the millions upon millions of those who have believed and are "the faithful."

O Come, All Ye Faithful

*"Let us go over to Bethlehem and see this thing that has happened,
which the Lord has made known to us."*

LUKE 2:15

A - des - te, fi - de - les, læ - ti tri - um - phan - tes;
1. O come, all ye faith - ful, joy - ful and tri - um - phant,
2. God of___ God,___ Light_ of___ Light;___
3. Sing, choirs of an - gels, sing in ex - ul - ta - tion,
4. Yea, Lord, we greet Thee, born this hap - py morn - ing:

Ve - ni - te, ve - ni - te in Beth - le - hem.
O come ye, O come_ ye to Beth - le - hem;
lo, He ab - hors__ not the Vir - gin's womb:
sing, all ye cit - i - zens of heav'n__ a - bove;
Je - sus, to Thee_ be all glo - ry giv'n;

Na - tum vi - de - te, Re - gem an - ge - lo - rum.
come and be - hold Him born the King of an - gels;
ver - y__ God, be - got - ten, not cre - a - ted;
glo - ry to God__ glo - ry in the high - est;
Word of the Fa - ther, now in flesh ap - pear - ing;

Ve - ni - te a - do - re - mus, ve - ni - te a - do - re - mus,
O come, let us a - dore Him, O come, let us a - dore Him,

Ve - ni - te - a - do - re - mus__ Do - mi - num.
O come, let us a - dore Him,_ Christ__ the Lord.

TEXT: Latin Hymn, attr. to John Francis Wade
TUNE: John Francis Wade's *Cantus Diversi,* 1751

ADESTE FIDELES

TEXT: Traditional French carol ‖

No one knows who wrote the words to this carol. It was first sung in nine-teenth-century France, but the chorus is in Latin, suggesting that it was written much earlier. Hymnologists agree that the author had an excellent knowledge of the Scripture and the skill to shape biblical text into verse. All this suggests that it might have been written by a monk in the early Roman Catholic Church.

The text first appeared in print in French in 1855, but it is known to have been sung at least fifty years earlier in France. It was translated into English by a priest named James Chadwick.

Of course, it was the angels themselves who first sang some of the hymn's words on the night Jesus was born. *Excelsis* (pronounced "egg-shell-cees") means "highest." *Deo* means "God." So *Gloria in excelsis Deo* means "glory to God in the highest."

TUNE: arr. Edward S. Barnes, 1937 ‖

GLORIA is a traditional French melody. However, the simplicity of this tune may reflect the time of the very early church. The melody of the stanzas has only a five-note range and is chant-like. The modern arrangement we sing was adapted by Edward S. Barnes, an American organist.

As you sing this hymn . . . imagine the shepherds trying to retell their experience of see-ing a host of angels appear over their Bethlehem field one dark night. Words would be inadequate. But one gifted shepherd puts it to song, and they all sing it together. Most amazing, he remembers the angel's song, and he repeats it in the refrain! No, that is not the true story, but perhaps it is what the person who wrote the hymn imagined. How would you respond if even one angel appeared to tell you about Jesus' birth? Would you tell the world? Would you sing a song? Maybe it would be this one!

Because the refrain of "Gloria in Excelsis Deo" is so wonderfully familiar, a counter melody is offered for lower voices. If you are singing with a group, learn it alone first as its own melody, then combine the two as a growing host of angels praising God in this beautiful carol written and sung in the heavens!

Angels We Have Heard on High

*"Glory to God in the highest, and on earth peace
among those with whom He is pleased!"*

LUKE 2:14

1. An - gels we have heard on high, sweet - ly sing-ing o'er the plains,
2. *Shep- herds, why this ju - bi - lee? Why your joy - ous strains pro - long?*
3. Come to Beth-le - hem and see Him whose birth the an - gels sing;

and the moun-tains in re-ply ech - o back their joy - ous strains.
Say what may the tid - ings be, which in - spire your heav'n - ly song?
come, a - dore on bend - ed knee Christ the Lord, the new - born King.

Glo - - - - - - - ri - a

in ex - cel - sis De - o, Glo - - - -

- - - ri - a in ex - cel - sis De - - o.

TEXT: Traditional French carol

GLORIA

TUNE: Traditional French melody, arr. Edward S. Barnes

TEXT: Anonymous ||

Since "Away in a Manger" was passed down through generations as a folk song, the original author is not known. For many years the words were attributed to Martin Luther. But most experts now believe that an American probably wrote at least the first two verses in the middle of the nineteenth century.

The Evangelical Lutheran Church was the first to publish this hymn in its *Little Children's Book: For School and Families* (1885). Two years later hymn writer James R. Murray published it in *Dainty Songs for Little Lads and Lassies*. He must have heard the legend of Luther's authorship since he titled it "Luther's Cradle Hymn" and claimed that Luther had written it and sang it to his children every night. (Luther did write a Christmas carol to teach his children about Jesus' coming to earth. It is called "From Heaven Above to Earth I Come.")

The third verse appeared in a collection called *Vineyard Songs* published in 1892 by Charles Gabriel, who discovered it among the many circulating versions at that time.

TUNE: James R. Murray, MUELLER || b. March 7, 1841, Ballard Vale, Andover, Massachusetts
d. March 10, 1905, Cincinnati, Ohio

TUNE: William James Kirkpatrick, || b. February 27, 1838, Duncannon, Pennsylvania
CRADLE SONG || d. September 20, 1921, Germantown, Pennsylvania

There are two tunes commonly used for this carol. Perhaps most used is the tune MUELLER. It is attributed to James Murray. The other tune is called CRADLE SONG, possibly written by William Kirkpatrick, a hymn writer from Pennsylvania. No one is sure. The latter has the beauty and simplicity of a folk song, but both tunes could be called lullabies—soothing songs, simple and repetitive, usually sung to help young children sleep.

As you sing this hymn . . . you may not be trying to go to sleep, but the poem and melody bring a comforting picture of baby Jesus' birth. Was baby Jesus so perfectly contented that it is true "no crying he makes"? We know Jesus the man got hungry and that Jesus the man wept. Whether or not the newborn cried, we ask this Jesus, fully human and fully God, to be near us and to bless all children, fitting them by His grace to live with Him in heaven forever.

Away in a Manger

*And she gave birth to her firstborn son and wrapped Him
in swaddling cloths and laid Him in a manger, because there was
no place for them in the inn.*

LUKE 2:7

1. A - way in a man - ger, no crib for a bed,
2. *The cat - tle are low - ing, the ba - by a - wakes,*
3. Be near me, Lord Je - sus, I ask Thee to stay

the lit - tle Lord Je - sus laid down His sweet head;
but lit - tle Lord Je - sus no cry - ing He makes;
close by me for - ev - er, and love me, I pray;

the stars in the sky____ looked down where He lay,
I love Thee, Lord Je - sus! Look down from the sky,
bless all the dear chil - dren in Thy ten - der care,

the lit - tle Lord Je - sus, a - sleep on the hay.
and stay by my cra - dle till morn - ing is nigh.
and fit us for heav - en, to live with Thee there.

TEXT: Anonymous
TUNE: James R. Murray

MUELLER

He is the image of the invisible God,
the firstborn of all creation.

For by Him all things were created, in heaven
and on earth, visible and invisible, whether thrones
or dominions or rulers or authorities—all things
were created through Him and for Him.

And He is before all things, and in Him all things hold together.
And He is the head of the body, the church.
He is the beginning, the firstborn from the dead,
that in everything He might be preeminent.
For in Him all the fullness of God was pleased to dwell,
and through Him to reconcile to Himself all things,
whether on earth or in heaven,
making peace by the blood of His cross.

COLOSSIANS 1:15–20

Away in a Manger

"Let the children come to Me; do not hinder them, for to such belongs the kingdom of God." . . . And He took them in His arms and blessed them, laying His hands on them.

MARK 10:14, 16

1. A - way in a___ man - ger, no___ crib for a bed,
2. *The cat - tle are___ low - ing, the___ ba - by a - wakes,*
3. Be near me, Lord_ Je - sus, I___ ask Thee to stay

the___ lit - tle Lord Je - sus lay___ down His sweet head;
but___ lit - tle Lord Je - sus, no___ cry - ing He makes;
close_ by me for - ev - er and___ love me I pray;

the___ stars in the___ bright sky looked down where He lay,
I love Thee, Lord_ Je - sus, look___ down from the sky
bless all the dear_ child - ren in___ Thy ten - der care,

the___ lit - tle Lord Je - sus a - sleep on the hay.
and___ stay by my cradle un - til___ morn - ing is nigh.
and___ fit us for heav - en to___ live with Thee there.

TEXT: Anonymous
TUNE: William J. Kirkpatrick

CRADLE SONG

| TEXT: Joseph Mohr | b. December 11, 1792, Salzburg, Austria |
| | d. December 4, 1848, Wagrain, Austria |

Joseph Mohr grew up in poverty with his mother and grandmother. His father, a soldier, was absent from his life. The choirmaster of his church saw potential in Joseph and served as his foster father. He saw to it that Joseph, an excellent honor student, was well educated. Joseph was ordained as a priest in 1815 and became a greatly loved pastor by the people he served in several parishes throughout Austria. When he died, he was as poor as he had been as a child, having given away all of his money to educate the children and care for the elderly of his parish. Today, if you visit the Alpine village of Wagrain, his last parish and where he is buried, you will see the Joseph Mohr School, a memorial from the townspeople.

While serving at Mariapfarr a year after his ordination, Joseph Mohr wrote a poem entitled *"Stille Nacht, Heilige Nacht"* ("Silent Night, Holy Night").

| TUNE: Franz Gruber | b. November 25, 1787, Unterweizberg, Austria |
| | d. June 7, 1863, Hallein, Austria |

Two years later he was serving in Oberndorf where Franz Gruber was organist. There is much speculation as to why the two partnered in writing the carol. But on December 24, 1818, Gruber wrote the music for the words "Silent Night," to be sung at the midnight mass. It was to be accompanied by a guitar.

As you sing this hymn . . . sing it quietly and calmly. Have you ever been present at the birth of a baby? It can be an atmosphere of hurry, nervousness, even panic! But this carol paints a different picture of the birth of Jesus. The overall feeling is one of calm and peace. Why? Not because Mohr knew that Jesus' birth was particularly peaceful, but because Jesus' birth alone would bring true peace and rest to the world.

If we were planning the Son of God's entrance into the world, we would have chosen a palace, or at least a well-heated, clean, and elegant room. But not God. God placed the newborn King in a crude, hidden place. Yet isn't this how God often works? He chooses "what is low and despised in the world, even things that are not, to bring to nothing things that are, so that no human being might boast in the presence of God" (1 Cor. 1:28–29). Sure enough, the hymn moves from the picture of an infant to a picture of a beaming face of holiness and the royal pronouncement that Jesus is Lord. True peace and rest do not come through the frenzied gift-giving of Christmas or any religious act. It comes through the birth, life, death, and resurrection of Christ. So sing and meditate on the surprising wisdom of God, who offers us peace and love's pure light through a babe in a manger.

Silent Night! Holy Night!

*And they went with haste and found Mary and Joseph,
and the baby lying in a manger.*

LUKE 2:16

Stil - le Nacht! Hei - li - ge Nacht! Al - les schläft
1. Si - lent night! Ho - ly night! All is calm,
2. Si - lent night! Ho - ly night! Shep - herds quake
3. Si - lent night! Ho - ly night! Son of God,
4. Si - lent night! Ho - ly night! Won - drous star,

ein - sam wacht nur das trau - te, hoch hei - li - ge Paar
all is bright 'round yon vir - gin moth - er and Child.
at the sight! Glo - ries stream_ from heav - en a - far,
love's pure light, ra - diant beams_ from Thy ho - ly face,
lend thy light; with the an - gels let____ us sing

hold - er Kna - be im lock - i - gen Haar, schlaf in himm - lisch - er
Ho - ly in - fant, so ten - der and mild, sleep in heav - en - ly
heav'n - ly hosts_ sing al - le - lu - ia; Christ, the Sav - ior, is
with the dawn of re - deem - ing grace, Je - sus, Lord, at Thy
al - le - lu - ia to____ our King; Christ, the Sav - ior, is

Ruh,____ schlaf_ in himm - lisch - er Ruh!
peace,____ sleep_ in heav - en - ly peace.
born!____ Christ, the Sav - ior, is born!
birth,____ Je - sus, Lord, at Thy birth.
born!____ Christ, the Sav - ior, is born!

TEXT: Joseph Mohr

STILLE NACHT

TUNE: Franz Gruber

Christmas Let All Mortal Flesh Keep Silence

TEXT: Liturgy of St. James (ca. 5th c.),
adapt. Gerard Moultrie ‖

The words of this carol are a translation from a Greek Christmas Eve service of worship used as early as the fourth or fifth century called the Liturgy of St. James. Some scholars believe this carol dates back to AD 60, the same time that Paul was writing Romans. This liturgy is believed to be perhaps the oldest liturgy developed for the church and is still used today in the Eastern Orthodox Church. In 1864, Gerard Moultrie translated this text into English.

The word *liturgy* means the public work of the congregation and refers to the words they use in worship, often repeatedly each week. With the words of this song, the congregation expresses profound awe and wonder at a majestic picture of the incarnation of Jesus and the whole story of salvation. This is different from the narrative or folksy description of many carols. The text points to Jesus offering the "gift of Himself as heavenly food," making it appropriate for a communion service. It concludes with a trilogy of "Alleluias" to the Lord Most High.

TUNE: Traditional French melody, 17th c. ‖

PICARDY is a tune based on a French carol and thought to be named for the province in France where it was first used. Ralph Vaughan Williams arranged it for this text in 1906. It has a chant-like style in a modal or minor key similar to the sound from ancient worship you might hear in cathedrals. Notice that the text was written 1,200 years earlier!

As you sing this hymn . . . you may remember a time you were so afraid that you were completely silent. Perhaps you were quiet on the outside, but inwardly you could feel your heart pounding so loudly you wondered if everyone could hear it. We all know that God loves us, and we often think of Him as our "friend." But if we were suddenly in His actual physical presence, we would be awestruck and stunned into silence. There is a kind of fear that is right and good. It is called "awe," a great feeling of reverence, admiration, and wonder when encountering something sublime or extremely powerful. The minor key and mysterious melody create an emotion of awe as you "in fear and trembling stand." There is a time for joy, but there is also a time for silence. Perhaps after you sing the "Alleluias," it would be appropriate simply to stop and keep silence before the Lord.

Let All Mortal Flesh Keep Silence

The LORD is in His holy temple;
let all the earth keep silence before Him.

HABAKKUK 2:20

1. Let all mor-tal flesh keep__ si-lence, and with fear and
2. *King of kings, yet born of__ Ma-ry, as of old on*
3. Rank on rank the host of__ heav-en spreads its van-guard
4. *At His feet the six - winged ser-aph; cher-u-bim, with*

trem-bling__ stand; pon-der noth-ing earth-ly__ mind-ed,
earth He__ stood, Lord of lords, in hu-man__ ves-ture,
on the__ way, as the Light of light de-scend-eth
sleep-less__ eye, veil their fac-es to the__ Pres-ence,

for with bless-ing in His__ hand, Christ our God to earth de-
in the bod-y and the__ blood, He will give to all the
from the realms of end-less__ day, that the pow'rs of hell may
as with cease-less voice they__ cry, "Al-le-lu-ia, al-le-

scend - eth, our full hom-age to de - mand.
faith - ful His own self for heav'n-ly__ food.
van - ish as the dark-ness clears a - way.
lu - - ia, al-le-lu-ia, Lord Most__ High!"

TEXT: Liturgy of St. James, 5th c., adapt. Gerard Moultrie
TUNE: Traditional French melody 17th c.

PICARDY

TEXT: Polish carol ‖

This very old Polish carol is of unknown origin. First published in 1908, it was translated into English thirteen years later, in 1921, by Edith Reed (1885–1933). Reed worked as an associate for the Royal College of Organists in London and was the editor of its music magazine, *Music and Youth*, in which the carol appeared.

TUNE: Traditional Polish melody ‖

The composer of the tune W Zlobie Lezy is also unknown. The name is Polish for "in a manger lies." It follows the rhythmic pattern of a mazurka, a Polish folk dance in triple meter. Two eighth notes precede two quarter notes, with the accent on the second beat, the first quarter note. This entire melody follows this pattern, occurring sixteen times. (The famous Polish composer Frédéric Chopin made mazurkas well-known to the Polish ear, having composed fifty-seven of them.)

As you sing this hymn . . . imagine you are watching a painting in progress. Each time the rhythmic pattern repeats, it is like a painter's brushstroke, adding a new aspect of the picture.

First and foremost, in the very center, lies the infant in a cattle stall. He is surrounded by animals, which you can almost smell and hear. Above the manger, cherubic angels are flying overhead. Through a window you see on a nearby hillside the sleeping shepherds with their flocks of sheep. The glorious song of the angels suddenly awakens them. Now the painting is placed in a frame, and a plaque on the bottom reads, "Christ the babe is Lord of all."

Although the story of Christmas cannot be reduced to a two-dimensional painting, it helps to picture the gospel in its simplest form. "Unless you turn and become like children, you will never enter the kingdom of heaven," Jesus said (Matt. 18:3). The manger scene helps children, and everyone who is childlike, visualize the baby and ponder why He was born—to become the perfect man, the crucified King, and the risen Redeemer of the world.

Infant Holy, Infant Lowly

You will find a baby wrapped in swaddling cloths and lying in a manger.
He is Lord of lords and King of kings.

LUKE 2:12, REVELATION 17:14

1. In - fant ho - ly, in - fant low - ly, for His bed a cat - tle stall;
2. *Flocks were sleep - ing, shep-herds keep - ing vig - il till the morn- ing new*

ox - en low - ing, lit - tle know- ing Christ, the babe, is Lord of all.
saw the glo - ry, heard the sto - ry, tid - ings of a gos- pel true.

Swift are wing - ing an-gels sing - ing, no - ëls ring - ing, tid-ings bring- ing:
Thus re - joic - ing, free from sor - row, prais-es voic - ing, greet the mor - row:

Christ the babe is Lord of all. Christ the babe is Lord of all.
Christ the babe was born for you. Christ the babe was born for you.

TEXT: Polish carol paraphrased, Edith Reed

W ZLOBIE LEZY

TUNE: Traditional Polish melody

TEXT: Phillips Brooks ǁ b. December 13, 1835, Boston, Massachusetts
ǁ d. January 23, 1893, Boston, Massachusetts

Phillips Brooks, called by some the greatest preacher of the nineteenth century, was born in Massachusetts. He attended the Boston Latin School, then Harvard University. The Phillips Brooks House at Harvard is named for him. He attended the Episcopal Theological Seminary in Virginia, and became an Episcopal priest in 1860, just prior to the Civil War. He preached in support of freeing the slaves and giving them a vote. He also gave the funeral message for Abraham Lincoln.

This carol was written by Reverend Brooks for the children in his Sunday school when he was rector of Holy Trinity Church in Philadelphia. It was inspired by a trip he had taken to Israel in 1865. Wanting to get away from all of the other travelers there for the holidays, he borrowed a horse and rode from Jerusalem to Bethlehem to assist with the Christmas Eve service. He describes it thus:

> I remember standing in the old church in Bethlehem, close to the spot
> where Jesus was born, when the whole church was ringing hour after
> hour with splendid hymns of praise to God, how again and again it
> seemed as if I could hear voices I knew well, telling each other of the
> wonderful night of the Savior's birth.[5]

TUNE: Lewis H. Redner ǁ b. December 15, 1830, Philadelphia, Pennsylvania
ǁ d. August 29, 1908, Atlantic City, New Jersey

Mr. Brooks asked the organist at his church to write a tune for his hymn text. The story goes that Lewis Redner, who was also the Sunday school superintendent, was having difficulty writing it. Then on Christmas Eve, the tune finally came to him. It was first performed December 24, 1868. The tune's name is St. Louis. It is possible that this comes from the first name of the composer, Lewis, and that Mr. Brooks chose it as a play on words.

As you sing this hymn . . . imagine you are one of the children in Reverend Brooks' Sunday school class 150 years ago. What an ideal description he painted of the little town and of the nativity event. Sadly, today the city of Bethlehem is not so inviting, as Arab and Jewish conflict has made it a dangerous place to visit. What is the solution for Bethlehem today and for all the world without peace? "Where meek souls will receive Him still," Brooks asks us to sing, speaking of those who can admit they need help, "the dear Christ enters in." And when Christ enters, He imparts the blessings of heaven—forgiveness from sin and His continual sustaining presence for troubled people in a troubled world. Your last sentence is the prayer: "Abide with us, Emmanuel."

O Little Town of Bethlehem

11

But you, O Bethlehem Ephrathah, who are too little
to be among the clans of Judah, from you shall come forth
for Me One who is to be ruler in Israel.

MICAH 5:2

1. O lit - tle town of Beth - le - hem, how still we__ see thee lie;
2. *For Christ is born of Mar - y and gath - ered__ all a - bove,*
3. How si - lent - ly, how si - lent - ly, the won - drous gift is giv'n!
4. *O Ho - ly Child of Beth - le - hem, de - scend to__ us, we pray;*

a - bove thy deep and dream-less sleep the si - lent_ stars go by:
while mor - tals sleep, the an - gels keep their watch of__ won - d'ring love.
So God im - parts to hu - man hearts the bless - ings_ of His heav'n.
cast out our sin and en - ter in; be born in__ us to - day.

yet in thy dark streets shin - eth the ev - er - last - ing Light:
O morn - ing stars, to - geth - er pro - claim the ho - ly birth!
No ear may hear His com - ing, but in this world of sin,
We hear the Christ-mas an - gels the great glad tid - ings tell;

the hopes and fears of all the years are met in thee to - night.
And prais - es sing to God the King, and peace to men on earth.
where meek souls will re - ceive Him still, the dear Christ en - ters in.
O come to us, a - bide with us, our Lord Em - man - u - el.

TEXT: Phillips Brooks
TUNE: Lewis H. Redner

ST. LOUIS

Christmas Joy Has Dawned upon the World

TEXT: Stuart Townend ‖ b. June 1, 1963, West Yorkshire, England
(for more on Townend, see No. 26, 34, 62, 65, and 99)

Stuart Townend was a literature major at the University of Sussex in Brighton, England. His songs reflect this scholarship. They are spiritually deep and filled with Scripture. He states, "Worship begins with God. . . . We live in an alarmingly self-oriented society, where the bottom line to every choice we make, from relationships to religion, seems to be: '. . . but does it make me happy?' If we're not careful we can bring this attitude into church, and even into our worship. We can come looking for the experience, for the 'warm feelings' . . . Although we have many new songs that effectively describe our feelings as we worship and respond to God, we need more songs that are about HIM."[6]

Mr. Townend and Mr. Getty wrote this song while working on a larger project entitled "Creed," referring to the Apostle's Creed. (The Apostle's Creed was written by early church fathers and restates the foundational truths of the Christian church as set forth by Christ's apostles.) They realized that there is a shortage of newer hymns on some important Christian foundations such as the Incarnation, God coming into our world through Jesus as a human being.

TUNE: Keith Getty ‖ b. December 16, 1974, Lisburn, Northern Ireland
(for more on Getty, see No. 34, 62, 65, and 99)

Keith Getty characterizes this hymn as a Christmas version of "In Christ Alone."[7] It tells the story of Christmas, from prophecy to Wise Men, just as "In Christ Alone" tells the whole gospel story. When performing this hymn in concert, Getty and his wife, Kristyn, often pair it with the refrain *Gloria in excelsis Deo* from "Angels We Have Heard on High."

As you sing this hymn . . . think about what a wonderful thing that dawn is. Nighttime darkness, terrors, and fear are all shattered at that very first ray of light. It occurs every twenty-four hours as a constant reminder that in the dark, oppressive world of the first century BC, one tiny wail in a dark and lonely manger would crush forever sin and the dominion of darkness! Did everyone know and see it then? No, but we can now look back and wonder at the unfolding mystery of God since creation. The light has dawned, and it continues to dawn upon people in whom God's Spirit reveals Himself.

This is a Christmas carol because it is a narrative of Jesus' birth story, including Mary, a manger, shepherds, angels, wise men, and the deeper meaning of their gifts. But it could be sung year-round as it declares what God was doing—paying a ransom, reconciling, becoming Champion over sin and death, and becoming our Savior and even our Friend! There have been great men, great leaders, and great rulers in history, but here we declare that Jesus is the Lord of history. The simplicity of the story may puzzle you, the humility of God in Christ will astound you, but the truth of what Jesus came to earth to do should change you forever.

Joy Has Dawned upon the World

12

*And we have the prophetic word more fully confirmed, to which
you will do well to pay attention as to a lamp shining in a dark place,
until the day dawns and the morning star rises in your hearts.*

2 PETER 1:19

1. Joy has dawned up - on the world, pro - mised from cre - a - tion:
2. *Sounds of won - der fill the sky with the songs of an - gels,*
3. Shep-herds bow be - fore the Lamb, gaz - ing at the glo - ry;
4. *Son of A - dam, Son of heav'n, giv - en as a ran - som;*

God's sal - va - tion now un - furled, hope for e - v'ry na - tion.
as the migh - ty Prince of Life shel - ters in a sta - ble.
Gifts of men from dis - tant lands proph - e - sy the sto - ry.
re - con - cil - ing God and man, Christ our migh - ty Champ - ion!

Not with fan-fares from a - bove, not with scenes of glo - ry,
Hands that set each star in_ place, shaped the earth in dark - ness,
Gold, a King is born to - day, in - cense, God is with_ us,
What a Sav - ior! What a_ Friend! What a glo - rious myst - 'ry:

but a hum-ble gift of love, Je - sus born of Ma - ry.
cling now to a moth - er's breast, vul - nera-ble and help - less.
myrrh, His death will make a way, and by blood He'll win_ us,
Once a babe in Beth - le - hem, now the Lord of hist - 'ry.

TEXT AND TUNE: Stuart Townend, Keith Getty

TEXT: Cecil F. Alexander	b. 1818, Ballykean House, Redcross, Wicklow, Ireland d. October 12, 1895, Londonderry (for more on Alexander, see No. 48)

Cecil Alexander started writing poetry at a young age. As an adult she published some of her poetry in *Dublin University Magazine* under pseudonyms (names not her own). Her poem "Burial of Moses" caused Alfred, Lord Tennyson to say it was one of the few poems by another author he wished he had written.[8] Alexander is probably best known for the hymn text "All Things Bright and Beautiful," where she describes the first phrase of the Apostles' Creed.

"Once upon a time" begins many stories. "Once in Royal David's City" begins the truest story of all. Royal David's city is Bethlehem, where Christ was born. In this carol, Mrs. Alexander addresses the words from the Apostles' Creed, "conceived by the Holy Ghost, born of the Virgin Mary." The hymn was written for children but is often labeled in hymnals "suitable also for adults."[9]

TUNE: Henry J. Gauntlett	b. July 9, 1805, Wellington, Shropshire, England d. February 21, 1876, London, England

Henry J. Gauntlett wrote this tune for this text. He was a gifted musician in England in the nineteenth century but was also a lawyer, author, organ designer, and organ recitalist. The tune first appeared in his book *Christmas Carols*, published in 1849. The tune's name, IRBY, is the name of a village in Lincolnshire, England.

As you sing this hymn . . . you begin with a creedal declaration of what Christians believe about Jesus. It is a kind of theological sermon. But in the third stanza, you declare what these truths mean to you personally. He is your pattern for life. He is a friend who understands your feelings of weakness or helplessness, your fears and tears, and who joins in when you are glad.

Best of all, the hymn declares in the final stanza that someday Christians will meet Him! Because of His redeeming love, this One whom we regard at Christmas as a child has ascended to heaven to prepare our eternal home with Him. Never will the phrase "they lived happily ever after" be truer.

If you are a child who knows and trusts Jesus, this Christmas hymn speaks to and for you. It should be one of the Christmas carols you know and love the best because its truth will be your hope for the rest of your life.

Once in Royal David's City

13

Christ Jesus, who, though He was in the form of God, . . . emptied Himself,
by taking the form of a servant, being born in the likeness of men.

PHILIPPIANS 2:5–7

1. Once in roy - al Da - vid's cit - y stood a low - ly cat - tle
2. *He came down to earth from heav - en Who is God and Lord of*
3. Je - sus is our child - hood's pat - tern, day by day like us He
4. *And our eyes at last shall see Him, through His own re - deem - ing*

shed, where a moth - er laid her ba - by in a
all, and His shel - ter was a sta - ble, and His
grew, He was lit - tle, weak, and help - less, tears and
love; for that Child, so dear and gen - tle, is our

man - ger for His bed: Ma - ry was that moth - er
cra - dle was a stall: with the poor and meek and
smiles like us He knew: and He feels for all our
Lord in heav'n a - bove, and He leads His chil - dren

mild, Je - sus Christ her lit - tle child.
low - ly lived on earth, our Sav - ior ho - ly.
sad - ness, and He shares in all our glad - ness.
on to the place where He is gone.

TEXT: Cecil F. Alexander
TUNE: Henry J. Gauntlett

IRBY

TEXT: Traditional English carol ||

This text is known in Great Britain as Sussex Carol. It was first published by Luke Wadding, a seventeenth-century Irish bishop, in 1684. It is not known whether he wrote it or merely copied it from an earlier writing. It was rediscovered over 200 years later by musicologists in England who were studying the folk music of Great Britain. Cecil Sharp (1859–1924), the leader of the folklore revival in England, is responsible for finding, writing down, and preserving much of the folk music and traditional dances of that culture. And here, he restored and preserved for us one of the most joyous of Christmas poems.

TUNE: Traditional English carol, || arr. Ralph Vaughan Williams ||

The tune is also a folk song from England. Another famous musicologist and composer of the early twentieth century, Ralph Vaughan Williams, heard it sung by a lady named Harriet Verrall at Monk's Gate in Sussex, England. He wrote it down, arranged it, and published it in 1919, under the name SUSSEX CAROL. It is a favorite carol in Great Britain and is regularly used at Cambridge in the King's College "Service of Nine Lessons and Carols."

As you sing this hymn . . . notice the meter or pulse of the rhythm. It sparkles with joy, giving the melody a joyous, lilting feeling appropriate to the "mirth" of a birth. It makes you smile and dance and sing. It appropriately asks, "Why be so sad, when our Redeemer made us glad?" Sometimes, people find Christmas difficult because they are lonely or have difficult memories that make it hard to be "merry." The fourth stanza, however, declares that Jesus is light for darkness, building on John 1:5: "The light shines in the darkness, and the darkness has not overcome it." Jesus' birth brings hope and power over darkness to this world, not only to the world but also to each of us who personally trusts Him as Redeemer.

If you are singing this carol as a family or in a group, you may add to the joyous experience by dividing into two groups. One group sings the first phrase, and the other echoes the repeated phrase. Then both groups sing together the last two phrases of each stanza. Take a fast enough tempo to express the joyful mood of the carol text. And remember, be glad—not sad!

On Christmas Night All Christians Sing 14

*The angel said to them, "Fear not, for behold, I bring you good news
of great joy that will be for all the people."*

LUKE 2:10

1. On Christ - mas night all Christ - ians sing, to hear the news_ the
2. *Then why should all on earth_ be sad, since our Re - deem - er*
3. When sin de - parts be - fore_ His grace, then life and health come
4. *All out of dark - ness we__ have light, which made the an - gels*

an - gels bring; on Christ - mas night all Christ - ians sing, to
made us glad, then why should all on earth_ be sad, since
in its place; when sin de - parts be - fore_ His grace, then
sing this night; all out of dark - ness we__ have light, which

hear the news___ the an - gels bring:
our Re - deem - er made us glad,
life and health___ come in its place;
made the an - gels sing this night:

news of great joy,___ news of__ great mirth,
when from our sin___ He set___ us free,
heav - en and earth_ with joy__ may sing,
"Glo - ry to God__ and peace__ to men,

news of our mer - ci - ful_ King's birth.___
all for to gain our lib - er - ty?_____
all for to see the new - born King.___
now and for - ev - er - more._ A - men."___

TEXT: Traditional English carol
TUNE: Traditional English carol

SUSSEX CAROL

TEXT AND TUNE: Geoffrey Ainger ‖ b. 1925, Mistley, Essex, England
d. 2013, England

Geoffrey Ainger was born and raised in England. He went to Richmond College in London and Union Theological Seminary in New York City. He returned to England as a Methodist minister, where he served churches in Loughton, Essex, and Notting Hill. While he was at Loughton in 1964, he wrote this hymn.

Ainger did not write many hymns, but this one has become a favorite for many. Using modern language and imagery, it brings the ancient story to the streets of our world. It expresses a modern encounter, a prayer from today to the child born long ago of Mary.

Shorter than most carols, MARY'S CHILD tune employs a gentle jazz syncopation and a triplet riff, a "hook" that causes you to remember the tune. It helps to sing this tune with ascending key changes in each stanza to create a heightened earnestness to the prayer. You will be able to sing these key changes if your accompanist uses the supplementary piano accompaniment book, *Our Hymns, Our Heritage Piano Accompaniment Book.*

As you sing this hymn . . . you are speaking directly to the infant, Jesus, and with a dawning realization of the profound significance of His coming. There is also a sense of irony that grows with each verse. The dictionary defines *irony* as incongruity between what might be expected and what actually occurs. The Creator of the universe is born in a borrowed room. A child's face brings light to a dark world. A good God sends His only Son to a cross of wood. Rebels like us ask this King to walk in our streets again. Why would He when the world rejected and crucified Him?

It is even ironic that such a simple carol of relatively few words and only five notes in the melody portrays the wonder of the gospel, the most profound truth in all the universe and in all of history. The Son of God came from heaven to live, die, and rise from the dead so that whoever believes in Him will live.

This is an unusual Christmas carol with minimal references to the events of Christmas. Rather, its focus is on what that story means and how we need this child of Mary.

Mary's Child

The Word became flesh and dwelt among us.
And being found in human form, He humbled himself by
becoming obedient to the point of death, even death on a cross.

JOHN 1:14, PHILIPPIANS 2:8

1. Born in the night, Mar-y's Child,__ a
2. *Clear shin-ing light, Mar-y's Child,__ Your*
3. Truth of our life, Mar-y's Child,__ You
4. *Hope of the world, Mar-y's Child,__ You're*

long way from Your home;___
face lights up our way;___
tell us God is good;___
com-ing soon to reign;___

Com-ing in need, Mar-y's Child,__
Light of the world, Mar-y's Child,__
Prove it is true, Mar-y's Child,__
King of the earth, Mar-y's Child,__

born in a bor-rowed room.
dawn on our dark-ened day.
go to your cross of wood.
walk in our streets a-gain.

TEXT: Geoffrey Ainger
TUNE: Geoffrey Ainger

MARY'S CHILD

Christmas   Lo, How a Rose E'er Blooming

TEXT: German hymn, ca. 1500 ‖

First written in German around AD 1500, this beautiful poem was translated into English by three different people at three different times. This particular translation was created by Theodore Baker in 1894. The poem uses imagery from the prophet Isaiah to describe Jesus as the "rose" and "stem of Jesse." Some translations of Isaiah use the words crocus or lily, but these flowers are both known as roses of the desert. Jesus came like a rose to a dry, barren land.

To say He is the stem of Jesse means He descends from the line of Jesse, who was King David's father. The "men of old" in the song are the prophets, particularly Isaiah. The imagery continues: perhaps "cold of winter" refers to the Roman occupation and the 400 years of silence of the prophets. It was into this darkness for Israel that Jesus came. And what do you suppose "when half-spent was the night" means? Some think it means that Jesus was born in the middle of the night. It could refer to the middle of human history as expressed by our calendar in the division of BC and AD—before and after Christ.

Like a sermon, the first two stanzas tell a story with delightful metaphors. Here the metaphors are about flowers. The final stanza explains the meaning of the imagery. The flower is Christ—"true man, yet very God."

TUNE: German melody, 16th c. ‖

Es Ist Ein' Ros' Entsprungen is a German melody from the fifteenth century. Without knowing German, you might guess it means "a rose has sprung up." The prolific German organist, composer, and musicologist Michael Praetorius arranged the tune for congregational worship in about 1602. The rhythm of the melody is not a strict meter, so a quarter note is what you focus on in counting instead of a bar line.

As you sing this hymn . . . enjoy the beautiful, poetic ways that the birth of Jesus is portrayed. What are some of your favorite images in this carol? Here are some to consider:

Rose e're blooming	Christ is born
Sprung from tender stem	From the family tree
Flower of fragrance tender	Goodness of Jesus
Sweetness fills the air	Holy Spirit pervades
Dispels glorious splendor	Light of the world
Darkness everywhere	Sin ruling over the earth
Lightens every load	Righteousness brings peace

Because we have no actual pictures of Jesus, these images help us picture His splendor in our world both then and now.

Lo, How a Rose E'er Blooming 16

The wilderness and the dry land shall be glad;
the desert shall rejoice and blossom like the crocus;
it shall blossom abundantly and rejoice with joy and singing.

ISAIAH 35:1–2

1. Lo, how a Rose e'er bloom - ing from ten - der stem hath sprung,
2. *I - sa - iah 'twas fore - told it, the Rose I have in mind;*
3. This flow'r, whose fra-grance ten - der with sweet-ness fills the air,

of Jes - se's lin-eage com - ing, as men of old have sung.
with Ma - ry we be - hold it, the Vir - gin Moth - er kind.
dis - pels with glo-rious splen - dor the dark-ness ev - ery-where.

It came a flow'r - et bright, a - mid the cold of
To show God's love a - right, she bore to us a
True man, yet ver - y God, from sin and death He

win - ter, when half - spent was the night.
Sav - ior, when half - spent was the night.
saves us and light - ens ev - ery load.

TEXT: German hymn, ca. 1500
TUNE: German melody, 16th c.

ES IST EIN' ROS' ENTSPRUNGEN

TEXT: Spiritual
adapt. John Wesley Work Jr.   ‖

The spirituals from the African American tradition provide a rich contribution to hymnody. Often the slaves created these songs in the fields as they worked and then passed them on from generation to generation. This created a body of music that is one-hundred percent of American origin. Much of it was preserved through the effort of John Wesley Work and his two sons, John Jr. and Frederick, together with the Jubilee Singers of Fisk University. John Sr. was an African American church choir director in Nashville, Tennessee, after the Civil War. John Jr. graduated from Fisk University, where he later taught Latin and Greek. He is credited with compiling and adapting the text we sing as "Go, Tell It on the Mountain."

TUNE: Spiritual   ‖

As with the texts, slaves created and improvised on their tunes. Most are simple and follow the pentatonic (five-note) scale. This is what you hear, for instance, if you play only the five black keys on the piano. They can be sung in canon without ever producing dissonance. The rhythm of this particular tune is strong and energetic, using a "jazz shuffle." This pattern uses dotted eighth connected to sixteenth notes rather than successive, even eighth notes. The tune is named for its first words, Go Tell It.

The Fisk Jubilee Singers introduced this music to the nation and the world. They sang before Queen Victoria and President Arthur. The famous composer Antonín Dvořák said of this music, "In the Negro melodies of America I discover all that is needed for a great and noble school of music. They are pathetic [moving, heart-rending], tender, passionate, melancholy, solemn, religious, bold, merry, gay. . . . It is music that suits itself to any mood or purpose."[10]

As you sing this hymn . . . you are doing what every family does after a new baby is born: they tell all their friends! Joy kept to yourself is incomplete. Sharing it completes it. If you see a beautiful sunset, you want to say to those around you, "Look at this!" Now think of the shepherds after they saw the newborn Jesus. The Bible says they spread the word of the angels' message, and that all who heard it were amazed (Luke 2:17–18). They couldn't keep their mouths shut. This baby was the Savior, the long-awaited Messiah! In the same way, this song gives us the chance to spread the word of the real meaning of Christmas. It allows us to share our joy, so that all may be amazed and worship Jesus, making Him their Savior.

Go, Tell It on the Mountain

*When they saw it, they made known the saying that
had been told them concerning this Child.*

LUKE 2:17

Go, tell it on the moun - tain, o - ver the hills and ev - 'ry - where;

go, tell it on the moun - tain that Je - sus Christ is born.

1. While shep-herds kept their watch-ing o'er si - lent flocks by night,
2. *The shep - herds feared and trem - bled when, lo! a - bove the earth*
3. Down in a low - ly man - ger our hum - ble Christ was born,

be - hold, through-out the heav-ens there shone a ho - ly light.____
rang out the an - gel cho - rus that hailed our Sav - ior's birth.____
and God sent us sal - va - tion that bless-ed Christ-mas morn.____

TEXT: John W. Work Jr.

GO TELL IT

TUNE: Spiritual

Christmas Thou Who Wast Rich Beyond All Splendor

TEXT: Frank Houghton | b. 1894, Stafford, Staffordshire, England
d. January 25, 1972, Tunbridge Wells, Kent, England

Frank Houghton was an Anglican missionary, bishop, and author. He was educated at London University and ordained to the ministry in 1917. After holding pastoral positions in England, he went to China with the China Inland Mission (begun in 1865 by Hudson Taylor). He became general director of the mission in 1940, but in 1951, the mission was forced to leave China. He returned to England and served as a vicar.

In 1934, while serving as editorial secretary for CIM, he decided to visit China to see the work firsthand. At that time the civil war between Chinese government forces and the Communist Red Army had begun. This made it a difficult and dangerous time for the missionaries. Some had been captured and imprisoned. One young couple who had been there only a short time, John and Betty Stam, had been killed by the Red Army. News of their deaths shocked and saddened the entire mission. When word of the terrible incident reached CIM headquarters in Shanghai, Houghton decided to make a trip throughout the country to visit the mission outposts, even though it was risky. While traveling over the mountains of Szechwan, Houghton was reminded of 2 Corinthians 8:9, "For you know the grace of our Lord Jesus Christ, that though He was rich, yet for your sake He became poor, so that you by His poverty might become rich." These words, impressed into his mind, resulted in this beautiful, powerful, and comforting poem.

TUNE: French carol melody

QUELLE EST CETTE ODEUR AGREABLE (translated: Whence is that goodly fragrance flowing?) is a seventeenth-century French Christmas carol about the Nativity. The origin of the tune is anonymous. It was a popular tune used by John Gay in his famous *The Beggar's Opera* in 1728. The tune made its way from France to England, where it was matched with Houghton's poem.

As you sing this hymn . . . note the word *beyond*, the fifth word in all three stanzas. Each time Houghton is pointing to something beyond our comprehension—the splendor of heaven, the wonder of the Trinity, and the extent of Christ's love for us. However, we can comprehend what it means to be a poor human being. And the fact that Jesus would leave one extreme for the other leads to only one conclusion: He is worthy of our highest commitment ("Emmanuel, within us dwelling"), our complete trust ("make us what Thou would'st have us be"), and our deepest adoration ("Savior and King, we worship Thee"). Indeed, it was because they knew this Christ and His love that missionaries like the Stams could give their all.

Thou Who Wast Rich Beyond All Splendor 18

For you know the grace of our Lord Jesus Christ,
that though He was rich, yet for your sake He became poor,
so that you by His poverty might become rich.

2 CORINTHIANS 8:9

1. Thou Who wast rich be - yond all splen - dor,
2. Thou Who art God be - yond all prais - ing,
3. Thou Who art love be - yond all tell - ing,

all for love's sake be - cam - est poor;
all for love's sake be - cam - est man;
Sav - ior and King, we wor - ship Thee.

thrones for a man - ger didst sur - ren - der,
stoop - ing so low, but sin - ners rais - ing,
Em - man - u - el, with - in us dwell - ing,

sap - phire - paved courts for sta - ble floor.
heav'n - ward by Thine e - ter - nal plan.
make us what Thou wouldst have us be.

Thou Who wast rich be - yond all splen - dor,
Thou Who art God be - yond all prais - ing,
Thou Who art Love be - yond all tell - ing,

all for love's sake be - cam - est poor.
all for love's sake be - cam - est man.
Sa - vior and King, we wor - ship Thee.

TEXT: Frank Houghton

TUNE: French carol melody

QUELLE EST CETTE ODEUR AGREABLE

Christmas Joy to the World! The Lord Is Come

TEXT: Isaac Watts

b. July 17, 1674, Southampton, England
d. November 25, 1748, Stoke Newington, England
(for more on Watts, see No. 24, 46, 52, and 71)

Evidently, Isaac Watts was never satisfied with the congregational singing in churches. In his later years, he wrote, "To see the dull indifference, the negligent and thoughtless air that sits upon the faces of a whole assembly, while the psalm is upon their lips, might even tempt a charitable observer to suspect the fervency of their inward religion."[11] To counter this indifference, he attempted to write hymns that elicited joy and zeal. "Joy to the World" certainly accomplished that purpose. It is probably one of the most recognized and commonly sung Christmas carols in the world. Interestingly, this hymn, based on Psalm 98:4–9, does not speak of Christmas at all! There is no baby in a manger, no angels, no shepherds or wise men. Rather, it presents a mighty, triumphant ruler coming to judge the earth with righteousness. The important word is "come." His first Advent is past. A second Advent is coming.

TUNE: Lowell Mason

b. January 8, 1792, Medfield, Massachusetts
d. August 11, 1872, Orange, New Jersey
(for more on Mason, see No. 24)

Lowell Mason was primarily responsible for introducing music into American public schools and is considered to be the first influential music educator in the United States. But he is also a leading figure in American church music, having written over 1,600 hymns. Like Watts, Mason sought better congregational singing. At his church, Fifth Avenue Presbyterian in New York City, he fired all of the hired musicians except the organist, and his church became known for having the finest congregational singing in the city.

Mason attributed the tune ANTIOCH to G. F. Handel since several parts of the melody can be found throughout Handel's *Messiah*. ANTIOCH is the name of the city in Syria mentioned in Acts 11:26 where Christ's followers were first called "Christians."

As you sing this hymn . . . do you understand this song is not about being joyous just at Christmas? Our joy should last far beyond Christmas because He reigns all year. One wonders what non-Christians think when they sing this carol! Yet Christians can sing with the psalmist, with heaven and nature, even with fields, floods, rocks, hills, and plains. We shout with joy that the baby Jesus came to the world to die, rise from the dead, and rule the world in justice and righteousness! He rules over sin, sorrow, and the thorns in our lives. He puts a stop to the curse of death that all mankind has been under since Adam and Eve. He rules with truth and grace, and one day "every knee should bow . . . and every tongue confess that Jesus Christ is Lord" (Phil. 2:10–11).

Joy to the World! The Lord Is Come   19

Make a joyful noise to the LORD, all the earth;
break forth into joyous song and sing praises!

PSALM 98:4

1. Joy to the world! The Lord is come: let earth re - ceive her
2. *Joy to the earth! The Sav - ior reigns: let men their songs em -*
3. No more let sins and sor - rows grow, nor thorns in - fest the
4. *He rules the world with truth and grace, and makes the na - tions*

King!___ Let ev - ery___ heart___ pre - pare___ Him___
ploy;___ while fields___ and___ floods,___ rocks, hills,___ and___
ground;___ He comes to___ make His bless - ings___
prove___ the glo - ries___ of___ His right - eous -

room,___ and heav'n and na - ture___ sing, and___ heav'n and na - ture___
plains___ re - peat the sound - ing___ joy, re - peat the sound - ing___
flow___ far as the curse is___ found, far___ as the curse is___
ness,___ and won - ders of His___ love, and___ won - ders of His___

sing, and___ heav'n and heav'n___ and na - ture sing.
joy, re - peat,___ re - peat___ the sound - ing joy.
found, far___ as,___ far as___ the curse is found.
love, and___ won - ders, won - ders of His love.

TEXT: Isaac Watts
TUNE: Lowell Mason

ANTIOCH

Epiphany What Child Is This?

TEXT: Traditional English carol, adapt. William Chatterton Dix

b. June 14, 1837, Bristol, England
d. September 9, 1898, Cheddar, Somerset, England
(for more on Dix, see No. 21)

William's father named him William Chatterton Dix after one of his own heroes, Thomas Chatterton, an English poet. He encouraged his son to follow after his namesake. William studied poets and poetry, read classic literature, and spent much time in college focusing on his writing ability. Although he became the manager of a marine insurance company, he made time to write. When a serious illness caused him to be bedridden for a year, he wrote his lengthy poem "The Manger Throne," the story of the men from the East who came to visit the baby Jesus (Matt. 2:1–12). This text is written from their perspective, which is why it is in the "Epiphany" section of this hymnal (see "As with Gladness Men of Old"). The poem was published and quickly became popular in England and America, where the Civil War was ending. An unknown Englishman put the poem's words to the beautiful English folk song GREENSLEEVES, creating this carol.

TUNE: English melody, 16th c.

GREENSLEEVES is an English folk melody of uncertain origin, dating back to the sixteenth century. Some attribute it to King Henry VIII as a gift to Anne Boleyn, but for reasons of style, that is not likely. In Shakespeare's *The Merry Wives of Windsor*, written around 1602, one character calls out, "Let the sky rain potatoes! Let it thunder to the tune of 'Greensleeves'!" It is truly one of the most hauntingly beautiful tunes ever written, and "What Child Is This?" is the reason it is well-known to this day.

As you sing this hymn . . . notice that the first two stanzas ask two profound questions, *Who?* and *Why?* The first question, "What child is this," is a way of asking, who is this one? It's a question that everyone feels. The apostle Paul said, "Great indeed, we confess, is the mystery of godliness: 'He was manifested in the flesh, vindicated by the Spirit, seen by angels, proclaimed among the nations, believed on in the world, taken up in glory'" (1 Tim. 3:16). But the "why" question follows: Why would God come to earth "in such a mean estate" (a lowly place, a barn)? And why would "nails, spear . . . pierce him through"? Of course, hiding behind Dix's question, "What child is this?" is an even more profound question: "What God is this?" Would anyone be able to imagine a God of such love and compassion if these things had not really happened?

The third stanza describes the right response: offer your highest treasures, enthrone Him as reigning Lord, and raise songs of praise. In short, the hymn offers a Q&A—a question and answer concerning a matter of more importance than all other mysteries in our universe. May this Christmas mystery never lose its wonder in your life.

What Child Is This?

20

They saw the child with Mary His mother,
and they fell down and worshiped Him.
Then, opening their treasures, they offered Him gifts.

MATTHEW 2:11

1. What Child is this,— Who, laid to rest,— on Mar-y's lap— is
2. *Why lies He in— such mean es-tate,— where ox and ass— are*
3. So bring Him in-cense, gold, and myrrh: come peas-ant, king,— to

sleep - ing? Whom an-gels greet— with an-thems sweet,— while
feed - ing? Good Chris-tian, fear;— for sin-ners here— the
own Him; the King of kings— sal-va-tion brings,— let

shep-herds watch— are keep-ing? This, this— is
si - lent Word— is plead-ing. Nails, spear,— shall
lov-ing hearts— en-throne Him. Raise, raise— the

Christ the King,— Whom shep-herds guard— and an-gels sing:
pierce Him through;— the cross be borne— for me, for you:
song on high,— the vir-gin sings— her lul-la-by:

haste, haste— to bring Him laud, the Babe,— the son— of Mar - y.
hail, hail— the Word made flesh, the Babe,— the son— of Mar - y.
joy, joy— for Christ is born, the Babe,— the son— of Mar - y.

TEXT: Traditional English carol, adapt. William C. Dix
TUNE: English melody, 16th c.

GREENSLEEVES

As with Gladness Men of Old

TEXT: William Chatterton Dix	b. June 14, 1837, Bristol, England
	d. September 9, 1898, Cheddar, Somerset, England
	(for more on Dix, see No. 20)

William Dix lived in England during the nineteenth century, when romantic poetry was at its height. Dix inherited a love for poetry from his father, particularly as it was used in worship. He wrote over forty hymns and poems. It was said of Dix, "Few modern writers have shown so single a gift as his for the difficult art of hymn-writing."[12]

Dix was struck with a serious and mysterious illness in his twenties that kept him in bed for months. He became severely depressed, but it was during this time that he explored the Scriptures and wrote many of his hymns. On Epiphany Day, January 6, 1865, while sick in bed, Dix read Matthew 2:1–12 and was inspired to write a lengthy poem—all in one day. He called it "The Manger Throne." Dix refers to the "men of old" in the story rather than "kings" or "magi" because those ideas come from tradition, not Scripture. "What Child Is This?," is derived from this same poem.

TUNE: Conrad Kocher	b. December 16, 1786, Dietzingen, Württemberg, Germany
	d. March 12, 1872, Stuttgart, Germany

The tune carries the name of the author of this text, DIX, but the tune itself was first written by a German man, Conrad Kocher. An Englishman, William Henry Monk, then adapted it for this carol. We sing another hymn to this melody. Can you name it?

As you sing this hymn . . . think of those men who came from the East to look for Jesus. They had studied astronomy and saw the star that God had used to mark the place where Jesus was born. They traveled for months, possibly years, to find Him. Just as these men were foreigners to ancient Israel, so were we, as Gentiles, foreigners. Up to that point in history, the Messiah was for the nation of Israel, God's people. The lesson of Epiphany is that God's salvation and His Son are for the entire world, not just for the Jews.

Dix's father told his son that he liked the way in which the conclusion of each stanza tells the singer how to respond to the birth of Jesus. Many other European carols simply leave us with a beautiful picture. As you sing, you are asking God to help you be like those early seekers, seeking, kneeling, offering gifts, praising for all eternity your heavenly King.

As with Gladness Men of Old

21

*Behold, the star that they had seen when it rose went before them
until it came to rest over the place where the Child was.
When they saw the star, they rejoiced exceedingly with great joy.*

MATTHEW 2:9–10

1. As with_ glad-ness men of old did the guid-ing star be-hold;
2. *As with_ joy - ful steps they sped to that low - ly man - ger bed,*
3. As they_ of -fered gifts most rare at that man -ger rude and bare,
4. *Ho - ly___ Je - sus, ev - ery day keep us in the nar - row way;*

as with_ joy they hailed its light, lead - ing on - ward, beam-ing bright,
there to___ bend the knee be - fore Him Whom heaven and earth a - dore,
so may_ we with ho - ly joy, pure and free from sin's al - loy,
and when_ earth - ly things are past, bring our ran - somed souls at last

so, most gra-cious Lord, may we ev - er-more be led to Thee.
so, may we with will - ing feet ev - er seek Thy mer - cy seat.
all our cost-liest treas - ures bring, Christ, to Thee, our heaven-ly King.
where they need no star to guide, where no clouds Thy glo - ry hide.

TEXT: William Chatterton Dix

TUNE: Conrad Kocher

Dix

Lent What Wondrous Love Is This

TEXT AND TUNE: American folk hymn ‖

From the rural folk of the southern Appalachian Mountains comes what some consider the finest and most beautiful of American folk hymns. Life was difficult for people in the mountains, but they came together to sing, dance, and worship. Their music was passed on from generation to generation orally, never being written down. This anonymous text first appeared in print in 1811, in *A General Selection of the Newest and Most Admired Hymns and Spiritual Songs Now in Use* (edited by Stith Mead, Lynchburg, Virginia: Virginia Conference of the Methodist Episcopal Church, 1811). The first person to write down the tune that is now called WONDROUS LOVE was James Christopher, a man from South Carolina.

William Walker (1809–1875) was a musically gifted young man also from South Carolina who collected and arranged folk songs from Appalachia and camp meetings. People called him "Singing Billy." Walker participated in the singing schools, which began in the early days of America by those who immigrated here for religious freedom. It was essential for them to train every churchgoer how to sing because of their strong convictions on congregational singing in Christian worship. In 1835, Walker published a collection called *Southern Harmony*, which contained the text and tune we now use. Walker's brother-in-law, Benjamin White (who started his musical career playing the fife in the War of 1812), also published this hymn in a hymnal called *The Sacred Harp* (1844).

As you sing this hymn . . . you are preaching to yourself! You are directing your own soul to heed the declarations and assurances of this song. Perhaps that is why the first five words of each stanza are repeated three times and the last phrase is repeated twice. Often, we have the hardest time convincing ourselves of something. We have to tell ourselves over and over.

The second stanza uses an unusual expression for guilt: "When I was sinking down beneath God's righteous frown." When we understand our sin, and what the righteous Judge demands, we want to hide, to sink down. We rightly feel guilty. But here's the good news: Christ stepped in, laid aside His crown as King, and died for everyone who repents and believes. What wondrous love!

Bert Polman, a hymnologist and author, notes that the hymn begins with a personal reflection by addressing your own soul. But as you sing, you realize that "millions join the theme," and when all sing together, it is "a great corporate sermon"! We will sing its theme throughout eternity!

What Wondrous Love Is This

See what kind of love the Father has given to us,
that we should be called children of God; and so we are.

I JOHN 3:1

TEXT AND TUNE: American folk hymn

WONDROUS LOVE

| TEXT: Bernard of Clairvaux | b. 1090, Fontaine-lès-Dijon, France |
| | d. August 20, 1153, Clairvaux Abbey, France |

Bernard was the son of a knight. He lost his mother at the age of nineteen, and his life was so filled with temptations that he decided to enter a monastery. He also convinced twelve friends, an uncle, and four brothers to join him. At the age of twenty-four, he founded his own monastery in a valley in France that he renamed *Clara Vallis* ("Beautiful Valley") from which comes his title, Bernard of Clairvaux. This monastery became famous, numbering among its students a pope, six cardinals, and thirty bishops. Although influential in his lifetime, Bernard is most remembered for the kind of devotion and love for his Savior that is expressed in this poem. Martin Luther said of him, "If there has ever been a pious monk who feared God, it was St. Bernard, whom alone I hold in much higher esteem than all other monks and priests throughout the world."[13]

Bernard originally wrote this poem in seven sections, each focusing on a different part of the Savior's suffering body. He wrote it in Latin, then the language of the church. Five hundred years later, Paul Gerhardt (1607–1676), whom some regard as the greatest of Lutheran hymnists, translated it into German. Almost 200 years after that, James Waddell Alexander (1804–1859) translated it into English. In short, this beautiful expression of God's love as shown in our suffering Savior has come to us through 700 years, three languages, and three traditions—Catholic, Lutheran, and Reformed. It is truly a masterpiece worth being memorized by every Christian.

| TUNE: Hans Leo Hassler | b. October 25, 1564, Nuremberg, Germany |
| | d. June 8, 1612, Frankfurt, Germany |

The tune also has a diverse history. It began as a German folk song, which Hans Leo Hassler employed for this hymn text. J. S. Bach wrote the current harmonization, which is now considered one of the world's masterpieces of sacred music. It was under Bach's hand that it came to its current name, PASSION CHORALE.

As you sing this hymn . . . you behold Jesus on the cross covered in grief and shame. Bernard does not try to gloss over our Savior's agony. Yet the question is, Why would Jesus be weighed down with shame if He never sinned? Answer: because He took the blame for our sins upon Himself. So sing with stanza 2, "Mine, mine was the transgression, but Thine the deadly pain." There is little to say in response to such self-giving love. Stanza 3 gets it right: "What language shall I borrow to thank Thee, dearest Friend?" All of the words in every language could never be enough to say thank you to Jesus Christ for receiving the punishment that we deserve, that we might be reconciled to God.

O Sacred Head, Now Wounded

23

He was pierced for our transgressions; He was crushed for our iniquities.

ISAIAH 53:5

1. O sa - cred Head, now wound - ed, with grief and shame weighed down,
2. *What Thou, my Lord, hast suf - fered was all for sin - ners' gain:*
3. What lan-guage shall I bor - row to thank Thee, dear - est Friend,

now scorn-ful-ly sur-round - ed with thorns, Thine on - ly crown,
mine, mine was the trans - gres - sion, but Thine the dead - ly pain.
for this, Thy dy - ing sor - row, Thy pit - y with - out end?

O sa - cred Head, what glo - ry, what bliss till now was Thine!
Lo, here I fall, my Sav - ior! 'Tis I de - serve Thy place;
O make me Thine for ev - er; and should I faint - ing be,

Yet, though de-spised and gor - y, I joy to call Thee mine.
look on me with Thy fa - vor, vouch-safe to me Thy grace.
Lord, let me nev - er, nev - er out - live my love to Thee.

TEXT: Bernard of Clairvaux, trans. James W. Alexander   PASSION CHORALE
TUNE: Hans Leo Hassler, arr. Johann Sebastian Bach

Lent When I Survey the Wondrous Cross

TEXT: Isaac Watts

b. July 17, 1674, Southampton, England
d. November 25, 1748, London, England
(for more on Watts, see No. 19, 46, 52, and 71)

Isaac's father, a schoolmaster, was a leader in the Nonconformist State Church movement and was imprisoned repeatedly for his views. His son, too, did not follow traditions. It was clear that Isaac was very bright, learning Latin by age four, Greek at nine, French at eleven (so that he could talk to refugee neighbors), and Hebrew at thirteen. Friends offered to pay for his university education at Oxford or Cambridge, but Isaac refused, and at sixteen he went to London to study at a leading Nonconformist academy. In 1702, he became pastor of London's Mark Lane Independent Chapel, then one of the city's most influential independent churches.

This hymn is considered by many to be Isaac Watts' finest hymn, and some say it is the greatest hymn ever written because it so eloquently combines revelation and response. Watts wrote the hymn to be sung while taking communion.

TUNE: Lowell Mason

b. January 8, 1792, Medfield, Massachusetts
d. August 11, 1872, Orange, New Jersey
(for more on Mason, see No. 19)

Lowell Mason wrote HAMBURG in 1824. Its source was a Gregorian chant, a melody style that developed in the Middle Ages, named after Pope Gregory the Great. Chants are sung without a meter or rhythm and usually without interval skips. So the melody of this hymn, like a chant, moves up or down only one step at a time, and the range of the melody is only five notes!

As you sing this hymn . . . you are asked to approach the cross of Jesus in your mind's eye. You look and see the Prince of Glory dying. You survey the scene. You measure it. Just like you might survey a piece of land or measure a road, so now you survey and measure this gruesome scene.

What is it? And what is it worth? It is nothing other than the grandest demonstration of God's love in history, and it is more valuable than all the world. Boasting should stop here. Worldly desire should stop here. Christ's love is worth more than all that. It covers your sin and mine. It covers the past, the present, and the future. Most of all, it brings us to God. The cross changes everything in our lives; it makes us new.

What is your decision about the cross? Have you carefully measured how long, wide, high, and deep is the love of the suffering Savior as shown on the cross? Has looking to His sacrifice changed you? Does your heart respond, "Love so amazing, so divine, demands my soul, my life, my all"? If not, look again.

When I Survey the Wondrous Cross

24

But far be it from me to boast except in the cross of our Lord Jesus Christ, by which the world has been crucified to me, and I to the world.

GALATIANS 6:14

1. When I survey the wondrous cross
2. Forbid it, Lord, that I should boast,
3. See, from His head, His hands, His feet,
4. Were the whole realm of nature mine,

on which the Prince of glory died,
save in the death of Christ my God:
sorrow and love flow mingled down:
that were a present far too small;

my richest gain I count but loss,
all the vain things that charm me most,
did e'er such love and sorrow meet,
love so amazing, so divine,

and pour contempt on all my pride.
I sacrifice them to His blood.
or thorns compose so rich a crown?
demands my soul, my life, my all.

TEXT: Isaac Watts
TUNE: Lowell Mason

HAMBURG

Hallelujah! What a Savior

TEXT AND TUNE: Philip Bliss ‖ b. July 9, 1838, Clearfield County, Pennsylvania
d. December 29, 1876, Ashtabula, Ohio

Philip Bliss was born to a father who loved both God and music. His father encouraged his son to develop a love for singing. At age ten Philip first heard a piano, which captured his own love for music. At the age of twenty-two, Bliss became an itinerant music teacher and travelled from community to community on horseback carrying a melodeon (a small accordion). His wife's grandmother lent him $30 to attend the Normal Academy of Music of New York, where he developed his love for composing. At age twenty-six, he moved to Chicago, where he met the famed evangelist D. L. Moody, who encouraged him to give up teaching and become a music evangelist. Bliss wrote dozens of hymns, including the tune for "It Is Well with My Soul." He was one of the nineteenth century's most prominent American hymn writers. Bliss and his wife tragically perished when their train was crossing a bridge, the bridge collapsed, and the train plunged into a river.

Ira Sankey, soloist for the Moody Crusades, relates this about the hymn:

> This was the last hymn I heard Mr. Bliss sing. It was at a meeting in Chicago. . . . A few weeks before his death Mr. Bliss visited the State prison at Jackson, Michigan, where, after a very touching address on "The Man of Sorrows," he sang this hymn. Many of the prisoners dated their conversion from that day. When Mr. Moody and I were in Paris, holding meetings in the old church which Napoleon had granted to the Evangelicals, I frequently sang this hymn as a solo, asking the congregation to join in the single phrase, "Hallelujah, what a Savior," which they did with splendid effect as the word "Hallelujah" is the same in all languages.[14]

As you sing this hymn . . . consider the "man of sorrows" in Isaiah 53. Read the chapter as you prepare to sing this hymn. It points to Christ's sufferings. "He was despised and rejected by men, a man of sorrows and acquainted with grief" (v. 3). Isaiah observes that He suffered in our place: "Surely He has borne our griefs and carried our sorrows" (v. 4).

The hymn makes this remarkable chapter our testimony through personal pronouns, for those who are Christians. Isaiah writes, "He was pierced for our transgressions; He was crushed for our iniquities" (v. 5). The hymn puts it like this: "In my place condemned He stood," and He "sealed my pardon."

As in Isaiah 53, the hymn concludes on a note of triumph. The suffering servant becomes the glorious King, and He returns to bring His ransomed ones—us!—home with Him. Our faces should break into a smile as we sing, "Hallelujah! What a Savior!"

Hallelujah! What a Savior

*He was despised and rejected by men, a man of sorrows
and acquainted with grief.*

ISAIAH 53:3

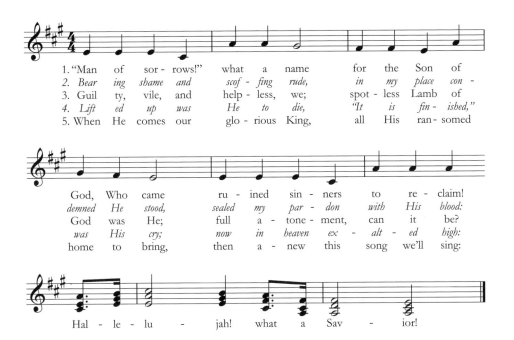

1. "Man of sor - rows!" what a name for the Son of God, Who came ru - ined sin - ners to re - claim!
2. Bear ing shame and scof - fing rude, in my place con - demned He stood, sealed my par - don with His blood:
3. Guil ty, vile, and help - less, we; spot - less Lamb of God was He; full a - tone - ment, can it be?
4. Lift ed up was He to die, "It is fin - ished," was His cry; now in heaven ex - alt - ed high:
5. When He comes our glo - rious King, all His ran - somed home to bring, then a - new this song we'll sing:

Hal - le - lu - jah! what a Sav - ior!

TEXT AND TUNE: Philip P. Bliss

HALLELUJAH! WHAT A SAVIOR

Lent How Deep the Father's Love for Us

TEXT AND TUNE: Stuart Townend | b. June 1, 1963, West Yorkshire, England
(for more on Townend, see No. 12, 34, 62, 65, and 99)

S tuart Townend has written about Christian music:

There are probably more hymns and worship songs being written today
than in any period of church history. But relatively few will stand the
test of time. And that has always been the case: for every "Amazing
Grace" or "And Can It Be," you can bet there are several hundred trite,
interminably dull ditties that did the rounds at the time, but have now
thankfully faded into blissful obscurity.[15]

He then offers six guidelines for writing an excellent Christian song: 1) Study the
Scriptures; 2) Be poetic, not pompous; 3) Combine objective truth and subjective
response; 4) Look for musical dynamics; 5) Make every line count; and 6) Prune it
mercilessly.[16]

Townend gives insight into his writing of "How Deep the Father's Love for Us":

I'd been meditating on the cross, and in particular what it cost the
Father to give up His beloved Son to a torturous death on a cross. And
what was my part in it? Not only was it my sin that put him there, but
if I'd lived at that time, it would probably have been me in that crowd,
shouting with everyone else "crucify him." It just makes his sacrifice all
the more personal, all the more amazing, and all the more humbling.

As I was thinking through this, I . . . began to sing the melody, and it
flowed in the sort of way that makes you think you've pinched it from
somewhere! So the melody was pretty instant, but the words took quite
a bit of time, reworking things, trying to make every line as strong as I
could.[17]

The meter, or time signature, is in 5/4 time—the only such one in all 120 hymns in
this book. We are used to hearing **1–2–3–4, 1–2–3–4**; or **1–2–3, 1–2–3**; not **1–2–3–
4–5**! The extra beat in each measure takes us away from "feeling a beat" and into a free
flowing movement. This assists in the narrative, meditative quality of the words.

As you sing this hymn . . . notice the series of powerful and passionate words like *vast,
wretch, treasure, searing loss, ashamed, scoffers,* and *accomplished,* words not often found
in hymns. These tell the story of deep love. They help us consider the awfulness of the
cross and the extent of both the Father's and the Son's sacrifice.

How does this impact you? How do you respond? The third stanza is an expression
of Galatians 6:14: "But far be it from me to boast except in the cross of our Lord Jesus
Christ." Such amazing, sacrificial love is humbling. We don't deserve it. Why did He
die? There is no answer. We can only respond with our love in return.

How Deep the Father's Love for Us

That you . . . may have strength to comprehend with all the saints what is
the breadth and length and height and depth, and to know the love of Christ
. . . that you may be filled with all the fullness of God.

EPHESIANS 3:17–19

1. How deep the Fa-ther's love for us, how vast be-yond all meas - ure,
2. Be - hold the Man up - on the cross, my sin up - on His shoul - ders.
3. I will not boast in an - y thing: no gifts, no pow'r, no wis - dom.

that He should give His on - ly Son to make a wretch His treas - ure.
A - shamed, I hear my mock-ing voice call out a - mong the scof - fers.
But I will boast in Je - sus Christ; His death and res - ur - rec - tion.

How great the pain of sear-ing loss. The Fa - ther turns His face a-way
It was my sin that held Him there un - til it was ac - com - plished;
Why should I gain from His re- ward? I can - not give an an - swer.

as wounds which mar the Cho-sen One bring man - y sons to glo - ry.
His dy - ing breath has brought me life. I know that it is fin - ished.
But this I know with all my heart: His wounds have paid my ran - som.

TEXT AND TUNE: Stuart Townend

TEXT: George W. Kitchin ‖ b. December 7, 1827, Naughton, Suffolk, England
d. October 13, 1912, Durham, England

George Kitchin, the son of a minister, was educated at King's College and Oxford University. He served as Dean of Winchester, Dean of Durham Cathedral, and then as Chancellor of Durham University. He is best remembered as the author of "Lift High the Cross."

His hymn focuses on a primary symbol of Christianity, the cross. It is the symbol of gruesome death as well as the greatest victory. On this "tree of pain," Jesus Christ triumphed over mankind's two worst enemies, sin and death. The hymn describes it as "victorious," "healing," "glorious," "triumphant," and "conquering." The one lifted up on the cross is not just a dying Savior, but a triumphant King who draws the world to Himself in total victory. It reminds us of the bronze serpent lifted up by Moses in the wilderness, to which all Israelites bitten by poisonous snakes could look and live (Num. 21:4–9). Jesus then compared His own crucifixion to the lifting up of this bronze snake (John 3:14–15). Whoever looked to Him would not die but have eternal life.

TUNE: Sydney H. Nicholson ‖ b. May 30, 1947, Kent, England
d. February 9, 1975, London, England

Some churches begin their service by having a person carry a cross atop a long staff down the center aisle—a processional. At the end of the service, the cross is carried out during the recessional. The person carrying the cross is called a *crucifer*. This word comes from two Latin words, *crux*, which means "cross," and *ferre*, which is "to carry." *Crucifer* means "cross-bearer." Sydney Nicholson, who wrote this tune, named it Crucifer, since the text instructs all Christians to be cross-bearers.

Nicholson was the church organist in several prestigious churches, including Eton College, Manchester Cathedral, and Westminster Abbey, where he is buried. His tune begins with the chorus and returns to it following each verse, giving the sense of perpetual motion. The melody and harmonies are high and majestic, as befits a grand processional. Notice the melody matches the words on "lift high" by going up.

As you sing this hymn . . . consider how people at athletic events or political rallies lift up signs and banners to tell everyone what is important to them. Here, we are not being asked to lift up literal crosses but to "proclaim" Jesus Christ with our mouths and lives. When we do, people will be drawn to Him in adoration. Like the Israelites, they will be saved from the snake bites of sin and death.

Lift High the Cross

And I, when I am lifted up from the earth,
will draw all people to Myself.

JOHN 12:32

Lift high the cross, the love of Christ pro - claim
till all the world___ a - dore___ His sa - cred name.

Fine

1. Come, Chris - tians, fol - low where our Sav - ior trod,
2. *All new - born ser - vants of the Cru - ci - fied*
3. O Lord, once lift - ed on the tree of pain,
4. *Let ev - ery race and ev - ery lan - guage tell*
5. So shall our song of tri - umph ev - er be:

D.C.

our King vic - to - rious, Christ, the Son of God.
bear on their__ brows the seal of Him who died.
draw all the__ world to seek You once a - gain.
of Him who__ saves our souls from death and hell.
praise to the__ Cru - ci - fied for vic - to - ry!

TEXT: George W. Kitchin, rev. Michael R. Newbolt CRUCIFER
TUNE: Sydney H. Nicholson

TEXT: Jeannette Threlfall || b. March 24, 1821, Blackburn, Lancs, England
d. November 30, 1880, Westminster, England

Jeannette Threlfall was called a "sweet singer of hymns and other sacred poems."[18] Her parents died when she was quite young, and she lived out her childhood with relatives who referred to her as their "beloved inmate." Later in life she endured two bad accidents. The first left her lame, the second a total invalid. Yet it was said that "she bore her long slow sufferings brightly, and to the end retained a gentle, loving, sympathetic heart, and always a pleasant word and smile, forgetful of herself."[19] Threlfall was an avid reader, which led her to write many poems and hymns of her own. She published a collection of them that she titled *Sunshine and Shadow* (1873).

The word *hosanna* as used in the Old Testament means "save us" or "help us!" But in the story of Jesus' entry into Jerusalem on Palm Sunday, the story that is told by this hymn, the word *hosanna* is spoken in jubilation and praise. The first two stanzas focus specifically on the children singing, following, and waiting upon Jesus. Evidently, they followed Him into the temple and continued to sing "Hosanna to the Son of David" (Matt. 21:15). This angered the priests, prompting Jesus to remind them of Psalm 8:2: "They said to Him, 'Do you hear what these are saying?' And Jesus said to them, 'Yes; have you never read, "Out of the mouth of infants and nursing babies You have prepared praise"?'"(Matt. 21:16). This biblical episode defines the purpose of the hymnal you are holding in your hands: that children may praise God by singing hymns to Him.

TUNE: *Gesangbuch der Herzogl, Hofkapelle*
Württemberg, Germany, 1784

Ellacombe, named for a village in Devonshire, England, was first written for the Duke of Württemberg and published in a chapel hymnal in 1784. It was edited in 1868 by Henry Monk for inclusion in the historically significant English hymnal, *Hymns Ancient and Modern*. Still available today, the hymnal has sold over 170 million copies worldwide.

As you sing this hymn . . . never forget Jesus' tender love for children. One day He said to His disciples, "'Let the children come to Me; do not hinder them, for to such belongs the kingdom of God. Truly, I say to you, whoever does not receive the kingdom of God like a child shall not enter it.' And He took them in His arms and blessed them, laying His hands on them" (Mark 10:14–16). Jesus points to the example of little children because of their open and trusting hearts. Anyone who would follow Jesus, whether old or young, must have such a heart. Does your heart trust Him? If so, then you will want to sing with stanza 3, "Hosanna in the highest!" Christ is our Redeemer and King.

Hosanna, Loud Hosanna

28

The children crying out in the temple, "Hosanna to the Son of David!"...
"Do you hear what these are saying?" And Jesus said to them, "Yes; have you never
read, 'Out of the mouth of infants and nursing babies You have prepared praise'?"

MATTHEW 21:15–16

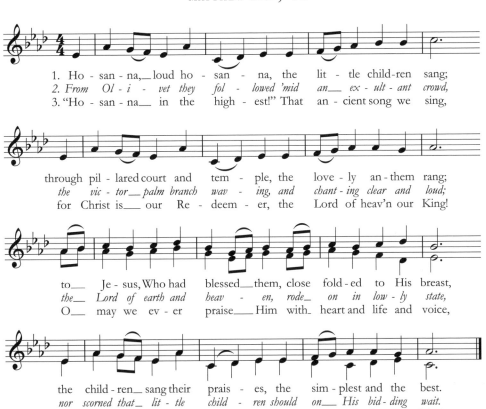

1. Ho-san-na,—loud ho-san-na, the lit-tle child-ren sang;
2. *From Ol-i-vet they fol-lowed 'mid an— ex-ult-ant crowd,*
3. "Ho-san-na— in the high-est!" That an-cient song we sing,

through pil-lared court and tem-ple, the love-ly an-them rang;
the vic-tor— palm branch wav-ing, and chant-ing clear and loud;
for Christ is— our Re-deem-er, the Lord of heav'n our King!

to— Je-sus, Who had blessed—them, close fold-ed to His breast,
the— Lord of earth and heav-en, rode— on in low-ly state,
O— may we ev-er praise— Him with— heart and life and voice,

the child-ren— sang their prais-es, the sim-plest and the best.
nor scorned that— lit-tle child-ren should on— His bid-ding wait.
and in His— bliss-ful pres-ence e-ter-nal-ly re-joice!

TEXT: Jeannette Threlfall
TUNE: *Gesangbuch der H.W.K. Hofkapelle,* 1784

ELLACOMBE

TEXT: Theodulph of Orleans ‖ b. 760, Italy
d. 821, Angiers, France

Theodulph knew kings! The first king he knew was Charlemagne, who brought him from Spain to help him build schools and reform the clergy. While serving this earthly king, Theodulph began writing hymns for his heavenly King. Theodulph also knew Charlemagne's son and successor, King Louis. But when Louis tried to divide the kingdom among his sons, Theodulph got caught in the family dispute and was falsely accused of conspiring with Louis's nephew, King Bernard of Italy. Theodulph was placed in prison, where he wrote the seventy-eight verses of "All Glory, Laud, and Honor . . . to Thee, Redeemer *King*." It is said that King Louis freed Theodulph upon hearing him sing this hymn from outside the prison window.

We would not know this hymn were it not for John Mason Neale (1818–1856), who lived a thousand years after Theodulph and translated the text from Latin to English. Neale lost his father at the age of five and was schooled at home by his mother. A student of classic Greek and Roman culture and language, he became part of a movement that researched Roman liturgy and hymnody for English use. This revolutionized English church music and ultimately American as well. Other hymns translated by Neale include "O Come, O Come, Emmanuel," "Good Christian Men, Rejoice," and "Of the Father's Love Begotten."

TUNE: Melchior Teschner ‖ b. April 29, 1584, Prussia
d. December 1, 1635, Prussia

The tune is called ST. THEODULPH, the author of the text. But it was written by Melchior Teschner, a German hymn writer born in 1584, 700 years after Theodulph.

As you sing this hymn . . . if you are at your church, it will most likely be the Sunday before Easter, or Palm Sunday, since it recalls Jesus' triumphal entry into Jerusalem. The week before He was crucified, Jesus entered Jerusalem, riding on a donkey. People laid palm branches before Him and shouted, "Hosanna!" which means, "please, save us!"

Have you noticed how people in a parade always smile and wave at the crowds? Do you think Jesus did that as He entered Jerusalem? He was not on an elegant float or a decorated horse. Instead He sat humbly on a donkey, aware that people who shouted "Hosanna!" five days later would shout, "Crucify Him!" Yet, Theodulph's hymn offers no hint of irony. It simply asks us to smile and sing with joy because we know the end of the story. Jesus triumphed over death! He is our reigning King. "Hosanna! Blessed is He who comes."

All Glory, Laud, and Honor

29

The next day the large crowd . . . heard that Jesus was coming to Jerusalem.
So they took branches of palm trees and went out to meet Him, crying out, "Hosanna!
Blessed is He who comes in the name of the Lord, even the King of Israel!"

JOHN 12:12–13

All glo - ry, laud and hon - or to Thee, Re-deem-er, King, to

Fine

whom the lips of chil - dren made sweet ho - san - nas ring!

1. Thou art the King of Is - rael, Thou Da - vid's roy - al Son,
2. *The peo - ple of the He - brews with palms be - fore Thee went;*
3. To Thee, be - fore Thy pas - sion, they sang their hymns of praise;
4. *Thou didst ac - cept their prais - es, ac - cept the prayers we bring,*

D.C.

Who in the Lord's name com - est, the King and bless - ed One!
our praise and prayer and an - thems be - fore Thee we pre - sent:
to Thee, now high ex - alt - ed, our mel - o - dy we raise:
Who in all good de - light - est, Thou good and gra - cious King!

TEXT: Theodulph of Orleans, trans. John Mason Neale   ST. THEODULPH
TUNE: Melchior Teschner

TEXT: Willard F. Jabusch, 1966

b. 1930, Chicago, Illinois
d. December 12, 2018

When Willard Jabusch was in the seventh grade, he watched while a priest visited his dying grandmother. The gravity of the occasion, combined with the man's work of pointing to spiritual realities, prompted Willard to think, "This is something very important, and I want to do this, too."[20] He then studied ministry and music, and was ordained for ministry in 1956. He served in several Midwestern churches and taught in several seminaries. He wrote four books, several articles, and many hymns that are in use today. This hymn, based on Psalm 24, is probably his best known.

TUNE: Israeli folk song,
arr. John Ferguson, 1973

The appeal of this hymn lies in its joyous, minor, syncopated tune, which is similar to the Jewish *hora* dance. It is an Israeli folk tune, probably of Hasidic origin, associated with the folk song *Gilu Hagalilim*, which was brought by Zionist settlers to Israel after World War I.

John Ferguson adapted the folk tune to Jabusch's text and named it PROMISED ONE for the promised Messiah. Ferguson is a well-known organist and composer. He was a professor of music at St. Olaf College from 1983 to 2012.

As you sing this hymn . . . you tell the world to receive the coming Savior, Jesus Christ. The refrain, unusually placed at the hymn's beginning and adapted from Psalm 24:7–10, declares as much: "The King of glory comes . . . Open the gates before Him." The first stanza then asks the important question, "Who is this King of glory?" The following stanzas give answers from the New Testament.

This hymn has been placed in the Lenten section of the hymnal—even though it has an upbeat tune—because it is appropriate for Palm Sunday worship. You can imagine the children standing on the roadside, like children at a parade, on that day when Jesus entered Jerusalem on a donkey. And can you hear them shouting? "Look, here He comes! Who is He? He is the King of glory!"

The syncopated rhythm (the reason you like this song) makes you want to clap and dance. Go ahead! In fact, as in the typical Israeli *hora* dance, you may want to start the tempo more slowly and gradually increase the speed to the end. This is a song of celebration and joy for the triumphant King.

The King of Glory Comes

30

Lift up your heads, O gates! And be lifted up, O ancient doors,
that the King of glory may come in.

PSALM 24:7

TEXT: Based on Psalm 24, Willard F. Jabusch

TUNE: Israeli folk song

PROMISED ONE

Easter   Christ the Lord Is Risen Today

TEXT: Charles Wesley ‖ b. December 18, 1707, Epworth, England
‖ d. March 29, 1788, London
‖ (for more on Wesley, see No. 2, 4, 37, 41, 63, 86, and 103)

If there is a most commonly sung hymn on Easter, in all churches of all denominations, it is "Christ the Lord Is Risen Today." It is easily sung. It is quickly understood and learned. And it resounds with joy and exuberant cheer. When it was first published in 1739, it contained eleven verses. It would be rare to find any hymnal that does not include this wonderful Easter hymn.

Though the hymn was popular, its author, Charles Wesley, was not. Neither was his brother John. They were shunned by many of the Anglican ministers of their day who did not like their evangelistic preaching. A friend of theirs, George Whitefield, was having the same problem. Since he was not welcome in the churches, Whitefield began preaching in the streets and fields and invited John and Charles to join him. This began the "open-air" preaching of the Wesleys, by which they reached thousands with the gospel.

The word "Alleluia," which is the Greek form of the Hebrew "Hallelujah," is generally never used outside of religion. It's preserved for praising God! The Hebrew word means, "Let us praise Yah (God)."

TUNE: *Lyra Davidica*, London, 1708 ‖

During the Middle Ages, singing in the church was largely confined to the clergy. Fortunately, desire for the congregation to sing resulted in the rise of what are called "sequences." The cantor, or song leader, would chant a hymn text. The congregation responded with a sequence, or "Alleluia." This evolved with melismas (multiple notes on the same syllable), which continued to evolve as full texts for the congregation were added. One of the hymns from this period is the Easter carol "Jesus Christ Is Risen Today, Alleluia!" It was first printed in English in the collection *Lyra Davidica* (1708), but in 1739, Wesley added his own text. A similar hymn of Alleluia sequences from this era is "All Creatures of Our God and King."

As you sing this hymn . . . let your voice soar on the Alleluias. If you are singing in a group, sing antiphonally by having someone sing the text, the others singing the Alleluias, and joining together at the end. Think carefully and deeply about all the reasons stated as to why the resurrection is an Alleluia! The final stanza, which begins with the words "Soar we now where Christ has led," paints a glorious picture of the final resurrection when the souls of all those in Christ soar from this earth to our eternal home in heaven. Imagine that! Doesn't it make your heart soar even now? Alleluia!

Christ the Lord Is Risen Today

31

But thanks be to God, who gives us the victory
through our Lord Jesus Christ.

I CORINTHIANS 15:57

1. Christ, the Lord, is ris'n to-day,— Al - le - lu - ia!
2. *Lives a-gain our glo-rious King,— Al - le - lu - ia!*
3. Love's re-deem-ing work is done,— Al - le - lu - ia!
4. *Soar we now where Christ has led,— Al - le - lu - ia!*

Sons of men and an-gels say:— Al - le - lu - ia!
Where, O death, is now thy sting?— Al - le - lu - ia!
Fought the fight, the bat-tle won,— Al - le - lu - ia!
Fol-lowing our ex-alt-ed head,— Al - le - lu - ia!

Raise your joys and tri-umphs high, Al - le - lu - ia!
Dy-ing once He all doth save, Al - le - lu - ia!
Death in vain for-bids Him rise, Al - le - lu - ia!
Made like Him, like Him we rise, Al - le - lu - ia!

Sing, ye—heav'ns and earth re-ply:— Al - le - lu - ia!
Where thy— vic-to-ry, O grave? Al - le - lu - ia!
Christ has— op-ened Par-a-dise,— Al - le - lu - ia!
Ours the— cross, the grave, the skies,— Al - le - lu - ia!

TEXT: Charles Wesley
TUNE: *Lyra Davidica*, 1708

EASTER HYMN

TEXT: Edmond Budrey	b. August 30, 1854, Vevey, Switzerland
	d. November 12, 1932, Vevey, Switzerland

Budrey, a pastor of a free church in Switzerland, wrote this hymn in 1884. It is reported that he was inspired to write it by the death of his wife. Today it is sung at Easter and for funerals. Budrey not only wrote hymns but also translated many others from German, English, and Latin into French, his native tongue. Originally in French, it was translated into English by Richard Hoyle in 1923, for the hymnal of the World's Student Christian Federation, *Cantate Domino*.

TUNE: George Frederick Handel	b. February 23, 1685, Halle, Germany
	d. April 14, 1759, London, England

It was Budrey who chose this triumphant, victorious tune of George Frederick Handel, one of the greatest composers of the Baroque era. It is adapted from a chorus in the oratorio *Judas Maccabeus*, which is why it is called MACCABEUS. In the oratorio the title is "See, the Conquering Hero Comes." Baroque composers like Handel and Bach wrote music that pictured the words, a technique called "word painting." For instance, what direction does the melody move on the word "risen"? Up. What does it do on the word "victory"? It leaps up. With a strong rhythm and harmony, the music alone fairly shouts, "Easter!"

As you sing this hymn . . . picture what the return of a hero looks like. Do you see a parade? A crowd? Celebration, light, and noise? What happy words would sound forth on such an occasion? And what music would be suitable? Triumphant music! "Thine Be the Glory" is a hymn about the resurrection and the glorified Christ. It honors the risen, conquering, victorious Son. So often the resurrection is mentioned only in the last stanza of a hymn, but here an entire hymn exalts the risen Lord who greets us as He rises from the grave.

This hymn tells about a hero greater than any we can imagine, conquering a foe greater than any we can face—sin, death, and hell. It tells of a victory that only God could accomplish through Jesus Christ. Yet, if we are Christians, His victory is our victory. When we sing this hymn, we foreshadow the true celebration that awaits us, a day when the conquering hero will return to earth to complete what He has begun and set all things right.

How do we honor One who has done something no one in history has ever done—rise from the grave to conquer death? By singing with all our might to honor Him and tell the world of this conquering hero! Hallelujah!

Thine Be the Glory

Blessed be the God and Father of our Lord Jesus Christ! According to His great mercy, He has caused us to be born again to a living hope through the resurrection of Jesus Christ from the dead.

I PETER I:3

1. Thine be the glo - ry, ris - en,__ con-qu'ring Son;
2. *Lo! Je - sus meets us, ri - sen__ from the tomb;*
3. No more we doubt Thee, glo - rious Prince of life;

end - less__ is the vic - tory Thou o'er death hast won;
lov - ing - ly He greets us, scat - ters fear and gloom;
life__ is__ naught with - out Thee: aid us in our strife;

an - gels__ in bright rai - ment rolled the stone a - way,
let__ the__ church with glad - ness, hymns of tri - umph sing,
make us__ more than con - qu'rors thro' Thy death-less love;

kept__ the__ fold - ed grave clothes, where Thy bod - y lay.
for__ her__ Lord now liv - eth, death has__ lost its sting.
bring us__ safe to Jor - dan, to Thy__ home a - bove.

Thine be the glo - ry, ris - en,__ con-qu'ring Son;

end - less__ is the vic - tory Thou o'er death hast won.

TEXT: Edmond Budrey
TUNE: George Frederick Handel

MACCABEUS

| TEXT: Samuel Medley | b. June 23, 1738, Cheshunt, Hertfordshire, England |
| | d. July 17, 1799, Liverpool, Lancashire, England |

As a young sailor in the Royal Navy, Samuel Medley led a selfish and sinful life. At the age of twenty-one, he was badly wounded in a sea fight, and a doctor told him that his leg had to be amputated. He knew he didn't deserve God's mercy, but he prayed earnestly. Before the operation, the leg healed, surprising even the doctor. Medley returned home to recuperate, where a godly grandfather read him a sermon by Isaac Watts. He listened at first with indifference; then his heart softened at the grace and mercy of the Lord. Medley fell to his knees, repented, and was converted. He moved to London, where he became a Baptist minister. He also pastored for many years in Liverpool, where his past experiences helped him to minister to many sailors. Medley also wrote over 200 hymns for his church. "I Know That My Redeemer Lives" is one of the most well-known.

The hymn title comes from the story of Job. In the midst of his pain and loss, Job, filled with faith, reflects, "For I know that my Redeemer lives, and at the last He will stand upon the earth" (Job 19:25).

| TUNE: John Hatton | b. Date unknown; christened September 25, 1710, Lancashire, England |
| | d. December, 1793, Lancaster, England |

Very little is known of John Hatton except that he lived on Duke Street in Windle, from which the name of the tune comes. DUKE STREET is one of hymnody's grandest of tunes and is also used for "Jesus Shall Reign."

As you sing this hymn . . . do not take for granted the resurrection of Jesus Christ. If He had not been raised from the dead, our salvation would not exist. All we believe would be a lie. The Bible and all of God's promises would be meaningless. The resurrection is the power of the gospel. Christ, risen from the dead, is our promise that we, too, will live eternally, and that we have a Savior who right now intercedes for us. Look at all of the results of Christ's resurrection in the stanzas of this song. How many can you find? Other stanzas not commonly found in hymnals today list more:

He lives to silence all my fears,
He lives to wipe away my tears;
He lives to calm my troubled heart,
He lives all blessings to impart.
He lives and grants me daily breath;
He lives, and I shall conquer death:
He lives my mansion to prepare;
He lives to bring me safely there.

I Know That My Redeemer Lives

33

For I know that my Redeemer lives,
and at the last He will stand upon the earth.

JOB 19:25

1. I know that my Re - deem - er____ lives!
2. He lives tri - um - phant____ from the____ grave;
3. He lives to bless me____ with His____ love;
4. He lives, my kind, wise,____ heav - enly____ friend;
5. He lives, all glo - ry____ to His____ name!

What joy this blest as - sur - ance gives!
He lives e - ter - nal - ly to save;
He lives to plead for me a - bove;
He lives and loves me to the end;
He lives, my Sav - ior, still the same;

He lives, He lives,____ Who____ once____ was____ dead;
He lives ex - alt - ed,____ throned_ a - bove;
He lives my hun - gry____ soul____ to____ feed;
He lives, and while____ He____ lives,____ I'll____ sing;
what joy this blest____ as - sur - ance____ gives:

He lives, my ev - er - liv - ing Head!
He lives to rule His church in love.
He lives to help in time of need.
He lives, my Proph - et, Priest, and King!
I know that my Re - deem - er lives!

TEXT: Samuel Medley
TUNE: John Hatton

DUKE STREET

TEXT AND TUNE: Stuart Townend, Keith Getty, and Kristyn Getty
(for more on Gettys and Townend, see No. 12, 26, 62, 65, and 99) ||

In 1995, Keith Getty earned his advanced music degree from Durham University in northeast England, which included rare conducting opportunities at the Canford Summer School of Music in 1994 and in 1995 at the Tanglewood Music Center, home of the Boston Symphony in Massachusetts. Keith was introduced to his wife, Kristyn, by her uncle, John Lennox, an esteemed professor and author at Oxford University. Kristyn graduated from Queen's University, Belfast, and is a singer and lyricist. They began to write songs together and were married on June 16, 2004. Keith and Kristyn and family divide their time between homes in both the United States and Northern Ireland. Much of their time is spent on concert tours with Kristyn as vocal soloist and Keith accompanying and leading an ensemble of top instrumentalists in Irish and American folk music. They introduce their hymns and encourage the audience to learn them and sing along.

As you sing this hymn . . . recognize there is one word that makes all the difference in how you will accept the invitation to come—the word *risen*. If Jesus had not risen from the dead, why would we come to sing about Him? The apostle Paul said, "And if Christ has not been raised, then our preaching is in vain and your faith is in vain" (1 Cor. 15:14). So this is an invitation to celebrate Easter, but we should sing it year-round! As much as any glorious truth about God, the resurrection should cause us to sing the chorus: "Rejoice!"

Stuart Townend says the following about this hymn:

> It's so easy for us, especially after a difficult week, to be so aware of our failures, our weaknesses and our disappointments that we 'keep our distance' from God, feeling like we don't deserve to enjoy His closeness or experience His love. At this point we need to remember that we can NEVER come to God on the basis of our own worth–we ALWAYS come on the basis of what Christ has done. It is His righteousness, His total obedience that ushers us into the Father's presence and enables us to enjoy all the blessings that Jesus deserves because we are "in Christ."[21]

As you sing this hymn, imagine every Christian of every church around the world singing along with you. Now try to imagine every Christian from all centuries past and future singing together in heaven, "our God is all in all!" It's unimaginable!

Come, People of the Risen King

34

But let all who take refuge in You rejoice; let them ever sing for joy
. . . that those who love Your name may exult in You.

PSALM 5:11

1. Come, peo - ple of the ri - sen King, who de - light to bring Him praise.
2. *Come, those whose joy is morn - ing sun and those weep - ing through the night;*
3. Come, young and old from ev - ery land, men and wo - men of the faith.

Come, all and tune your hearts to sing to the Morn - ing Star of grace.
come, those who tell of bat - tles won, and those strug - gling in the fight.
Come, those with full or emp - ty hands, find the rich - es of His grace.

From the shift - ing shad-ows of the earth we will lift our eyes to Him,
For His per - fect love will nev - er change, and His mer - cies nev - er cease,
Ov - er all the world His peo - ple sing, shore to shore we hear them call,

where stea - dy arms of mer - cy reach to___ ga - ther chil-dren in.
but fol - low us through all our days with the cer - tain hope of peace.
the truth that cries through ev - ery age; "Our___ God is all in all."

Re - joice! Re - joice! Let ev - 'ry tongue re - joice!___

One heart, one voice; O Church of Christ, re - joice!

TEXT AND TUNE: Stuart Townend,
Kristyn Getty, Keith Getty

TEXT AND TUNE: Natalie Sleeth   ‖ b. October 29, 1939, Evanston, Illinois
d. March 21, 1992, Denver, Colorado

Natalie Sleeth began piano lessons at the age of four. She kept on going, all the way through a music degree from Wellesley College, then an honorary doctorate from West Virginia Wesleyan College. With over 180 published works, she is considered one of the twentieth century's most beloved composers for children. She worked for many years at Highland Park United Methodist Church in Dallas, Texas.

This hymn about the resurrection is probably her best known, appearing in at least twelve hymnals. Natalie wrote about its inspiration:

> I [was] pondering the death of a friend (life and death, death and
> resurrection), pondering winter and spring (seeming opposites), and a
> T. S. Eliot poem which had the phrase, 'In our end is our beginning.'
> These seemingly contradictory 'pairs' led to the thesis of the song and
> the hopeful message that out of one will come the other whenever God
> chooses to bring that about.[22]

Her husband, Dr. Ronald Sleeth, a professor of homiletics, first heard his wife's hymn shortly before his death and asked that it be sung at his funeral.

The tune has a wonderful name: PROMISE. Unlike many older hymns which begin as poems written by one person and are then joined with music composed by another, sometimes years apart, this tune was written by Mrs. Sleeth for her text.

As you sing this hymn . . . you will notice many riddles or ironies. Is there actually a flower in a bulb, or a tree in a seed? If you didn't already know, would you guess that beautiful flowers would grow from dry, brown bulbs? Would you expect that a large tree could grow from a tiny seed? How amazing is God's creation!

Yet even more remarkable is the fact that God means to reveal something about our lives and salvation through these very things. A seed must first go into the ground and die, said Jesus. It appears that God has left clues for understanding eternal life and death within the very fabric of nature.

Consider all the opposites: song/silence, dawn/darkness, past/future, doubt/believing. It is the last opposite that tells us what the song is about: "in our end is our beginning, at the last a victory." What is the meaning of this phrase? It is through our earthly death that we gain eternal life with God. Hallelujah!

Hymn of Promise

Behold! I tell you a mystery . . . we shall all be changed.

I CORINTHIANS 15:51

1. In the bulb there is a flow - er; in the seed, an ap - ple tree;
2. There's a song in ev - ery si - lence, seek-ing word and mel - o - dy;
3. In our end is our be - gin - ning; in our time, in - fin - i - ty;

in co - coons, a hid-den prom - ise: but - ter - flies will soon be free!
there's a dawn in ev - ery dark - ness bring-ing hope to you and me.
in our doubt there is be - liev - ing; in our life, e - ter - ni - ty;

In the cold and snow of win - ter there's a spring that waits to be,
From the past will come the fu - ture; what it holds, a mys - ter - y,
in our death, a res - ur - rec - tion; at the last, a vic - to - ry,

un - re - vealed un - til its sea - son, some-thing God a - lone can see.
un - re - vealed un - til its sea - son, some - thing God a - lone can see.
un - re - vealed un - til its sea - son, some-thing God a - lone can see.

TEXT AND TUNE: Natalie Sleeth   PROMISE

Pentecost Spirit of God, Descend upon My Heart

TEXT: George Croly || b. August 17, 1780, Dublin, Ireland
d. November 24, 1860, Holborn, England

George Croly was the son of a doctor. But he chose a different vocational path, and upon graduating from the University of Dublin was ordained as a minister. At the age of thirty, he began to pastor a small church in London. He eventually became known for his excellent poems, novels, biographies, and plays. Much to his surprise, his book *Salathiel* became a popular bestseller. He would say, "To look at me you would not think me capable of writing a sensational book, would you now?"[23]

Croly was asked to reopen a church in the poorest area of London that had closed one hundred years before. His preaching soon attracted large crowds. In a hymnal he prepared for his congregation, this hymn appears. It was titled "Holiness Desired."

TUNE: Frederick Atkinson || b. August 21, 1841, Norfolk, England
d. November 30, 1896, Norfolk, England

Frederick Atkinson originally wrote this melody for the hymn "Abide with Me." It is named MORECAMBE after a town on Morecambe Bay in western England near where Atkinson grew up. Like many church musicians in the United Kingdom, Atkinson received his first musical training in a boys' choir. He was a chorister at Norwich Cathedral. He later graduated from Cambridge University and became the organist and choir director in several churches. He also composed sacred music for chorus, piano, and organ.

As you sing this hymn . . . you learn about the purpose and work of the third member of the Trinity, the Holy Spirit. Very few hymns are written directly to Him. Here you find not only what He does, but also what He does not do. He works to draw us toward God and away from our love for worldliness. Stanza 2 teaches that we don't need to seek after dramatic experiences. Instead, the Holy Spirit works within us, turning on God's light so that we can begin discerning the true nature of things. He helps us to seek and find God, and then to cling to Him. When we feel far from God, or fear He doesn't hear our prayers, the Holy Spirit brings God's comfort, offering to God "groanings too deep for words . . . according to the will of God" (Rom. 8:26–27).

You will spend a lifetime learning about the work of the Holy Spirit, but this hymn provides an excellent start. The last line offers one of the most beautiful figures of speech in hymnody: "My heart an altar, and Thy love, the flame." As you give your heart to God and ask Him to be the Lord of your life, His Holy Spirit enflames it with love for Him, His good and perfect will, and His glory.

Spirit of God, Descend upon My Heart   36

If we live by the Spirit, let us also keep in step with the Spirit.

GALATIANS 5:25

1. Spir - it of God, de - scend up - on my heart;
2. *I ask no dream, no proph - et ec - sta - sies,*
3. Hast Thou not bid us love Thee, God and King,
4. *Teach me to feel that Thou art al - ways nigh;*
5. Teach me to love Thee as Thine an - gels love,

wean it from earth, through all its puls - es move;
no sud - den rend - ing of the veil of clay,
all, all Thine own, soul, heart and strength and mind?
teach me the strug - gles of the soul to bear,
one ho - ly pas - sion fill - ing all my frame;

stoop to my weak - ness, might - y as Thou art,
no an - gel vis - i - tant, no o - p'ning skies;
I see Thy cross, there teach my heart to cling:
to check the ris - ing doubt, the reb - el sigh;
the bap - tism of the heav'n - de - scend - ed Dove,

and make me love Thee as I ought to love.
but take the dim - ness of my soul a - way.
O let me seek Thee, and O let me find.
teach me the pa - tience of un - an - swered prayer.
my heart an al - tar, and Thy love the flame.

TEXT: George Croly
TUNE: Frederick Atkinson

MORECAMBE

Pentecost Love Divine, All Loves Excelling

TEXT: Charles Wesley

b. December 18, 1707, Epworth, England
d. March 29, 1788, London, England
(for more on Wesley, see No. 2, 4, 31, 41, 63, 86, and 103)

Charles Wesley was the eighteenth child born into the family of Samuel and Susanna Wesley. He was born prematurely and was not expected to live, but God had plans for him. Wesley was homeschooled and then attended Westminster School and Oxford University, where he received a master's degree in classical languages and literature. In 1735, he travelled as a missionary to America with his older brother John, but only later came to understand what it meant to be a Christian. Wesley rode on horseback and preached all over England and America. He carried note cards in his pocket and wrote down ideas for hymns as he went. He is credited with writing over 6,000 hymns.

TUNE: John Zundel

b. December 10, 1815, Hochdorf, Germany
d. July 1882, Cannstadt, Germany

John Zundel composed the tune BEECHER in 1870. He was the organist at the Pilgrim Congregational Church of Brooklyn, New York. His minister was the famous Henry Ward Beecher, for whom Zundel named this tune.

As you sing this hymn . . . you are singing about the process of sanctification, which is God's work to make us holy and complete. Sanctification begins when we become Christians; it ends when we are in heaven. Follow the progression: Stanza 1 describes becoming a Christian. The word *visit* used here is stronger than we think of it today. It means to come and stay, correct, and protect. Psalm 106:4 uses it in this same way: "O visit me with thy salvation" (KJV). Stanza 2 asks the Holy Spirit to free us from sin: "Take away our bent to sinning . . . set our hearts at liberty." The third stanza speaks of delivering us throughout life as we "glory in Thy perfect love." The fourth stanza asks God to "finish" His new creation work in us. The final phrase of the hymn anticipates that incredible moment when all the praises in all the hymns in all the hymnals of the world will culminate: "Till we cast our crowns before Thee, lost in wonder, love, and praise!"

Just before returning to heaven, Jesus prayed for all believers, "Sanctify them in the truth; Your word is truth"(John 17:17). Jesus wants His children to become holy in an unholy world. Read the entire prayer in John 17 to see what Jesus asks God to do for you, if you are a Christian. He wants your heart to be like His. He wants you to be not only saved from sin, but also freed from the power of sin. Such sanctification is the proof that we belong to God, and this hymn is your personal prayer that God would continue the work of proving you are His.

Love Divine, All Loves Excelling   37

And I am sure of this, that He who began a good work in you will
bring it to completion at the day of Jesus Christ.

PHILIPPIANS 1:6

1. Love di - vine, all loves ex - cel - ling, Joy of heav'n to earth come down:
2. *Breathe, O breathe Thy lov - ing__ Spir - it in - to ev - 'ry trou - bled__ breast;*
3. Come, Al-might -y to de - liv - er, let us all Thy life re - ceive;
4. *Fin - ish then, Thy new cre - a - tion; pure and spot - less let us__ be:*

    fix in us Thy hum - ble__dwell-ing, all Thy faith-ful mer - cies__crown.
    let us all in Thee in - her - it, let us find the prom - ised__ rest.
    sud-den - ly re - turn, and__ nev - er, nev - er-more Thy tem - ples__ leave.
    let us see Thy great sal - va - tion per - fect - ly re - stored in__ Thee;

    Je - sus,Thou art all com - pas - sion, pure, un-bound-ed love Thou art,
    Take a - way our bent to__ sin - ning, Al - pha and O - me - ga__ be,
    Thee we would be al - ways bless-ing, serve Thee as Thy hosts a - bove,
    changed from glo - ry in - to__ glo - ry, till in heav'n we take our__place,

    vis - it us with Thy sal - va - tion, en - ter ev - ery trem - bling heart.
    end of faith, as its be - gin - ning, set our hearts at lib - er - ty.
    pray, and praise Thee with - out__ ceas-ing, glo - ry in Thy per - fect__ love.
    till we cast our crowns be - fore Thee, lost in won - der, love, and__praise.

TEXT: Charles Wesley   BEECHER
TUNE: John Zundel

Lord, You have been our dwelling place in all generations.
Before the mountains were brought forth,
or ever You had formed the earth and the world,
from everlasting to everlasting You are God.

PSALM 90:1–2

God Is

TRINITY

KING

SOVEREIGN

CREATOR

I AM

OMNIPOTENT

FAITHFUL

SHEPHERD

THE WORD

SAVIOR

LOVE

OUR HOPE

PROTECTOR

TEXT: Reginald Heber ‖ b. April 21, 1783, Cheshire, England
d. April 3, 1826, Trichinopoly, India

The poet Alfred, Lord Tennyson called this the world's greatest hymn.[24] Erik Routley called it a complete theology of the Trinity.[25]

Reginald Heber was born into an ancient Yorkshire family and was Oxford-educated. He lived in the time when English Romantic poetry was blossoming. Surrounded by the beautiful lines of Wordsworth, Coleridge, Shelley, Keats, and Byron, Heber wrote fifty-seven poems, most of which remain in print today, a tribute to his skill.

Heber could read the Bible fluently at the age of five; his command of it astonished his parents. After winning a prize for his poem on Palestine when he was seventeen, his parents found him on his knees in fervent prayer. Heber loved Christian missions, as expressed in his hymn "From Greenland's Icy Mountains." After ministering as a pastor for many years at a local parish, he pursued his love for missions by moving to India at the age of forty. He died there two years later after preaching to a large crowd one afternoon in the hot sun. After his death, his widow discovered his hymns in a trunk and compiled them in a book she entitled *Hymns Written and Adapted to the Weekly Service of the Church Year*. Among those poems was "Holy, Holy, Holy."

TUNE: John B. Dykes ‖ b. March 10, 1823, Hull, England
d. January 22, 1876, Sussex, England

In 1861, a publisher rediscovered Heber's poem and challenged Dykes to write a tune. John had been a church organist since he was ten years old. He was cofounder and president of the Cambridge University Musical Society. Within thirty minutes of receiving the challenge, he wrote NICAEA, named after the Nicene Creed, an early church creed that affirms the Trinity's doctrine.

As you sing this hymn . . . count the series of threes. Without naming the Father, Son, and Spirit, "Holy, Holy, Holy" creates a picture of the Trinity. You will find three "Holies," three names (Lord, God, Almighty), three worshippers (saints, cherubim, seraphim), three places (earth, sky, sea), three divine perfections (power, love, purity), three times (wert, art, evermore), and the first three notes that form a triad (D, F#, A).

This hymn describes a God of such perfect purity that standing before Him would cause us to fall down in fear. Our sin, too, creates darkness, so we cannot fully see Him. Yet we sing with joy that He is merciful. How wonderful that our holy God is also perfect in love—which casts out fear! This high and holy God is *transcendent* (standing above) but also *immanent* (close), inviting us to worship and love Him.

Holy, Holy, Holy

38

"Holy, holy, holy, is the Lord God Almighty, who was and is and is to come!"
. . . [And the elders] cast their crowns before the throne.

REVELATION 4:8, 10

1. Ho - ly, ho - ly, ho - ly! Lord__ God Al - might - y!
   Ear - ly in the morn - ing our song shall rise to Thee.
   Ho - ly, ho - ly, ho - ly! Mer - ci - ful and might - y!
   God in three Per - sons, bless - ed Trin - i - ty.

2. *Ho - ly, ho - ly, ho - ly! All the saints a - dore Thee,*
   cast - ing down their gold - en crowns a - round the glass - y sea;
   cher - u - bim and ser - a - phim fall - ing down be - fore Thee,
   Who wert and art, and ev - er - more shalt be.

3. Ho - ly, ho - ly, ho - ly! Though the dark-ness hide Thee,
   though the eye of sin - ful man Thy glo - ry may not see,
   on - ly Thou art ho - ly; there is none be - side Thee
   per - fect in pow'r, in love, and pur - i - ty.

4. *Ho - ly, ho - ly, ho - ly! Lord__ God Al - might - y!*
   All Thy works shall praise Thy name, in earth, and sky, and sea.
   Ho - ly, ho - ly, ho - ly! Mer - ci - ful and might - y!
   God in three Per - sons, bless - ed Trin - i - ty!

TEXT: Reginald Heber
TUNE: John B. Dykes

NICAEA

Trinity   Holy God, We Praise Your Name

TEXT: Attributed to Ignaz Franz,   b. October 12, 1719, Protzau, Schlesien (Silesia)
trans. Clarence Walworth (1829–1900)   d. August 19, 1790, Breslau, Silesia

The words of this hymn are based on the *Te Deum laudamus*, a text that has been used as a worship liturgy by Christians since the fourth century—for over 1,600 years! It means "Thee, O God, we praise." The first *Te Deum* was dated AD 387 and is attributed to Bishop Ambrose in Milan, Italy, a prominent figure in the early development of church music. Paraphrases were written in many languages through the centuries, including this one, believed to have been written in German by Ignaz Franz, a Roman Catholic priest. He was author of ten books, perhaps the most important one being the hymnal *Katholisches Gesangbuch* (ca. 1774). It was translated by an American priest, Clarence Walworth, in 1853.

The fourth stanza strongly affirms the doctrine of the Trinity. A fourth-century priest named Arius (ca. AD 250–336) had taught that the Son was not fully divine but was the first of the Father's creations. Therefore, claimed Arius, He should not be worshipped as God. This view became known as Arianism, which the Council of Nicaea condemned as heresy. This hymn text affirms clearly that all three—Father, Son, and Holy Spirit—are divine persons who are to be worshipped as one God.

TUNE: *Katholisches Gesangbuch*, Vienna, 1774

Grosser Gott, Wir Loben Dich, German for *Te Deum laudamus*, first appeared in *Katholisches Gesangbuch*. Most hymn tunes are sixteen measures in length. This one is extended to twenty-four by repeating the first eight. The result is a gloriously majestic musical setting that pictures the triumphant procession of all the saints through the ages approaching the throne of God and waiting only for the church to finish the song. It presents an example of an excellent marriage between text and tune.

As you sing this hymn . . . picture standing before the throne of the Most High God. The prophets are there; the apostles are there; believers from every nation and century are there. Add to this all of the angels. How much sound does it take to "fill the heavens"? It's unimaginable! We will see God as we could never see Him on earth. All the nations in all their diversity will be unified in one song, sung in one language, joined by the angelic host. We will sing of His holiness, His reign over every dominion, and the marvelous mystery of the Holy Trinity.

Earth but prepares us for heaven. So let this hymn be your rehearsal. Let these words bind your heart together with all those whom God has called. Bend the knee—humble yourself as you sing this great and ancient *Te Deum*.

Holy God, We Praise Your Name

39

Above Him stood the seraphim. . . . And one called to another and said:
"Holy, holy, holy is the LORD of hosts; the whole earth is full of His glory!"

ISAIAH 6:2–3

1. Ho - ly God, we praise Your name.
2. Hark, the loud ce - les - tial hymn
3. Lo! the ap - os - tol - ic train
4. Ho - ly Fa - ther, Ho - ly Son,

Lord of all, we bow be - fore You.
an - gel choirs a - bove are rais - ing:
join Your sa - cred name to hal - low;
Ho - ly Spir - it, Three we name You;

All on earth Your scep - ter claim,
cher - u - bim and ser - a - phim
proph - ets swell the glad re - frain,
while in es - sence on - ly One,

all in heav'n a - bove a - dore You.
in un - ceas - ing cho - rus prais - ing,
and the white - robed mar - tyrs fol - low:
un - di - vid - ed God we claim You,

In - fi - nite Your vast do - main,
fill the heav'ns with sweet ac - cord:
and from morn to set of sun,
and a - dor - ing bend the knee,

ev - er - last - ing is Your reign.
"Ho - ly, ho - ly, ho - ly Lord."
through the Church the song goes on.
while we sing this mys - ter - y.

TEXT: Based on the *Te Deum*, 4th c., attr. to Ignaz Franz

GROSSER GOTT, WIR LOBEN DICH

TUNE: *Katholisches Gesangbuch*, ca. 1774

Trinity   Come, Thou Almighty King

TEXT: Anonymous

This hymn appeared in George Whitefield's *Hymn Book* (1757), with the author listed as "Unknown." Some believe that Charles Wesley wrote it in response to the song newly written for the English monarch, "God Save Our Gracious King," to remind people that God is the *true* King. This theory is supported by the fact that the two songs were originally sung to the same tune (which Americans know as "My Country, 'Tis of Thee").

There is a story from the Revolutionary War that tells of a band of British soldiers who entered a colonial American church one Sunday morning and demanded that the people sing allegiance to the King of England with "God Save Our Gracious King." The people responded by singing the right tune, but with the words from "Come, Thou Almighty King."

TUNE: Felice de Giardini

b. April 12, 1716, Turin, Italy
d. June 8, 1796, Moscow, Russia

Felice de Giardini was born in Italy in the Baroque era. He sang in a boys' choir in Milan and learned to play violin. He was a popular solo violinist and composer and had a very successful tour of Europe. This brought him to England, where he worked for the Duke of Gloucester and was commissioned to write the tune for this text. He named it ITALIAN HYMN. Sadly, his success did not last. At the age of eighty, he moved to Moscow, Russia, where he died in poverty.

Curiously, three times the melody outlines a triad chord. There is a descending triad twice *(sol-mi-do)* and an ascending triad once *(do-mi-sol)*. Is it possible that Giardini composed it as a word-painting to illustrate the Trinity?

As you sing this hymn . . . you will learn about the doctrine of the Trinity. The first three stanzas name and describe each of the persons of the Godhead. The Father is the Almighty King who reigns over all. The Son is the Incarnate Word, God in the flesh who hears and answers our prayers. The Holy Spirit comes to us as the Holy Comforter. He is the witness of God who remains with us in the world today. The fourth verse summarizes the first three: "To Thee, great One in Three." The wonder of the Trinity is that all three are One, yet distinctively deserving of our love and adoration. Therefore, when we sing this hymn, we must always sing all of the verses. Please, never leave one stanza out!

Come, Thou Almighty King

40

*The grace of the Lord Jesus Christ and the love of God and the
fellowship of the Holy Spirit be with you all.*

2 CORINTHIANS 13:14

1. Come, Thou Al - might - y King, help us Thy
2. *Come, Thou In - car - nate Word,* *gird on Thy*
3. Come, Ho - ly Com - fort - er, Thy sa - cred
4. *To Thee, great One in Three,* *e - ter - nal*

name to sing, help us to praise:
might - y sword, *our prayer at - tend:*
wit - ness bear in this glad hour:
prais - es be hence, ev - er - more!

Fa - ther, all glo - ri - ous, o'er all vic - to - ri - ous,
come, and Thy peo - ple bless, and give Thy Word suc - cess:
Thou who al - might - y art, now rule in ev - ery heart,
Thy sov - ereign maj - es - ty may we in glo - ry see,

come and reign o - ver us, An - cient of Days.
Spir - it of ho - li - ness, on us de - scend.
and ne'er from us de - part, Spir - it of power.
and to e - ter - ni - ty love and a - dore.

TEXT: Source unknown, ca. 1757

TUNE: Felice de Giardini

ITALIAN HYMN

King   Rejoice, the Lord Is King

TEXT: Charles Wesley

b. December 18, 1707, Epworth, England
d. March 29, 1788, London, England
(for more on Wesley, see No. 2, 4, 31, 37, 63, 86, and 103)

Charles Wesley and his brother John are known for starting a movement in England called "the Methodist movement," which today remains one of the largest Christian denominations. They were called Methodists because they did everything according to strict rules, or methodically. However, the state Church of England did not like this new group and severely persecuted them. Wesley wrote hymns to help these believers survive and even grow through their hardships by singing praises. This text encourages its singers in the same way that the apostle Paul, sitting in prison, encouraged his Philippian readers: "Rejoice in the Lord always; again I will say, rejoice" (Phil. 4:4).

Thomas Jackson, Wesley's biographer, says of him, "In the composition of hymns, adapted to Christian worship, he certainly has no equal in the English language, and is perhaps superior to every other uninspired man that ever lived. It does not appear that any person besides himself, in any section of the universal church, has either written so many hymns, or hymns of such surpassing excellence."[26]

TUNE: John Darwall

Baptized on January 13, 1731, Haughton, Staffordshire, England
d. December 18, 1789, Walsall, West Midlands, England
(for more on Darwall, see No. 87)

This tune was originally called DARWALL'S 148TH because it was written by John Darwall and was sung to Psalm 148. Darwall, an English pastor, composer, and poet, was considered only an amateur musician. The tune's unusual melody ends with an ascending octave scale, a picture of lifting our praise heavenward.

As you sing this hymn . . . follow the opening melody upward and consider where it lands in each of the four verses: on the words "King," "reigns," "not fail," and "hope!" The upward ascent is telling us to lift our hearts and voices to God at all times, even when life is hard. Our courage comes because we know the King who reigns, who never fails, and who gives us hope. He even owns the keys that release us from death and hell! His Kingdom cannot and will not fail. Ultimately, He will come and take us home. Are you discouraged about anything in life? Look upward to God. Then sing this joyful melody with its powerful words of promise.

Rejoice, the Lord Is King

*Sing to the LORD a new song . . . Let Israel be glad in his Maker;
let the children of Zion rejoice in their King!*

PSALM 149:1–2

1. Re - joice, the Lord is King! Your Lord and King a - dore!
2. *Je - sus the Sav - ior reigns, the God of truth and love;*
3. His King-dom can - not fail, He rules o'er earth and heaven;
4. *Re - joice in glo - rious hope! Our Lord, the Judge, shall come,*

Re - joice, give thanks, and sing, and tri - umph ev - er - more.
when He had purged our stains, He took His seat a - bove.
the keys of death and hell are to our Je - sus giv'n.
and take His ser - vants up to their e - ter - nal home.

Lift up your heart, lift up your voice! Re -

joice, a - gain I say, *(melody)* re - joice!

TEXT: Charles Wesley

TUNE: John Darwall

DARWALL

King   All Hail the Power of Jesus' Name!

| TEXT: Edward Perronet; | b. 1726, Kent, England |
| John Rippon, stanza 5 | d. 1792, Kent, England |

Edward Perronet wrote other hymns, but it is for this one that he is called "the bird of a single song."[27] It has been called the "National Anthem of Christendom." Perronet's grandparents had fled from France to England for religious freedom. Perronet and his father, a vicar (minister), were devoted to the Church of England until they were drawn to the revivals of George Whitefield and the Wesleys. They left the established church and joined the evangelical movement, even though it meant enduring opposition. Opponents of the gospel once threw Perronet from his horse and rolled him in the mud.

There is a wonderful story connected with this hymn that involves a missionary to India named E. P. Scott. With his violin under his arm, Scott traveled to a certain violent tribe. Many had warned him not to go. When he arrived at their village, a large party of tribesmen surrounded him and pointed their spears at his heart. Assuming he would die at any moment, he took out his violin, closed his eyes, and began playing and singing this hymn. At the words "every kindred, every tribe," he opened his eyes to see spears lowered and tears in the eyes of the tribesmen. Scott remained with them for the next two and a half years and led many to Christ.[28]

| TUNE: Oliver Holden | b. September 18, 1765, Shirley, Massachusetts |
| | d. September 4, 1844, Charlestown, Massachusetts |

In 1793, Holden, a carpenter, realtor, music educator, legislator, and pastor in Charlestown, Massachusetts, composed this melody and called it CORONATION. A coronation is the occasion for placing a crown upon the head of a king or queen. Holden was also known for writing the music which was played to receive George Washington on his visit to Boston in 1789. As Holden neared death in 1844, he said, "Such beautiful themes! Such beautiful themes! But I can write no more."[29]

As you sing this hymn . . . picture in your mind's eye a coronation attended by every Christian believer who has ever lived. Add all the angels and heavenly beings to the picture. They all join in this great cry of acclamation to Jesus as each lays crowns before Him. Everyone praises Him because He created everything, sacrificed everything, loved and redeemed His own, and rules forever. He is crowned King of kings and Lord of lords. Do you picture yourself there? If you belong to Christ through repentance and faith, you will be! This hymn is known as the church's great coronation hymn. It has been said that Christians will sing this hymn as long as there are Christians on earth, and after that, it will be sung in heaven.

All Hail the Power of Jesus' Name!   42

He has a name written, King of kings and Lord of lords.

REVELATION 19:16

1. All hail the pow'r of Je - sus' name! Let an - gels pros-trate fall;
2. *Ye cho - sen seed of Is - rael's race, ye ran - somed from the fall,*
3. Sin - ners whose love can ne'er for - get the worm-wood and the gall,
4. *Let ev - ery kin - dred ev - ery tribe, on this ter - res - tial ball,*
5. O that with yon - der sa - cred throng we at His feet may fall!

bring forth the ro - yal di - a - dem, and crown Him
hail Him who saved you by His grace and crown Him
go, spread your tro - phies at His feet and crown Him
to Him all maj - es - ty a - scribe, and crown Him
We'll join the ev - er - last - ing song, and crown Him

Lord of all; bring forth the ro - yal di - a - dem,
Lord of all; hail Him Who saves you by His grace,
Lord of all; go spread your tro - phies at His feet
Lord of all; to Him all maj - es - ty a - scribe
Lord of all; we'll join the ev - er - last - ing song,

and crown Him Lord of all!

TEXT: Edward Perronet   CORONATION
TUNE: Oliver Holden

King   Crown Him with Many Crowns

TEXT: Matthew Bridges   b. July 14, 1800, Essex, England
d. October 6, 1894, Quebec, Canada

In early nineteenth-century England, there was much conflict between Roman Catholic and Anglican churches. But with this hymn they found something they both liked. Matthew Bridges was born into the Anglican Church. As a gifted poet and author, he published a hymnal in 1847. At one point he wrote a book condemning Catholic theology, but at age forty-eight he converted to the Roman Church. Three years later (1851) he wrote "Crown Him with Many Crowns," which he titled "The Song of the Seraphs," based on Revelation 19:12.

Godfrey Thring (1823–1903), an Anglican clergyman, said that some of Bridges' six original verses were not appropriate for a Protestant service and asked Bridges if he could add more. Bridges wrote another six. Today, you will discover various versions of the hymn, depending on the hymnal you are using.

TUNE: Sir George J. Elvey   b. March 27, 1816, Canterbury, England
d. December 9, 1893, Windlesham, Surrey, England
(for more on Elvey, see No. 93)

This tune was written for this text and first published in 1868. The name DIADEMATA comes from *diadem*, a Latin word for a crown worn by royalty. The composer, Sir George Elvey, also wrote the tune for "Come, Ye Thankful People, Come." Mr. Elvey was born into a musical family and received his training in the boys' choir of Canterbury Cathedral and later at the Royal Academy of Music. For over fifty years, he served as organist and Master of the Boys at St. George's Chapel in Windsor, England. He was knighted in 1871 for writing *Festival March*, which was played at the wedding of the Princess Louise. You can hear a royal march in this hymn tune as well.

As you sing this hymn . . . think of the common expression, "so-and-so wears many hats." It means a person has many roles or jobs. So we learn about Jesus with this hymn. It declares Him to be the Lamb on the throne, the Lord of love, the Lord of peace, the Lord of life, and the Potentate of time (a potentate is someone with unquestionable authority). Revelation 19:12 says that on Christ's head are many diadems, indicating that He is King of kings and Lord of lords. The question for you is, Do you crown Him as your Savior and King? Do you acknowledge that He is worthy of all your praise, honor, and obedience?

Crown Him with Many Crowns

43

His eyes are like a flame of fire, and on His head are many diadems.

REVELATION 19:12

1. Crown Him with man - y crowns, the Lamb up - on His throne;
2. *Crown Him the Lord of love; be - hold His hands and side,*
3. Crown Him the Lord of peace; whose pow'r a scep - ter sways
4. *Crown Him the Lord of life, Who tri - umphed o'er the grave.*
5. Crown Him the Lord of years, the Po - ten - tate of time;

hark! how the heav'n-ly an - them_drowns all mu - sic but its own:
rich wounds, yet vis - i - ble a - bove, in beau - ty glo - ri - fied:
from pole to pole, that wars may_ cease ab -sorbed in prayer and praise:
Who rose vic - to - rious in the__ strife for those He came to save.
Cre - a - tor of the roll - ing_spheres, in - ef - fa - bly sub - lime:

a - wake, my soul, and sing of Him who died for thee,
no an - gels in the sky can ful - ly bear that sight,
His reign shall know no end; and round His pierc - ed feet
His glo - ries now we sing, Who died and rose on high,
All hail, Re - deem - er, hail! for Thou hast died for me:

and hail Him as thy match-less King through all e - ter - ni - ty.
but down - ward bend their burn - ing eyes at mys - ter - ies so bright.
fair flow'rs of par - a - dise ex -tend their fra-grance ev - er sweet.
Who died e - ter - nal life to bring, and lives that death may die.
Thy praise shall ne - ver, ne - ver fail through - out e - ter - ni - ty.

TEXT: Matthew Bridges
TUNE: George J. Elvey

DIADEMATA

King Christ Triumphant, Ever Reigning

TEXT: Michael Saward   ‖   b. May 14, 1932, Blackheath, Kent, England
d. January 31, 2015, Switzerland

An Anglican minister and hymn writer, Saward was one of the founders of Jubilate Hymns (see "O God Beyond All Praising"). He was an author, journalist, hymn writer, broadcaster, and lecturer. Of his poetry he said, "My style is deliberately punchy and I love to use strong, graphic illustration."[30] An example of this is in stanza 3, where with a burst of fourteen strong words he describes the passion of Christ. Of his nearly one hundred hymns, this hymn is the most well-known.

TUNE: John Barnard   ‖   b. 1948, London, England

The tune GUITING POWER was written by a German teacher who is also a professional musician: an organist, choral director, and composer, particularly of hymn tunes. His tunes are generally named after towns or villages in the United Kingdom, like GUITING POWER, which is a village in the Cotswolds. This melody is quite unusual and not easily sung because of its angularity and leaps. The melody covers an octave and a fourth. Like the text, it is a bold, confident, even courageous declaration of the King. In the refrain the tune uses a compositional technique known as word painting—where the melody paints a description of the words—as on the word *high*, the melody leaps up to the highest note of the entire tune.

As you sing this hymn . . . do not sing it casually. Some hymns permit a casual tone; you can sing them under a tree, lying on your back ("This Is My Father's World"); you can skip rope to some ("Blessed Assurance"). But to sing "Christ Triumphant" is to unwrap a package or open a series of windows to discover something wonderful to shout about! Each stanza peels back the layers of the verses as they declare both Christ's attributes and His actions. The stanzas are compounding lists of who Christ is, what happened to Him, and how we are impacted by Him, ending in the repeating refrain, "Yours [is] the glory, crown, high renown, and eternal name." *Renown* means fame. Christ's fame is the highest, the most enduring, the most honoring, the loudest, and the longest acclaim of anyone who has ever been or ever will be on earth. His name will never fade from the earth—it is eternal.

As you sing, imagine being in a grand cathedral, packed to the rafters with worshippers, accompanied by a roaring pipe organ, blasting brass, and thunderous timpani. Everyone is singing his very loudest. As the last note cuts off, the sound continues to reverberate for many seconds. This is triumphant! The King is here. For all ages, we will ceaselessly gaze upon Him and sing!

Christ Triumphant, Ever Reigning

44

Give glory and honor and thanks to Him
who is seated on the throne, who lives forever and ever.

REVELATION 4:9

1. Christ tri - um- phant, ev - er reign- ing, Sav - ior, Mas - ter, King!
2. *Word in - car - nate, truth re - veal - ing, Son of Man on earth!*
3. Suffer - ing Ser - vant, scorned, ill- treat - ed, vic - tim cru - ci - fied!
4. *Priest - ly King, en - throned for - ev - er high in heaven a - bove!*
5. So, our hearts and voic - es rais - ing through the a - ges long,

Lord of heaven, our lives sus - tain - ing, hear us as we sing:
power and maj - es - ty con - ceal - ing by Your hum - ble birth:
Death is through the cross de - feat - ed, sin - ners jus - ti - fied:
Sin and death and hell shall nev - er sti - fle hymns of love:
cease - less - ly up - on You gaz - ing, this shall be our song:

Yours the glo - ry and the crown, the high re - nown, the e - ter - nal name.

TEXT: Michael Saward
TUNE: John Barnard

GUITING POWER

TEXT: Timothy Dudley-Smith | b. December 26, 1926, Manchester, England
(for more on Dudley-Smith, see No. 55)

Timothy Dudley-Smith's father introduced him to poetry. When he was eleven, his father died, and Dudley-Smith began to feel that God was calling him to ministry. He was educated at Cambridge University, and eventually he served as Archdeacon of Norwich and then as Bishop of Thetford. He has written over 400 hymn texts, which have been published in more than 250 hymnals throughout the English-speaking world.

TUNE: Michael Baughen | b. June 7, 1930, Borehamwood, Hertfordshire, England

MAJESTAS is the name Michael Baughen gave to the tune he wrote for his friend and coworker, Dudley-Smith. It reflects his great love of majestic mountains. Before his retirement, Baughen held a number of posts in the Church of England, including Rector of All Souls, Langham Place, and Bishop of Chester.

As you sing this hymn . . . think of this amazing story. "Once upon a time" there was a magnificent King who lived in a faraway land with His Father and Spirit and many angels. He was so loved that the angels worshiped Him. The Father, Son, and Spirit then created a world and filled it with good and beautiful things, including people to take care of it. However, the people disobeyed the Father. They were now guilty and sinful, and the holy Father could not look upon them. The price of that guilt was eternal death. But Father, Son, and Spirit still loved them. So the Son, by the power of the Spirit, would travel to the faraway land, now a shadow of what had been created, and become just like the people. He came, was born a helpless infant, and grew up like all boys, except without sin. As a man He gradually revealed who He was. Some believed Him; some did not, and so called Him an imposter and killed Him. But this was part of the plan! His death paid the price of eternal death for all who would repent and follow Him. And then, as the true King, He rose victorious over death, proving that He had defeated sin and death! He was King over everything, even death and hell. Ultimately, all those who would repent and believe would be reunited with Him and His Father. They would die, but they, too, would rise in victory over death because they were united to the Son. They would go to live in the beautiful kingdom with the Father, the Son, and the Spirit, and join the angels in worship of the Son. They would truly live "happily ever after." Of course, this is not a fairy tale. This story is true. So sing at the top of your voice, "Jesus is Lord!"

Name of All Majesty

O Lord, our Lord, how majestic is Your name in all the earth!

PSALM 8:9

1. Name of all maj - es - ty, fa - thom-less mys - ter - y,
2. *Child of our des - ti - ny, God from e - ter - ni - ty,*
3. Sav - ior of Cal - va - ry, cost - li - est vic - to - ry,
4. *Source of all sov - ereign - ty, light, im - mor - tal - i - ty,*

King of the a - ges by an - gels a - dored;
love of the Fa - ther on sin - ners out - poured;
dark - ness de - feat - ed and E - den re - stored;
life ev - er - last - ing and heav - en as - sured;

power and au - thor - i - ty, splen - dor and dig - ni - ty,
see now what God has done send - ing His on - ly Son,
born as a man to die, nailed to a cross on high,
so with the ran - somed, we praise Him e - ter - nal - ly,

bow to His mas - ter - y, Je - sus is Lord!
Christ, the be - lov - ed One, Je - sus is Lord!
cold in the grave to lie, Je - sus is Lord!
Christ in His maj - es - ty, Je - sus is Lord!

TEXT: Timothy Dudley-Smith
TUNE: Michael Baughen and Noel Tredinnick

MAJESTAS

King Jesus Shall Reign

TEXT: Isaac Watts

b. July 17, 1674, Southampton, England
d. November 25, 1748, London, England
(for more on Watts, see No. 19, 24, 52, and 71)

The church in which Watts grew up sang only metrical Psalms. The texts were directly from Scripture, but rhymed, and the melodies were simple and plain. Isaac continually complained to his father about how boring and meaningless they were to him. His father, tired of his complaints, challenged him to write something better. The following week, the adolescent Isaac presented his first hymn to the church, which was received enthusiastically. The career of the "Father of English Hymnody" had begun. Watts did not reject metrical psalms; he simply wanted to see them more impassioned. "They ought to be translated in such a manner as we have reason to believe David would have composed them if he had lived in our day,"[31] he wrote. Watts created a psalter into which he inserted New Testament theology and language (*Psalms of David*, 1719). "Jesus Shall Reign" is his version of Psalm 72.

TUNE: John Hatton

b. ca. 1710, Warrington, Lancashire, England
d. December 13, 1793, St. Helens, Windle, England

DUKE STREET is the name of the street where the composer John Hatton lived. Little else is known about Hatton, but his stately tune is one of the best known tunes in hymnody.

As you sing this hymn . . . remember that there are Christians all around the world. The good news of Jesus Christ is not limited to our small part of the world. All people, young and old, poor and rich, "leap" in praise to God. If you are a Christian, you are part of an amazing worldwide church of worshippers whose songs "like sweet perfume" rise to give praise for our endless blessings.

"Jesus Shall Reign" is often sung as a missionary hymn because it describes the extent of God's work and His kingdom all around the world. It was a favorite hymn of Scottish Olympian Eric Liddell (who was featured in the movie *Chariots of Fire*). As he was leaving Scotland to be a missionary in China, he called to his friends, "Let our motto be 'Christ for the World, for the World Needs Christ!'" He then broke into song, singing two verses of "Jesus Shall Reign."[32]

Beyond Psalm 72 the hymn references Isaiah 45:23, Romans 14:11, and Philippians 2:10 to tell us who is important to this reigning King: the weary, the prisoner, the helpless infant, and the poor.

Originally, the final two words of the hymn were "long Amen" instead of the current "loud Amen." Sing His praises loud and long! People of the King should do both.

Jesus Shall Reign

May He have dominion from sea to sea, and from the River to the ends of the earth! . . . May all kings fall down before Him, all nations serve Him!

PSALM 72:8, 11

1. Je - sus shall reign wher - e'er the___ sun does its suc - ces - sive jour - neys run; His king-dom spread from___ shore___ to___ shore, till moons shall wax and wane no more.

2. To Him shall end - less___ prayer be___ made, and end - less prais - es crown His head; His name like sweet___ per - fume___ shall___ rise with ev - ery morn - ing sac - ri - fice.

3. Peo - ple and realms of___ ev - ery tongue dwell on His love with sweet - est song, and in - fant voic - es___ shall___ pro - claim their ear - ly bless - ings on His name.

4. Bless - ings a - bound wher - e'er He___ reigns; the pris - oners leap to lose their chains, the wea - ry find___ e - ter - nal___ rest, and all who suf - fer want are blessed.

5. Let all the peo - ple___ rise and___ bring their spe - cial hon - ors to our King; an - gels de - scend___ with___ songs___ a - gain, and earth re - peat the loud A - men.

TEXT: Isaac Watts
TUNE: John Hatton

DUKE STREET

Sovereign God Moves in a Mysterious Way

TEXT: William Cowper ‖ b. November 15, 1731, Hertfordshire, England
d. April 25, 1800, East Dereham, Norfolk, England

William Cowper (pronounced "Coo-per") is a well-regarded early British Romantic poet and the only one who also wrote hymns. Cowper's mother died when he was six years old, and his father sent him to a boarding school. It was not a happy situation, and he spent most of his life grieving for his mother. Though he was highly intelligent and learned multiple languages, he never sustained a job other than writing poetry or stories. Severe depression dominated his life, and often he did not want to live.

But God sustained Cowper. John Newton ("Amazing Grace") befriended and cared for him, which resulted in a close lifelong friendship and collaboration. Together they created the historically important hymnal _Olney Hymns_, named for the town in which they lived. "God Moves in a Mysterious Way," called by some the finest hymn ever written on God's providence, was included. Renowned British hymnologist Erik Routley compares this hymn text to a Rembrandt painting: its dark background sets off the bright light of truth in the foreground.[33] Over it Cowper wrote John 13:7: "What I am doing you do not understand now, but afterward you will understand."

TUNE: _Scottish Psalter_, 1615 ‖

The tune DUNDEE first appeared in the _Scottish Psalter_ of 1615, named after the city of Dundee, Scotland. The city was known as the "Scottish Geneva" during the Scottish Reformation. Written in a French style, it is sometimes called FRENCH.

As you sing this hymn . . . you may find it easy to understand God's ways in nature—His "footsteps in the sea" and riding "upon the storm." But then we sing of "fearful saints," "dreaded clouds," and "bitter taste." Are these also a part of God's way? Although not very many people know this hymn, you may occasionally hear the title quoted as a comfort for situations not easy to understand or accept.

The Bible teaches that God allows, even plans for, difficult trials to enter our lives. And it tells us in broad terms why: to produce faith, steadfastness, and hope (James 1:2–4). Yet it never speaks to _this_ or _that_ specific trial, and there will always be the temptation to judge God by our "feeble sense." But hold on, says this hymn. Know that God moves mysteriously and is performing _wonders_ even through the hardest trials: "His wonders to perform."

Are you in a time of sadness or grief? If you are a Christian, take courage. The trial tastes bitter now, but sweet will be the flower. You might not understand it today, but Jesus promised that one day God will "make plain" exactly what He's doing (see John 13:7). You will proclaim, "God, I would not have had it otherwise! You are amazing!"

God Moves in a Mysterious Way 47

Oh, the depth of the riches and wisdom and knowledge of God!
How unsearchable are His judgments and how inscrutable His ways!

ROMANS 11:33

1. God moves in a mys - ter - ious way His
2. *Deep in un - fath - om - a - ble mines of*
3. You fear - ful saints, fresh cour - age take; the
4. *Judge not the Lord by fee - ble sense, but*
5. His pur - pos - es will rip - en fast, un -
6. *Blind un - be - lief is sure to err and*

won - ders to per - form. He plants His foot - steps
nev - er - fail - ing skill, He trea - sures up His
clouds you so much dread are big with mer - cy
trust Him for His grace; be - hind a frown - ing
fold - ing ev - ery hour; the bud may have a
scan His work in vain; God is His own in -

in the sea, and rides up - on the storm.
bright de - signs, and works His sov - ereign will.
and shall break in bless - ings on your head.
pro - vi - dence He hides a smil - ing face.
bit - ter taste, but sweet will be the flower.
ter - pret - er, and He will make it plain.

TEXT: William Cowper
TUNE: *Scottish Psalter,* 1615

DUNDEE

Creator   All Things Bright and Beautiful

TEXT: Cecil F. Alexander | b. 1818, Ballykean House, Redcross, Wicklow, Ireland
d. October 12, 1895, The Palace, Londonderry
(for more on Alexander, see No. 13)

Even as a child, Cecil loved to write poetry. But she was so afraid that her father, an officer in the British Royal Marines, would not approve that she hid her poems under the carpet! She was wrong, however. When he discovered them, he set aside an hour every Saturday to read her poems aloud. When Cecil grew up, she loved teaching children through her poetry. Before she married, she published *Verses for Holy Seasons* and *Hymns for Little Children* (1848), the latter of which includes her most famous work, "All Things Bright and Beautiful."

Cecil married her parish minister, the Reverend William Alexander. He was appointed a bishop in Ireland and then the Primate of All Ireland. Although he was powerful and well-known in his lifetime, shortly before he died, he said that he would be remembered primarily as the husband of the poet who wrote "There Is a Green Hill Far Away" (her best-known poem of the time).[34]

In her lifetime Mrs. Alexander wrote over four hundred hymns. She founded a school for the deaf with her older sister. She also established the Girls' Friendly Society, an organization in the Episcopal Church which is still in operation around the world today.

Mrs. Alexander wrote "All Things Bright and Beautiful" to help children understand the first line of the Apostles' Creed, "I believe in God, the Father Almighty, Maker of heaven and earth." She is believed to have written this poem in a castle in Ireland called Markree Castle.

TUNE: English melody, 17th c.

ROYAL OAK is an English melody dating back to the seventeenth century that first appeared in *The Dancing Master* (1686). It was put to the words of this hymn by Martin Shaw, an English musician who worked in the theater and was a church organist at the well-known St. Martin-in-the-Fields.

As you sing this hymn . . . you cannot help but picture your favorite animals, birds, and many other creation details. The language is so beautiful that you can almost smell the flowers, hear the river, and feel the wind. Of all people who love creation, Christians should love it the most because, through God's Son, Jesus, they have a personal relationship with the Creator! So whenever you get a chance to spend time in the glories of nature, don't just say, "Wow!" but sing out loud, "All things bright and beautiful, O Lord, You made it all!"

All Things Bright and Beautiful

You have made heaven, the heaven of heavens,
with all their host, the earth and all that is on it, the seas
and all that is in them, and You preserve all of them.

NEHEMIAH 9:6

All things bright and beau - ti - ful, all crea-tures great and__ small,

Fine

all things wise and won - der - ful, the Lord God made them all.

1. Each lit - tle flow'r that__ o - pens, each lit - tle bird__ that sings,
2. *The pur - ple head - ed__ moun - tains, the riv - er run - ning by,*
3. The cold wind in the__ win - ter, the pleas - ant sum - mer sun,
4. *The tall trees in the__ green - wood, the mead - ows where we play,*
5. He gave us eyes to__ see them, and lips__ that we__ might tell

D.C.

He__ made their glow - ing__ col - ors, He__ made their ti - ny__ wings.
the__ sun - set, and the__ morn - ing that__ bright - ens up the__ sky.
the__ ripe fruits in the__ gar - den, He__ made them, ev - 'ry__ one.
the__ flow - ers by the__ wa - ter we__ gath - er ev - 'ry__ day.
how great is God Al - might - y, Who has made all things well.

TEXT: Cecil F. Alexander
TUNE: English melody, 17th c.

ROYAL OAK

Creator   This Is My Father's World

TEXT: Maltbie Davenport Babcock ‖ b. August 3, 1858, Syracuse, New York
‖ d. May 18, 1901, Naples, Italy

Maltbie Babcock loved to take long walks in the beautiful New York country-side between Lake Erie and Lake Ontario and would often tell his wife or coworkers, "I'm going out to see my Father's world!"[35] From those walks blossomed a sixteen-stanza poem, with each stanza beginning, "This is my Father's world."

Babcock was a gifted young man. He was an expert swimmer, the captain of a base-ball team, an excellent fisherman. A top student at Syracuse University, he directed the university orchestra and glee club, played several instruments, and composed music. He became a pastor, serving near Niagara Falls in New York, in Maryland, and The Brick Presbyterian Church in New York. While there, his congregation gave him the gift of a trip to Israel. En route to Italy, Babcock became ill and died. After his death, his wife Catherine collected his poems and published them. Babcock never knew that his poem would become the beloved hymn it is today.

TUNE: Franklin L. Sheppard ‖ b. August 7, 1852, Philadelphia, Pennsylvania
‖ d. February 15, 1930, Philadelphia, Pennsylvania

Sheppard was valedictorian of his 1872 graduating class at the University of Pennsylvania. In 1915, he edited a Presbyterian songbook called *Alleluia*. For the hymnal, Sheppard set to music the poem of his close friend, Rev. Babcock. Sheppard believed the tune was inspired by an English melody his mother sang to him as a child. TERRA BEATA means "blessed earth."

As you sing this hymn . . . ask yourself if God is your Father. Babcock writes, "This is *my* Father's world." To see the world as this poet does, God has to become *your* Father through repentance and faith in Christ. Everyone can see the beauty and wonder of nature, but some do not know the Father because they do not know the Son (John 14:6). The heavens declare the glory of God to the Christian and the non-Christian alike, but only Christians join with the heavens by giving glory to God, or clap their hands like the trees of the field (see Ps. 19:1; Isa. 55:12). He "speaks to us everywhere" only when we have ears that are tuned to God through Christ.

It is clear from stanza 3 that Babcock is under no illusions about this world's trials and sinful temptations. He is no head-in-the-clouds dreamer. Instead, he is confident the person and work of Christ will reconcile all things: "The battle is not done; Jesus who died shall be satisfied, and earth and heaven be one!" The God who creates is the God who redeems. It is all His.

This Is My Father's World

Sovereign Lord, who made the heaven and the earth
and the sea and everything in them.

ACTS 4:24

1. This is my Fa-ther's world, and to my lis-t'ning ears,
2. *This is my Fa-ther's world, the birds their car-ols raise,*
3. This is my Fa-ther's world, O let me ne'er for-get

all na-ture sings, and round me rings the mu-sic of the spheres.
the morn-ing light, the lil-y white, de-clare their Ma-ker's praise.
that though the wrong seems oft so strong, God is the Rul-er yet.

This is my Fa-ther's world: I rest me in the thought
This is my Fa-ther's world: He shines in all that's fair;
This is my Fa-ther's world: the bat-tle is not done;

of rocks and trees, of skies and seas; His hands the won-ders wrought.
in the rus-tling grass I hear Him pass, He speaks to me ev-ery-where.
Je-sus Who died shall be sat-is-fied, and earth and heav'n be one.

TEXT: Maltbie Davenport Babcock   TERRA BEATA
TUNE: Franklin L. Sheppard

TEXT: Stuart Hine ‖ b. July 25, 1899, London, England
d. March 14, 1989, Essex, England

Carl Boberg (1859–1940), a pastor in Sweden, found himself stuck in a thunderstorm while out in the country. After it passed and sunlight and singing birds again surrounded him, he wrote a poem, "O Store Gud," which means, "O Great God." Years later, he heard his poem being sung to a Swedish folk tune. In 1907, it was translated into German and then in 1912 into Russian, appearing with nine stanzas. An English missionary to Russia, Stuart Hine, heard it and was so moved he translated the first two stanzas, expanding the words using his own experience in the Carpathian Mountains of Eastern Europe. Hine also paraphrased the third stanza to reflect his joy in salvation and then added a fourth stanza on his return to Great Britain while contemplating his true home in heaven. The song eventually found its way to India, where a man named J. Edwin Orr heard it and brought it to California. It was there that it came to the attention of a music publisher called Manna Music, who got permission from Mr. Hine to publish it.

"How Great Thou Art" became well-known through the singing of George Beverly Shea of the Billy Graham Association. He sang it ninety-nine times at the 1957 New York Crusade. From there it spread throughout the world. It has been repeatedly selected as Great Britain's number-one favorite hymn.

TUNE: Swedish folk melody, arr. Stuart Hine, 1949 ‖

O STORE GUD, the original Swedish poem by Mr. Boberg, became connected to a Swedish folk melody sometime after the poem was written. Stuart Hine, who translated the song into English, also harmonized that melody. Hine had written many hymn tunes. This one, by far, became the most famous.

As you sing this hymn . . . you are first acknowledging that this world and its wonders are not here by accident. Some deny that God created the universe, but they do this to avoid submitting to Him (see Ps. 14:1). But with this hymn, you acknowledge God as Creator and Lord. You also declare Him as Savior through His Son Jesus, who died and rose for you. And finally, you affirm that He will one day stop history to return and bring His people to the place that is truly home.

In this song, you will repeat the phrase "How Great Thou Art" seventeen times! As you do, think of how fantastic creation is, the woods and the mountains, and then consider your salvation and the promise of glory. Now, sing not just *about* God, but directly *to* God. Let your own volume thunder and flow, as the chorus says, from your very soul.

How Great Thou Art

*Great is the L*ORD *and greatly to be praised.*

PSALM 48:1

1. O Lord my God, when I in awe-some won-der_____ con-sid-er
2. *When through the woods and for-est glades I wan-der_____ and hear the*
3. And when I think that God, His Son not spar-ing,_____ sent Him to
4. *When Christ shall come with shout of ac-cla-ma-tion_____ and take me*

all the *worlds Thy hands have made, I see the stars, I hear the roll-ing
birds sing sweet-ly in the trees, when I look down from loft-y moun-tain
die, I scarce can take it in, that on the cross, my bur-den glad-ly
home, what joy shall fill my heart! Then I shall bow in hum-ble a-do-

thun - der,_____ Thy power through-out the u-ni-verse dis-played.
gran - deur,_____ and hear the brook and feel the gen-tle breeze;
bear - ing,_____ He bled and died to take a-way my sin.
ra - tion,_____ and there pro-claim, my God, how great Thou art.

Then sings my soul, my Sav-ior God, to Thee;

how great Thou art,_____ how great Thou art!

Then sings my soul, my Sav-ior God, to Thee:

how great Thou art,_____ how great Thou art!

* Author's original words are "works," "mighty," and "shall I bow"

TEXT: Stuart K. Hine
TUNE: Swedish folk melody, adapt. and arr. Stuart K. Hine

O STORE GUD

I AM   The God of Abraham Praise

TEXT: Thomas Olivers | b. 1725, Tregynon, Montgomeryshire, Wales
d. March 1799, London, England

Having become an orphan at the age of four, Thomas Olivers grew up without direction and lived a rather wild life. But as an adult, he heard a sermon by the great preacher George Whitefield, was convicted of his sins, and became a Christian. Olivers later met John Wesley and joined the Wesleys' evangelical movement.

One night while in London, he attended a Jewish service to hear a famous singer named Leoni. There he heard a melody in a minor key that he loved and determined to write a hymn for it. Keeping with the Jewish source, he took an ancient Hebrew doxology, or *Yigdal*, and paraphrased it, giving it a Christian "character." His original poem has twelve verses.

TUNE: Synagogue melody

Olivers called the melody LEONI after the soloist he heard that night. The original tune is a synagogue melody and was arranged by Meyer Lyon around 1770.

As you sing this hymn . . . you are declaring praise to the same God that Abraham did so many centuries ago. You are addressing God with His unique name, I AM. When Moses asked God who He was, God replied, "I AM WHO I AM" (Ex. 3:14). What does that mean? It means God exists, and there is no reality behind Him that caused His existence, no one who created Him. Before there was a universe, He was there. He has no beginning or end, no boundaries of time or place. It is impossible to answer the question of how old God is because He has always existed.

God's eternal nature, praised throughout this hymn, is hard for us to understand. How do we grasp that God has no beginning and no end? We hear the words and know what they mean, but our human minds cannot comprehend them. We are finite. But this is one thing that makes God, God! All we can do is "bow and bless Him."

Yet God has also entered history and described Himself in a way that is connected to time. He calls himself the "God of Abraham, Isaac, and Jacob." It was with Abraham that God made a covenant to bless the world through his descendants. This hymn reminds us that, if we are Christians, we have been adopted into the family line of Abraham and are his descendants, even if we are not Jewish. God the Father, Son, and Holy Spirit is "Abraham's God and mine." The hymn ends with the only appropriate response to these unbelievable truths: we will join the angels in heaven to sing His praise forever.

The God of Abraham Praise

The princes of the peoples gather as the people of the God of Abraham.
For the shields of the earth belong to God; He is highly exalted!

PSALM 47:9

1. The God of A-braham praise, Who reigns en-throned a - bove,
2. *He by Him - self hath sworn, we on His oath de - pend;*
3. The God who reigns on high the great arch - an - gels sing,
4. *The whole tri - um - phant host give thanks to God on high;*

An - cient of ev - er - last - ing days, and God of love.
we shall, on ea - gles' wings up - borne, to heaven as - cend;
and "Ho - ly, ho - ly, ho - ly" cry, "Al - might - y King!
"Hail, Fa - ther, Son, and Ho - ly Ghost!" they ev - er cry.

Je - ho - vah, great I AM by__ earth and__ heaven con - fessed:
we shall be - hold His face, we__ shall His__ power a - dore,
Who was and is the same, and__ ev - er - more shall be:
Hail, A - braham's God and mine! With__ heaven our__ songs we raise;

we bow and bless the sa - cred__ name for__ ev - er blest.
and sing the won - ders of His__ grace for__ ev - er - more.
E - ter - nal Fa - ther, great I__ AM, we__ wor - ship Thee."
all might and maj - es - ty are__ Thine, and__ end - less praise.

TEXT: Thomas Olivers
TUNE: Hebrew melody, arr. Meyer Lyon

LEONI

TEXT: Isaac Watts

b. July 17, 1674, Southampton, England
d. November 25, 1748, Stoke Newington, England
(for more on Watts, see No. 19, 24, 46, and 71)

Both in the past and today, congregational songs have often created controversy. As the hymns of Isaac Watts grew in popularity toward the end of the seventeenth century, many argued that it was wrong to replace the singing of the Psalms with the new hymns. Over a century earlier the great theologian John Calvin had urged his followers to sing only metrical psalms, and many English Protestants had conceded. They called Watts's hymns "flights of fancy." Churches began to split over the issue. Watts was greatly affected by this dissent and had a mental or nervous breakdown in 1712, from which he never fully recovered.

Watts loved children and wrote many nursery rhymes that, for years, were among the most famous in the English language ("How doth the little busy bee," and "Let dogs delight to bark and bite"). In 1715, he published one of the first known hymn collections for children, *Divine Songs, Attempted in Easy Language for Children*. Alluding to the conflict over his hymns, the preface reads, "Children of high and low degree, of the Church of England or Dissenters, baptized in infancy or not, may all join together in these songs. And as I have endeavored to sink the language to the level of a child's understanding . . . to profit all, if possible, and offend none."[36] One of the hymns based on Psalm 19 was titled, "Praise for Creation and Providence." We know it as "I Sing the Almighty Power of God."

TUNE: Traditional English melody, arr. Ralph Vaughan Williams

b. October 12, 1872, Down Amprey, Gloucestershire, England
d. August 26, 1958, London, England

Ralph Vaughan Williams is one of the best known British composers of the twentieth century. He was the musical editor for *The English Hymnal* in 1906. It was at that time he arranged the traditional English melody for this hymn, which he named FOREST GREEN.

As you sing this hymn . . . ask yourself what "I sing" means and ask whether your soul is truly joining together with creation to praise God. Did you know creation praises Him? Note the verbs that describe nature's response in Psalm 19:1–4: "The heavens *declare* the glory of God, and the sky above *proclaims* His handiwork. Day to day pours out *speech*, and night to night *reveals* knowledge. There is no *speech*, nor are there *words*, whose *voice* is not heard" (emphasis added). Just as there is no place in creation we can travel that does not praise God, so we can proclaim that God is present with us everywhere and at all times. This hymn is a great song to sing for anyone who is looking for God. If you ever have doubts, sing this song, and hear creation singing with you.

I Sing the Almighty Power of God 52

It is He who made the earth by His power, who established the world by His wisdom, and by His understanding stretched out the heavens.

JEREMIAH 10:12

1. I sing th'al-might-y pow'r of__ God that made the__ moun-tains
2. *I sing the good-ness of__ the__ Lord that filled the__ earth with*
3. There's not a plant or flow'r be-low but makes Your glo-ries

rise, that spread the flow-ing seas__ a-broad and
food; He formed the crea-tures with__ His__ word, and
known; and clouds a-rise and tem-pests__ blow by

built the__ loft-y skies. I__ sing the wis-dom that__ or-dained the
then pro-nounced them good. Lord, how Your won-ders__ are__ dis-played wher-
or-der__ from Your throne; while all that bor-rows life__ from You is

sun to rule the day; the moon shines full at
e'er I turn my eye, if I sur-vey the
ev-er in Your care, and ev-ery-where that

His__ com-mand and all the__ stars o-bey.
ground__ I__ tread or gaze up-on the sky!
man__ can__ be, You, God, are__ pres-ent there.

TEXT: Isaac Watts   FOREST GREEN
TUNE: Traditional English melody, arr. Ralph Vaughan Williams

TEXT AND TUNE: Martin Luther   ‖   b. November 10, 1483, Eisleben, Germany
d. February 18, 1546, Eisleben, Germany

Martin Luther grew up hearing his mother sing. As a child, he was a member of a boys' choir. He also was skilled in playing the recorder. As an adult, Luther became a monk, a priest, a university professor, and a famous theologian. He translated the Bible into German because he wanted the German people to be able to read it! And he composed hymns so that people could sing the truths they learned. Luther's hymns helped revive congregational singing, and his Bible translation even helped solidify a standard version of the German language. Martin Luther is called "the Father of the Reformation" because he fought against church doctrines and practices that did not teach that "salvation is by faith alone in Christ alone," as the Bible teaches.

Many leaders in the established church persecuted Luther because of the reforms he sought. However, Luther knew that the worst enemy of God's people is not other people, but the devil, whom he called our "ancient foe." Luther found refuge in Psalm 46, which inspired him to write this hymn in 1527. Frederick H. Hedge translated it from German to English in 1852.

EIN' FESTE BURG literally means "A Firm Castle." Scholars assume that Luther either wrote it or adapted it from a folk song. The great composer J. S. Bach harmonized it as the hymn we know today. God is indeed our firm castle!

As you sing this hymn . . . you are doing one of the best things you can do to combat the devil and grow in faith. Luther didn't write the hymn because he always felt brave or courageous against the opposition. Just the opposite, he often felt afraid. Yet by singing the promises of God's Word, he placed these promises deep into his heart. When you feel scared and weak, one of the best things you can do is sing a song based on God's Word.

Luther believed that music was a powerful tool given to us by God for our use:

> Music is a gift and grace of God, not an invention of men. . . . I wish
> to compose sacred hymns so that the Word of God may dwell among
> the people also by means of songs. I would allow no man to preach or
> teach God's people without a proper knowledge of the use and power of
> sacred song.[37]

LORD *Sabaoth* is a Hebrew name for God which means "Lord of the Armies." He is the one who does battle. A *bulwark* is a solid wall built for defense against an enemy.

A Mighty Fortress Is Our God 53

The LORD of hosts is with us; the God of Jacob is our fortress.

PSALM 46:7

1. A might-y for-tress is___ our God, a bul-wark nev-er
2. Did we in our___ own strength con-fide, our striv-ing would be
3. And though this world, with dev-ils filled, should threat-en to un-
4. That Word a-bove___ all earth-ly pow'rs, no thanks to them, a-

fail - ing. Our help-er He,___ a-mid___ the flood of
los - ing, were not the right___ man on___ our side, the
do___ us, we will not fear,___ for God_ hath willed His
bid - eth; the Spir-it and___ the gifts___ are ours through

mor-tal ills pre-vail - ing. For still our an-cient
man of God's own choos - ing. Dost ask who that may
truth to tri-umph through___ us. The Prince of Dark-ness
Him who with us sid - eth. Let goods and kin-dred

foe doth seek to work us woe; his craft and pow'r are great, and
be? Christ Je-sus, it is He; Lord Sa-ba-oth His name, from
grim, we trem-ble not for him; his rage we can en-dure, for
go, this mor-tal life al-so; the bod-y they may kill; God's

armed with cru-el hate, on earth is not his e - qual.___
age to age the same, and He must win the bat - tle.___
lo! his doom is sure; one lit-tle word shall fell___ him.___
truth a-bid-eth still; His king-dom is for-ev - er.___

TEXT AND TUNE: Martin Luther   EIN' FESTE BURG

TEXT: Katharina A. von Schlegel,
trans. Jane L. Borthwick

b. October 22, 1697, Germany
d. Unknown, Germany
b. April 9, 1813, Edinburgh, Scotland
d. September 7, 1897, Edinburgh, Scotland

Looking at her full name, it may be assumed that Katharina Amalia Dorothea von Schlegel was born into an aristocratic German family. But little else is known about her—even the date of her death. Some think she may have been a Lutheran nun serving in the small court at Köthen (where J. S. Bach also served). Hymnologists consider her one of the leading female hymn writers of the German Pietistic Movement of the late 17th century.

Almost 100 years later, Jane Borthwick and her sister, Sarah, became drawn to the task of translating German hymns that they had discovered during a trip to Switzerland. Upon returning home to Scotland, her father persuaded her to translate these hymns. She named this hymn SUBMISSION.

TUNE: Jean Sibelius

b. December 8, 1865, Hämeenlinna, Finland
d. September 20, 1957, Ainola, Finland

Finland's most important and favorite composer's full name was Johan Julius Christian Sibelius. Jean Sibelius's music is credited with helping Finland gain its own identity as it struggled for independence from Russia. He wrote numerous symphonic works, but his most famous is called a tone poem (a symphonic work that tells a story) named *Finlandia*. The music is mostly turbulent and depicts the national struggle which eventually resolved into peace. To hear this hymn tune in its larger symphonic setting, please listen to one of many orchestral performances that can be found on YouTube. It will make you appreciate the contrast between turmoil and peace. Decades later, David Evans, a Welsh and Oxford-trained music professor, matched the text with the *Finlandia* tune for a 1927 British hymnal. It was first brought to America when used in *The Hymnal* (1933 Presbyterian USA). Evans also set the text of "Be Thou My Vision" (No. 112) to an ancient Irish folk tune.

Doesn't it seem to be an act of God's providence and sovereign guidance that brought together this remarkable hymn from Germany, Scotland, Finland, and Wales over a century of time? We believe it was divinely ordained and should definitely be one you know and sing.

As you sing this hymn . . . you are speaking to yourself from the truths of Scripture: "Why are you cast down, O my soul . . . Hope in God" (Ps. 42:5); "Though I walk in the midst of trouble, You preserve my life" (Ps.138:7); "For Your steadfast love is before my eyes, and I walk in Your faithfulness" (Ps. 26:3). There may be many experiences in your life that are hard to understand. This hymn will help you to express patience, trust, hope, and to "be still." The Lord is on your side!

Be Still, My Soul

54

*Surely I have stilled and quieted my soul; Like a weaned child with his
mother, Like a weaned child is my soul within me.*

PSALM 131:2 (ASV)

1. Be still, my soul! The Lord is on your side:
   bear pa - tient - ly the cross of grief or pain;
   leave to your God to or - der and pro - vide;
   in ev - ery change He faith - ful will re - main.
   Be still my soul! Your best, your heav'n - ly Friend
   thro' thorn - y ways leads to a joy - ful end.

2. *Be still, my soul! Your God will un - der - take*
   to guide the fu - ture as He has the past;
   your hope, your con - fi - dence let noth - ing shake;
   all now mys - te - rious shall be bright at last.
   Be still, my soul! The waves and winds still know
   His voice who ruled them while He dwelt be - low.

3. Be still, my soul! The hour is has - tening on
   when we shall be for - ev - er with the Lord,
   when dis - ap - point - ment, grief and fear are gone,
   sor - row for - got, love's pur - est joys re - stored.
   Be still my soul! When change and tears are past,
   all safe and bless - ed we shall meet at last.

TEXT: Katharina A. von Schlegel, trans. Jane L. Borthwick

TUNE: Jean Sibelius

FINLANDIA

TEXT: Timothy Dudley-Smith   ‖   b. December 26, 1926, Manchester, England
(for more on Dudley-Smith, see No. 45)

In the past fifty years, thousands of hymns have been written all over the world. Which ones will last for centuries, like the majority of hymns in this book? It is impossible to predict, but one modern hymn writer whose hymns have already received highest acclaim and been broadly published in 250 hymnals is Timothy Dudley-Smith. In 1997, he was named a Fellow in the Hymn Society of the United States and Canada, a rare accomplishment for anyone other than an American or a Canadian. In 2003, the Queen of England awarded him the OBE (Order of the British Empire) "for services to hymnody." In July 2009, he was awarded an honorary doctorate degree by Durham University.

TUNE: Norman L. Warren   ‖   b. July 19, 1934, London, England
d. June 19, 2019

Norman Warren is one of the founders of Jubilate Hymns. Like the others in the group, Warren was a minister as well as a hymn writer. He was educated at Ridley Hall, Cambridge, and was ordained in the Church of England, where he served as a curate, vicar, rector, and archdeacon. He worked closely with British hymn writer Michael Perry, composer of "O God Beyond All Praising." He has published over 100 hymn tunes and several books, including *Journey into Life*, which sold thirty million copies.

As you sing this hymn . . . you are personalizing Psalm 91 and declaring your trust in God to protect you. How can you be "safe in a shadow," as the hymn puts it? If you are in God's shadow, He must be close! We cannot see God, yet the psalmist says that it is possible to dwell in His shelter and abide in His shadow.

Normally a repeating refrain is found at the end of a hymn. The stanzas come first and then a refrain or chorus follows. But here, the refrain occurs within the stanzas—a quiet four-word exclamation of confidence: "I trust in Him." You will sing these words twelve times as your response to the many reasons Psalm 91 gives us for trusting God. Each revelation of His care should grow in your heart the conviction to trust Him.

This is not simply positive thinking. No, it is a declaration of faith that since "God is for us, who can be against us?" (Rom. 8:31).

Safe in the Shadow of the Lord

55

He who dwells in the shelter of the Most High will abide
in the shadow of the Almighty. I will say to the LORD, "My refuge
and my fortress, my God, in whom I trust."

PSALM 91:1–2

1. Safe in the sha - dow of the Lord,
2. *My hope is set on God a - lone,*
3. From fears and phan - toms of the night,
4. *His ho - ly an - gels keep my feet*
5. Strong in the ev - er - last - ing name,
6. *Safe in the sha - dow of the Lord,*

be - neath His hand____ and power.____
though Sa - tan spreads____ his snare.____
from foes a - bout____ my way.____
se - cure from ev - ery stone;____
and in my Fa - ther's care,____
pos - sessed by love____ di - vine,____

I trust in Him,____ I trust in Him,____

my for - tress and____ my tower.____
to keep____ me in____ His care.____
by dark - ness as____ by day.____
and un - a - fraid____ go on.____
Who hears____ and an - swers prayer.____
and meet____ His love____ with mine.____

TEXT: Timothy Dudley-Smith
TUNE: Norman Warren

CREATOR GOD

Faithful   Great Is Thy Faithfulness

TEXT: Thomas Obadiah Chisholm ‖ b. July 29, 1866, Franklin, Kentucky
d. February 29, 1960, New Jersey

Thomas Chisholm was born in a log cabin in Kentucky. Although he did not have a high school education, he became the teacher at the country schoolhouse he had attended. At the age of twenty, he became the editor of his hometown newspaper, *The Franklin Favorite*. After accepting Christ at the age of twenty-seven, he moved to Louisville to become the editor of a Christian magazine. Chisholm served as an ordained minister but left the pastorate due to poor health. He sold insurance for the rest of his working life but continued to write, producing around 1,200 poems and hymns. This hymn is autobiographical. In 1941, Chisholm wrote, "My income has not been large at any time due to impaired health. . . . I must not fail to record here the unfailing faithfulness of a covenant-keeping God and that He has given me many wonderful displays of His providing care, for which I am filled with astonishing gratefulness."[38]

TUNE: William Runyan ‖ b. January 21, 1870, Marion, New York
d. July 29, 1957, Pittsburg, Kansas

As a child Runyan loved music and by age twelve, he served as his church's organist. At twenty-one, he became a Methodist minister. In 1915, he wrote his first gospel song, and later was affiliated with Moody Bible Institute and became music editor of Hope Publishing Company. Chisholm, a friend of Runyan's, sent several poems to him. Captured by this text, Rev. Runyan wrote, "This particular poem held such an appeal that I prayed most earnestly that my tune might carry over its message in a worthy way, and the subsequent history of its use indicates that God answered prayer."[39] The tune is simply called FAITHFULNESS.

As you sing this hymn . . . remember a time when your life changed in a way that was difficult. God wants you to know that even when life changes, He remains constant. He is immutable, unchanging. The book of Lamentations declares that God shows His faithfulness as He renews His mercy "every morning" (Lam. 3:23). So Chisholm leads us to sing, "O God, my Father, there is no shadow of turning with Thee" (see James 1:17).

No one in the world is perfectly faithful. But God is. All His attributes make this possible. Since He is all-powerful, He can overcome any obstacle that would hinder Him from keeping His word. Since He is present everywhere, He can be faithful to you and everyone else in the world simultaneously. Since He is all-knowing, He is perfectly wise in what promises He makes. And best of all, since He is perfectly loving and always merciful, He remains faithful even when we are unfaithful.

Great Is Thy Faithfulness

The steadfast love of the LORD never ceases; His mercies never come to an end;
they are new every morning; great is Your faithfulness.

LAMENTATIONS 3:22–23

1. Great is Thy faith - ful - ness, O God my Fa - ther;
2. *Sum - mer and win - ter and spring - time and har - vest,*
3. Par - don for sin and a peace that en - dur - eth,

there is no shad - ow of turn - ing with Thee;
sun, moon, and stars in their cours - es a - bove,
Thine own dear pres - ence to cheer and to guide,

Thou chang - est not, Thy com - pas - sions, they fail not;
join with all na - ture in man - i - fold wit - ness
strength for to - day, and bright hope for to - mor - row,

as Thou hast been Thou for - ev - er wilt be.
to Thy great faith - ful - ness, mer - cy, and love.
bless - ings all mine, with ten thou - sand be - side!

Great is Thy faith - ful - ness! Great is Thy faith - ful - ness!

Morn - ing by morn - ing new mer - cies I see:

all I have need - ed Thy hand hath pro - vid - ed;

Great is Thy faith - ful - ness, Lord, un - to me!

TEXT: Thomas O. Chisholm
TUNE: William M. Runyan

FAITHFULNESS

Faithful   How Firm a Foundation

TEXT: Anonymous ‖

Curiously, some of our greatest hymns list the author as "Anonymous," which means the author is unknown. One of these is "How Firm a Foundation." An English Baptist minister named John Rippon, an authority on Isaac Watts, compiled a hymnal that he called *A Selection of Hymns from the Best Authors, Intended to Be an Appendix to Dr. Watts' Psalms and Hymns* (1787). This hymn was included, carrying the title "Exceedingly Great and Precious Promises." The author was listed only as "K." There were several "K's" in Mr. Rippon's life, but many believe it referred to his assistant, R. Keene. The hymnal was very popular and was reprinted twenty-seven times, selling 200,000 copies.

"How Firm a Foundation" became well-known in America. It was a favorite of President Andrew Jackson's wife, Rachel, and apparently, Jackson asked for it as he was dying. It was also sung at the funerals of General Robert E. Lee and Presidents Theodore Roosevelt and Woodrow Wilson. In the Spanish War of 1898, an entire regiment of American soldiers sang it on the hills of Cuba to the Christmas tune ADESTE FIDELES. Protestants, Catholics, North, and South all sang together, "Fear not I am with thee, O be not dismayed!"

TUNE: Traditional American melody ‖

Although it was first sung to an English tune, this hymn is now sung to a traditional American tune that hymn editors named FOUNDATION. A song labeled "traditional" means that it is a folk song that has been passed down verbally from generation to generation. The tune is pentatonic, which is a five-note scale commonly found in the folk music of Eastern Europe and Africa. Because there is no dissonance (clashing) of the notes, it can be sung in canon.

As you sing this hymn . . . think about the most essential part of a building. Is it the roof, the walls, the bricks? No, it is the foundation. Our lives, too, need a good foundation, as Jesus taught in Matthew 7 about the wise and foolish man. Just as the truest test of a building's foundation is how it endures storms, so we need the foundation of Jesus and His Word to weather the storms of life.

Stanza 1 is a declaration that God's excellent Word is our foundation, and we need to hear no more than what He has said in the Bible. In stanzas 2 through 4, God speaks directly to us in the first person. Stanza 2 comes from Isaiah 41:10; stanza 3 from Isaiah 43:2; stanza 4 draws from Isaiah 43:2 as well as Zechariah 13:9; and stanza 5 is the Christian's declaration based on John 10:27–29, Romans 8:38–39, and Hebrews 13:5–6. These are among the most comforting verses in the Bible. Look them up and make them your foundation as you sing this stirring melody with confidence and loud conviction. Believe God's promises; you can endure!

How Firm a Foundation

57

Everyone then who hears these words of Mine and does them will be like a
wise man who built his house on the rock.

MATTHEW 7:24–25

1. How__ firm a foun - da - tion, you saints of the Lord,
2. "Fear__ not, I am with you, O be not dis - mayed,
3. "When_ through the deep wa - ters I call you to go,
4. "When_ through fier - y tri - als your path - way shall lie,
5. "The__ soul that on Je - sus has leaned for re - pose,

is____ laid for your faith in His ex - cel - lent Word!
for___ I am your God, and will still give you aid;
the___ riv - ers of sor - row shall not o - ver - flow;
my___ grace, all suf - fi - cient, shall be your sup - ply;
I____ will not, I will not de - sert to its foes;

What more can He say than to you He has said,
I'll strength - en you, help you, and cause you to stand,
for I will be with you, your trou - bles to bless,
the flame shall not hurt you, I on - ly de - sign
that soul, though all hell should en - deav - or to shake,

to____ you who for ref - uge to Je - sus have fled?
up - held by my righ - teous, om - ni - po - tent hand.
and___ sanc - ti - fy to you your deep - est dis - tress.
your___ dross to con - sume and your gold to re - fine.
I'll___ nev - er, no, nev - er, no, nev - er for - sake."

TEXT: Anonymous, *Rippon's Selection of Hymns*, 1787
TUNE: Traditional American melody

FOUNDATION

Shepherd   The King of Love My Shepherd Is

TEXT: Henry W. Baker   ‖   b. May 27, 1821, London, England
d. February 12, 1877, Hertfordshire, England

Sir Henry Williams Baker was the son of a Navy admiral and was educated at Trinity College, Cambridge. He held the position of vicar his entire adult life and is credited with thirty-three published hymns. Baker worked for many years on a hymnal that he hoped would reflect the "grandeur of majestic worship."[40] It was finally printed in 1861 and named *Hymns Ancient and Modern*. This hymnal became the standard of the Anglican Church for many years, selling over 170 million copies. It is still in use in some parishes today. "The King of Love My Shepherd Is" first appeared in the 1868 revision.

The hymn is a beautiful paraphrase of the Twenty-Third Psalm. To "paraphrase" something is to put it in your own words, as when you retell a story that you just read. The last words of Henry Baker as he was dying were, "Perverse and foolish oft I strayed, but yet in love He sought me, and on His shoulder gently laid, and home rejoicing, brought me."[41]

TUNE: Traditional Irish melody   ‖

St. Columba, for whom the tune is named, was an Irish Christian in the sixth century who took Christianity to Scotland. George Petrie (1789–1866), a collector of ancient Irish music, helped found the Society for the Preservation and Publication of the Melodies of Ireland. This tune appeared in the *Complete Collection of Irish Music as Noted by George Petrie* (Charles Villers Stanford, 1902). ST. COLUMBA appears with this Twenty-Third Psalm text in *The English Hymnal* (1906).

As you sing this hymn . . . meditate on the goodness of Jesus Christ. The first and last stanzas tell us that His "goodness faileth never." Friends will fail us. Parents and teachers will fail us. Our favorite things will fail us. But Jesus' goodness will never fail. Jesus is good today, and He will be good every day hereafter.

How is Jesus good? The second stanza says He will feed us with the food of heaven. The third stanza says He seeks us out when we stray. The fourth stanza explains how He is our comfort even in the face of death. On and on, we could list examples of Christ's goodness.

Some words and phrases in this text are unfamiliar. To help, *verdant* means green with rich vegetation. *Celestial food* refers to food from heaven. *Vale* is an old word for valley. *Unction* refers to the act of anointing. There is one New Testament word in this paraphrase; can you find it? It is in the last phrase of stanza 4. It points to how Jesus, this best Shepherd, demonstrated His goodness most of all—by giving His life for the salvation of straying, weak sheep like us.

The King of Love My Shepherd Is

58

*The LORD is my shepherd, I shall not want . . . and I shall dwell
in the house of the LORD forever.*

PSALM 23:1, 6

1. The King of love my Shep - herd is,
   Whose good - ness fail - eth nev - er;
   I noth - ing lack if I am His,
   and He is mine for - ev - er.

2. Where streams of liv - ing wa - ter flow,
   my ran - somed soul He lead - eth,
   and where the ver - dant pas - tures grow,
   with food ce - les - tial feed - eth.

3. Per - verse and fool - ish oft I strayed,
   but yet in love He sought me,
   and on His shoul - der gen - tly laid,
   and home re - joic - ing brought me.

4. In death's dark vale I fear no ill,
   with Thee, dear Lord, be - side me:
   Thy rod and staff my com - fort still,
   Thy cross be - fore to guide me.

5. Thou spread'st a ta - ble in my sight,
   Thy unc - tion grace be - stow - eth,
   and O what trans - port of de - light
   from Thy pure chal - ice flow - eth!

6. And so through all the length of days
   Thy good - ness fail - eth ne - ver;
   Good Shep - herd, may I sing Thy praise
   with - in Thy house for - ev - er.

TEXT: Henry W. Baker
TUNE: Traditional Irish melody

ST. COLUMBA

Shepherd   The Lord's My Shepherd, I'll Not Want

TEXT: *Scottish Psalter*, 1650 || Francis Rous (1579-1659), Halton, Cornwall
Sir William Mure of Rowallan (1594–1657), Scotland

The Psalms are Hebrew poetry, and neither Hebrew poetry nor its English translations use the kind of literary conventions that people today use for singing, like rhyme or consistent meter. Many of the earliest English hymns are versifications of Psalms. Often the outcome was rather poor and difficult to sing.

The *Scottish Psalter* of 1650 was created to improve Psalm singing. This version of Psalm 23 was written for that collection by Sir William Mure, the knight of Rowallan, and Francis Rous. Sir William was an important seventeenth-century Scottish poet and writer as well as a soldier who fought under Oliver Cromwell. Francis Rous was a prominent Puritan who also supported Cromwell and was a Member of Parliament. How unusual for two authors of a hymn to have both been soldiers, politicians, and poets! Rous, who worked on the *Scottish Psalter* as a whole, had been disappointed with the versifications being sung at that time because he felt the meanings had been changed in order to make the rhyme fit.

The *Psalter* was the only authorized version for use in the Scottish Presbyterian Church until it was revised in 1929, almost 300 years after it was created.

TUNE: James Leith Macbeth Bain || b. November 21, 1860, Pitlochry, Scotland
d. September 19, 1925, Liverpool, England

James Bain was an English traveling preacher, healer, mystic, and poet who was often called "Brother James." He wrote this tune for a gospel tract that appeared in 1915. It is called BROTHER JAMES' AIR. "Air" is simply another name for a tune or melody.

As you sing this hymn . . . you can hear three musical phrases. The first two are identical while the third one is different. This is called an AAB form. The AA phrases firmly state the Scripture, while the B phrase repeats and emphasizes important words as if to say, "Don't pass over too quickly these important truths."

Since Psalm 23 is familiar, it might be easy to pass over essential truths that God wants you to know. What assurances might you need today? Maybe it is quiet waters of peace. Perhaps it's God's rod and staff. The Great Shepherd has many ways to lead and care for us.

Sometimes people will skip a stanza or two when singing hymns to save time. But be sure not to leave any verses out of this hymn. Sing the entire psalm.

The Lord's My Shepherd, I'll Not Want 59

He restores my soul. He leads me in paths
of righteousness for His name's sake.

PSALM 23:3

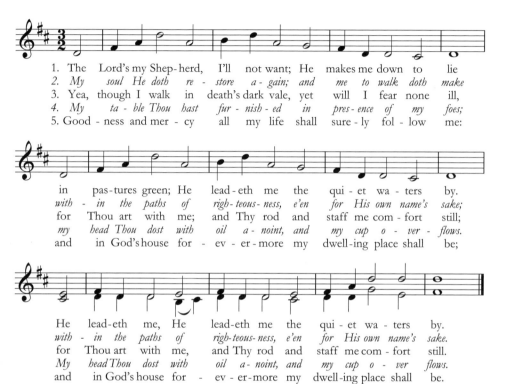

1. The Lord's my Shep-herd, I'll not want; He makes me down to lie
2. *My soul He doth re - store a - gain; and me to walk doth make*
3. Yea, though I walk in death's dark vale, yet will I fear none ill,
4. *My ta - ble Thou hast fur - nish - ed in pres - ence of my foes;*
5. Good - ness and mer - cy all my life shall sure - ly fol - low me:

in pas-tures green; He lead-eth me the qui - et wa - ters by.
with - in the paths of righ- teous- ness, e'en for His own name's sake;
for Thou art with me; and Thy rod and staff me com - fort still;
my head Thou dost with oil a - noint, and my cup o - ver - flows.
and in God's house for - ev - er-more my dwell-ing place shall be;

He lead-eth me, He lead-eth me the qui - et wa - ters by.
with - in the paths of righ- teous- ness, e'en for His own name's sake.
for Thou art with me, and Thy rod and staff me com - fort still.
My head Thou dost with oil a - noint, and my cup o - ver - flows.
and in God's house for - ev - er-more my dwell-ing place shall be.

TEXT: Psalm 23, Francis Rous, William Mure; *Scottish Psalter*, 1650   BROTHER JAMES' AIR
TUNE: J. L. Macbeth Bain

Savior, Like a Shepherd Lead Us

TEXT: Dorothy Thrupp ‖ b. June 20, 1779, Paddington, Middlesex, England
d. December 14, 1847, St. Marylebone, Middlesex, England

Little is known about Dorothy Thrupp except that she wrote many hymns for children. She often used the pseudonym "Iota," or the initials D. A. T. "Savior, Like a Shepherd Lead Us" was included in a book she edited for children called *Hymns for the Young*. It is based on Psalm 23 and John 10, where Jesus calls Himself "the good shepherd."

Ira Sankey, a famous nineteenth-century gospel singer, once sang this hymn at a Christmas Eve gathering. Afterward, a man approached him and told the story of how, as a Confederate soldier, he came upon a Union soldier and was preparing to shoot him. As he raised his gun, the Union soldier began to sing this hymn. Deciding to wait until he was finished to kill him, the Confederate soldier remembered his mother singing these words. At the end of the hymn, he could not pull the trigger. Now, on this Christmas Eve, he had just heard the song sung once again by the same Union soldier whose life he had almost taken—Sankey.[42]

TUNE: William B. Bradbury ‖ b. October 6, 1816, York, Maine
d. January 7, 1868, Montclair, New Jersey
(for more on Bradbury, see No. 68 and 72)

William Bradbury was a well-known composer, publisher, and piano manufacturer in New York City. During his lifetime, he published fifty-nine song collections, both sacred and secular. He gave this tune his own name, BRADBURY.

As you sing this hymn . . . you should consider the characteristics of sheep. They are not very intelligent and foolishly put themselves in peril. They are easily upset or spooked and can quickly get lost. They need constant care for water and food, cleanliness, or medical attention. Without a shepherd, they are helpless. Fortunately, they respond to the shepherd's voice and will follow it when he calls.

Think then of how Jesus looked on the crowds of people and had compassion because they were "like sheep without a shepherd" (Matt. 9:36). How we all need Christ as our Shepherd! And a sheep who knows its helplessness and listens to the shepherd is not so foolish after all. By singing this hymn, you acknowledge that you are a sheep in need of a Savior and that you belong to Him. The Good Shepherd will always listen. In fact, He laid down His life for His sheep (John 10:15). He has bought you, will hear you, will turn to you, and will love you forever.

Savior, Like a Shepherd Lead Us

60

I am the good shepherd. I know My own and My own know Me.

JOHN 10:14

1. Sav - ior, like a shep-herd lead_ us,__ much we need Thy ten - der care;
2. *We are Thine; do Thou be - friend us,__ be the guard-ian of our way;*
3. Thou hast prom-ised to re - ceive us,__ poor and sin -ful though we be;
4. *Ear - ly let us seek Thy fa - vor;__ ear - ly let us do Thy will;*

in Thy plea-sant pas-tures feed_ us,__ for our use Thy folds pre- pare:
keep Thy flock, from sin de - fend_ us,__ seek us when we go a - stray:
Thou hast mer - cy to re - lieve us,__ grace to cleanse, and pow'r to free:
bless - ed Lord and on - ly Sav - ior,__ with Thy love our be - ings fill:

Bless-ed Je - sus, bless-ed Je - sus, Thou hast bought us, Thine we are;
Bless - ed Je - sus, bless - ed Je - sus, hear, O hear us when we pray;
Bless-ed Je - sus, bless-ed Je - sus, ear - ly let us turn to Thee;
Bless - ed Je - sus, bless - ed Je - sus, Thou hast loved us, love us still;

bless-ed Je-sus, bless-ed Je - sus, Thou hast bought us, Thine we are.
bless - ed Je - sus, bless - ed Je - sus, hear, O hear us when we pray.
bless-ed Je-sus, bless-ed Je - sus, ear - ly let us turn to Thee.
bless - ed Je - sus, bless - ed Je - sus, Thou hast loved us, love us still.

TEXT: Dorothy Ann Thrupp
TUNE: William B. Bradbury

BRADBURY

Thy Word Is Like a Garden, Lord

TEXT: Edwin Hodder   ‖   b. December 13, 1837, Middlesex, England
d. March 1, 1904, Chichester, Sussex, England

Edwin Hodder worked for the British government, but in his spare time, he wrote hymns. In 1863, he published *The New Sunday School Hymn Book*, which contained twenty-three of his hymns, one of them entitled "Holy Scripture." That hymn is now named "Thy Word Is Like a Garden, Lord," taken from the poem's first line.

TUNE: Traditional Irish melody   ‖

CLONMEL is an ancient Irish tune, probably named for a town in Ireland by that name. It was adapted to these words in 1952 by William J. Reynolds, a Baptist publisher and musician.

As you sing this hymn . . . you are joining the psalmist who sang in Psalm 119:18, "Open my eyes, that I may behold wondrous things out of Your law." Psalm 119 is the longest chapter in the Bible. It is all about God's Word and the importance of reading, knowing, memorizing, and obeying it.

The Bible is a miracle book, written as God breathed His revelation into many authors over a period of approximately 1,500 years. Yet it all speaks of one theme, the plan of God from creation to magnify His Son until He establishes the new heavens and new earth.

This hymn uses similes as a means of describing the wonders and beauties of the Bible. It is "like" a garden, a mine, a galaxy, an armory. In our time we might use other similes such as a supermarket, a university, or an Internet search engine. Metaphors like these help us try to describe the amazing depth and breadth of the Bible. But of course, they all fall short because the Bible does one thing that nothing else does: it tells us truth that brings unconditional forgiveness and restores people to God.

Do you love your Bible? Do you treasure it? Today in most places, we have the freedom to have many copies of the Bible. People in the past have given their lives for a single copy, and people in some places today still risk their lives to smuggle it into nations that outlaw it. Never take the Bible for granted. Sing this beautiful hymn to remind you of the Bible's preciousness and treasure it as a most valued possession. The best way to keep it with you always, of course, is to memorize it!

Thy Word Is Like a Garden, Lord

61

*The law of the LORD is perfect, reviving the soul . . . the commandment
of the LORD is pure, enlightening the eyes; . . . More to be desired are
they than gold, even much fine gold.*

PSALM 19:7, 8, 10

1. Thy Word is like a gar - den, Lord, with flow - ers bright and fair;
2. Thy Word is like a star - ry host: a thou - sand rays of light
3. O may I love Thy pre - cious Word, may I ex - plore the mine,

and ev - 'ry - one who seeks may pluck a love - ly clus - ter there.
are seen to guide the trav - e - ler and make his path - way bright.
may I its fra - grant flow - ers glean, may light up - on me shine!

Thy Word is like a deep, deep mine; and jew - els rich and rare
Thy Word is like an arm - o - ry, where sold - iers may re - pair;
O may I find my ar - mor there! Thy Word my trust - y sword,

are hid - den in its might - y depths for ev - 'ry search - er
and find, for life's long bat - tle day, all need - ful wea - pons
I'll learn to fight with ev - 'ry foe the bat - tle of the

there, for ev - 'ry search - er there.
there, all need - ful wea - pons there.
Lord, the bat - tle of the Lord.

TEXT: Edwin Hodder
TUNE: Traditional Irish melody

CLONMEL

The Word   Every Promise of Your Word

TEXT AND TUNE: Stuart Townend, Keith Getty	b. June 1, 1963, West Yorkshire, England
	b. December 16, 1974, Lisburn, Northern Ireland (for more
	on Getty and Townend, see No. 12, 26, 34, 65, and 99)

Throughout the world and in almost every denomination, believers are discovering and singing the songs of these modern hymn writers. The musical and textual qualities of their hymns are some of the best of the twenty-first century. Although it is too soon to know how well they will endure through time, we believe they are certainly worth learning by students using this hymnal as a sourcebook of essential hymns. More of their hymns can be found on the Internet at:

www.gettymusic.com and www.stuarttownend.co.uk

This hymn text is a modern version of an older nineteenth-century song that your parents or grandparents might know called "Standing on the Promises of God." Ask them if they can sing it to you!

As you sing this hymn . . . consider: have you ever made a promise you didn't keep? Most of us have. Sometimes we don't keep our promises because we are negligent. Sometimes we don't keep them because of unforeseen events, and the ability to keep them is outside of our control.

Neither of these possibilities is true of God. He is omnipotent (all-powerful), so He always keeps His promises. He is omniscient (all-knowing), so He always knows what is ahead. He is also perfectly good and loving and will not fail us because He loses interest in keeping His promises or lacks the will. Joshua 21:45 declares, "Not one word of all the good promises that the LORD had made to the house of Israel had failed; all came to pass." It is through Jesus Christ that God keeps His promises to us, "For all the promises of God find their Yes in Him" (2 Cor. 1:20).

As you sing this hymn, think of how good you feel when your parents or a friend makes a promise to you. It makes you smile. Look at all the times this hymn reminds us that the promises of God are given. What a list! So sing it with a smile at God's love for you. Sing it with praise and thanksgiving. But most of all, sing it with a strong decision: "I will stand on every promise of Your Word." To "stand on a promise" is to fully rely on and trust that the promise will happen just as it has been given. Say to God, "I will read Your Word and learn Your promises and live by them."

Every Promise of Your Word

62

For the word of the LORD is upright, and all
His work is done in faithfulness.

PSALM 33:4

1. From the break-ing of the dawn to the set-ting of the sun,
2. *When I stum - ble and I sin, con - dem - na - tion press-ing in,*
3. When I'm faced with an-guished choice, I will lis-ten for your voice,
4. *Hope that lifts me from des - pair, love that casts out ev - 'ry fear,*

I will stand on ev-'ry pro-mise of your Word.
I will stand on ev-'ry pro-mise of your Word.
and I'll stand on ev-'ry pro-mise of your Word.
as I stand on ev-'ry pro-mise of your Word.

Words of po-wer, strong to save, that will ne-ver pass a-way;
You are faith-ful to for-give that in free-dom I might live,
Through this dark and troub-led land you will guide me with your hand
Not for-sak-en, not a-lone, for the Com-for-ter has come,

I will stand on ev-'ry pro-mise of your Word.
so I stand on ev-'ry pro-mise of your Word.
as I stand on ev-'ry pro-mise of your Word.
and I stand on ev-'ry pro-mise of your Word.

For your co-ve-nant is sure, and on this I am se-cure:
Guilt to in-no-cence re-stored, you re-mem-ber sins no more,
And you've pro-mised to com-plete ev-'ry work be-gun in me,
Grace suf-fi-cient, grace for me, grace for all who will be-lieve.

I can stand on ev-'ry pro-mise of your Word.
so I'll stand on ev-'ry pro-mise of your Word.
so I'll stand on ev-'ry pro-mise of your Word.
We will stand on ev-'ry pro-mise of your Word.

TEXT AND TUNE: Stuart Townend, Keith Getty

	b. December 18, 1707, Epworth, England
TEXT: Charles Wesley	d. March 29, 1788, London, England
	(for more on Wesley, see No. 2, 4, 31, 37, 41, 86, and 103)

We often hear about people who live selfish, depraved lives and then are transformed by their encounter with Christ. Charles Wesley, however, lived a righteous, ordered life. He even started a "holiness club" with his brother John at Oxford University and later traveled to America as a missionary. He returned to England, however, depressed by failure. Through all of his righteous living and sacrificial serving, Wesley still did not truly *know* Christ! He was godly on the outside only.

Back in England, Wesley found true salvation by faith in Christ. At the age of thirty, on May 21, 1738, he wrote, "I now found myself at peace with God and rejoiced in the hope of loving Christ. I saw that by faith I stood."[43] On May 23, he wrote, "I began a hymn upon my conversion."[44] Many believe that hymn was "And Can It Be."

| | b. July 27, 1777, Glasgow, Scotland |
| TUNE: Thomas Campbell | d. June 15, 1844, Boulogne, France |

Although Thomas Campbell wrote books, studied law, and helped found a university, he is mainly remembered as a composer, for which he won several prizes. SAGINA is one of twenty-three original tunes in his publication, *The Bouquet*. Sagina is a beautiful moss, commonly called Irish Moss, which grows profusely on thin, rocky soil. Campbell was honored by being buried at Westminster Abbey.

As you sing this hymn . . . notice that it is written in the first person—a personal testimony of Wesley's conversion. But it serves well as the testimony of all who come to Christ and are saved. The words "I" and "me" could stand for *you*. How amazing is the love of God that He left heaven to take the sin of His people?

Before salvation, everyone is bound by the "chains" of sin. Have you ever thought of sin that way? The apostle Paul said, "For freedom Christ has set us free; stand firm therefore, and do not submit again to a yoke of slavery" (Gal. 5:1). Sin enslaves us. You can imagine chains wrapped around your body or, actually, your soul. As you sing, "Amazing love! How can it be that Thou my God shouldst die for me," picture the chains breaking and finding yourself free! Sin enslaves us to the way of death, but because of Christ's sacrifice, God the Judge pronounces, "You are free. There is now no condemnation!"

This freedom has been given to you if you are God's child. Understanding the wonder of this freedom should make you want to shout this refrain: "Amazing love, how can it be that Thou my God shouldst die for me?"

And Can It Be That I Should Gain 63

*The Son of God, who loved me and gave Himself for me. . . .There is therefore
now no condemnation for those who are in Christ Jesus.*

GALATIANS 2:20, ROMANS 8:1

1. And can it be that I__ should gain an in - t'rest in the__
2. He left His Fa - ther's throne a - bove, so free,__ so__ in - fi -
3. Long my im - pris - oned spir - it__ lay fast bound in__ sin and__
4. No con - dem - na - tion now__ I__ dread: Je - sus,__ and__ all in__

Sav - ior's blood? Died He for me,__who caused His pain? For me,__ who
nite His grace! Emp - tied Him - self___ of all but love, and bled__ for
na - ture's night. Thine eye dif - fused__ a quick-'ning ray: I woke, the
Him, is mine! A - live in Him, my liv - ing Head, and clothed in

Him__ to death pur - sued? A - maz-ing love! How can__ it__
Ad - am's help - less race! 'Tis mer - cy all, im - mense and__
dun - geon flamed with light! My chains fell off, my__ heart was__
right - eous - ness di - vine, bold I ap - proach th'e - ter - nal__

be_____ that Thou,__ my God,__shouldst die____ for me.
free,_____ for, O_____ my God,__ it found____ out me.
free,_____ I rose,____ went forth,__ and fol - lowed Thee.
throne,_____ and claim____ the crown,__ through Christ,__ my own.

A - maz - ing love! How can it be that

A - maz - ing love! How can it be

Thou, my God, shouldst die for me.

that Thou, my God, shouldst die____ for__ me!

TEXT: Charles Wesley

TUNE: Thomas Campbell

SAGINA

| TEXT: Elizabeth Cecelia Clephane | b. June 18, 1830, Edinburgh, Scotland |
| | d. February 19, 1869, Bridgend House, Scotland |

Elizabeth Clephane lived in Scotland with two older sisters and a father who was the county sheriff. She was known in her town as "The Sunbeam," even though she was sickly and had a weak disposition. Elizabeth was very benevolent and used what money she had to help others. She wrote two hymns that remain, "Beneath the Cross of Jesus" and "The Ninety and Nine," but neither were published until after she died at the young age of thirty-nine. The editor who published Clephane's poems described her words as written by someone on the "edge of life" staring into eternity from the earth.[45] Perhaps the strength of her hymns is based on her excellent biblical knowledge, which is evident in the rich imagery found here. In the first stanza alone, we have the "mighty rock" from Isaiah 32:2; the "weary land" of Psalm 63:1; a "home within the wilderness," Jeremiah 9:2; "rest upon the way," Isaiah 28:12; "noontide heat," Isaiah 4:6; and the "burden of the day," Matthew 11:30.[46]

| TUNE: Frederick Charles Maker | b. 1844, Bristol, England |
| | d. January 1, 1927, Bristol, England |

Frederick Maker was a church musician who spent his entire life in Bristol, England, beginning as a chorister in the cathedral, then the organist and conductor, and ultimately a music professor at Clifton College. His organ teacher urged him to contribute his tunes to *The Bristol Song Book* (1881). Frederick wrote and named this tune St. Christopher after a third-century martyr. The date means that Elizabeth Clephane never heard her hymn sung to the music that made her hymn text famous.

As you sing this hymn . . . can you imagine yourself standing at the foot of the cross? The word *fain* in the first line is an archaic word that means happily or gladly. Would you gladly stand in such a gruesome place? In fact, there is a double meaning to "take a stand." It also refers to standing by your convictions or beliefs. How amazing that this instrument of torture and death becomes the mighty Rock where the weary can stand, where the sinful can find forgiveness, where the broken can find healing! The hymn declares that because of the cross, we see two opposites at once: the wonder of Christ's love and the depth of our unworthiness. Paul said the cross is "foolishness" to the world. But for Christians, it is glory because it is the greatest gift from God to humankind.

Beneath the Cross of Jesus

Each will be like a hiding place from the wind,
a shelter from the storm, like streams of water in a dry place,
like the shade of a great rock in a weary land.

ISAIAH 32:2

TEXT: Elizabeth Cecelia Clephane
TUNE: Frederick C. Maker

ST. CHRISTOPHER

Savior   In Christ Alone

TEXT: Stuart Townend ‖ b. June 1, 1963, West Yorkshire, England
(for more on Townend, see No. 12, 26, 34, 62, and 99)

Some of the most sung hymns written in the twenty-first century come from Great Britain, particularly from Stuart Townend and Keith and Kristyn Getty. "In Christ Alone" is one of their first hymns, written in 2001, and is a favorite hymn of people worldwide.

Townend, the youngest of four children born to a Church of England minister, committed his life to Christ at age thirteen. He began playing the piano at age seven, taught himself to play the guitar as a teenager, and began to compose songs at the age of twenty-two. He serves as a worship leader, recording artist, and seminar speaker.

Some have compared Townend's significance as a contemporary hymn writer to Watts and Wesley. He writes, "Sometimes great melodies are let down by indifferent or clichéd words. It's the writer's job to dig deep into the meaning of Scripture and express in poetic and memorable ways the truth he or she finds there. . . . Songs remain in the mind in a way sermons do not, so songwriters have an important role and a huge responsibility."[47] Townend received this melody from Getty before he wrote the text and knew immediately that the beautiful, haunting melody needed timeless lyrics that would be equal to it.

TUNE: Keith Getty ‖ b. December 16, 1974, Lisburn, Northern Ireland
(for more on Getty, see No. 12, 34, 62, and 99)

Keith Getty is a professional musician. His first instrument was the guitar, but he later excelled in the flute and piano. While taking a graduate-degree class with world-famous flutist Sir James Galway, Getty's ability was affirmed by the artist, which in turn opened up the music industry for him. Subsequently, Getty has worked on hundreds of projects for recording, concerts, theater, television, and film.

As you sing this hymn . . . you are singing the whole gospel: the birth, life, death, and resurrection of Jesus Christ. This hymn is full of theology. It is a complete description of our life in Christ, including how we are to respond to Him. Notice the phrase repeated at the end of stanzas: "Here in the love . . . here in the death . . . here in the [resurrection] power of Christ, I stand."

Although "here" may be different for everyone, Jesus Christ is always in the midst of our "here." Jesus commands all things, and He promises that nothing can "pluck us" from His hand. One American soldier serving in the Iraqi War emailed Stuart Townend and explained how he prayed through each stanza every day. He reported that these promises of God's protection and grace helped sustain him through the pressures and dangers of life in a war zone.

In Christ Alone

*Blessed be the God and Father of our Lord Jesus Christ! According to His
great mercy, He has caused us to be born again to a living hope through the
resurrection of Jesus Christ from the dead.*

I PETER 1:3

1. In Christ a - lone, my hope is found; He is my light, my strength, my song;
2. *In Christ a - lone, who took on flesh, full-ness of God in help - less babe!*
3. There in the ground His bod-y lay, Light of the World by dark - ness slain;
4. *No guilt in life, no fear in death, this is the power of Christ in me;*

this cor-ner-stone, this sol - id ground, firm through the fierc-est drought and storm.
This gift of love and right-eous-ness, scorned by the ones He came to save.
then burst-ing forth in glo-rious day, up from the grave He rose a - gain!
from life's first cry to fin - al breath, Je - sus com-mands my des - ti - ny.

What heights of love, what depths of peace, when fears are stilled, when striv-ings cease!
Till on that cross as Je - sus died, the wrath of God was sat - is - fied;
And as He stands in vic - to - ry, sin's curse has lost its grip on me;
No power of hell, no scheme of man, can ev - er pluck me from His hand;

My com-fort - er, my all in all, here in the love of Christ I stand.
for ev' - ry sin on Him was laid, here in the death of Christ I live.
for I am His, and He is mine, bought with the pre-cious blood of Christ.
till He re - turns or calls me home, here in the power of Christ I'll stand.

TEXT: Stuart Townend
TUNE: Keith Getty

Savior Lamb of God

TEXT AND TUNE: Twila Paris ‖ b. December 28, 1958, Ft. Worth, Texas

Twila Paris is known as a hymn writer, but she is also a solo performer and author. "Lamb of God," as well as her songs "We Will Glorify," "We Bow Down," "How Beautiful," and "He Is Exalted," are loved and sung by millions of Christians and included in many hymnals worldwide. She has produced over twenty albums and been given numerous Christian-music industry awards.

Paris grew up in Arkansas. She sang in a preschool church choir and started piano lessons at age six. When she was twelve, her father, a pastor and musician, challenged her to compose a song and continue the family tradition of ministry, dating back four generations. Her great-grandparents were traveling preachers, her grandfather was a church planter, and her grandmother a Christian songwriter.

Paris composed "Lamb of God" when she was twenty-two. She later said the experience was "like taking dictation."[48] After finishing it she thought, "Did I write that?"[49] She also said that watching the hymn spread worldwide felt like having a child grow up and go off to do things completely independently of you, something more gratifying than any award. "Lamb of God" is one of her favorite works since it meets her definition of excellent worship music—drawing people into delighting in Christ.

As you sing this hymn . . . do you see all the paradoxes in the text? Jesus had no sin, but God sent Him to this guilty earth. He is a gift of love, but we crucified Him. He is a humble King, but we called him a fraud. Our sin condemns us, but Jesus brings us to His side. Of course, the gospel itself is a paradox because it brings life out of death. What wonderful things to consider as you sing each chorus, giving you the chance to tell Jesus the Lamb how much you love Him.

Why is Jesus called a lamb? Centuries before Christ came, the Israelites had been taught to commemorate their escape from God's judgment upon all the land of Egypt through the Passover meal. In the original meal, God told them to sacrifice an unblemished, spotless lamb and then to smear its blood over the doorpost of their homes so that the angel of death would *pass over* them, sparing them from God's judgment. Yet, the real point of the meal was not to look back to the Exodus but to look forward to Jesus. He would become the real sacrificial "Lamb" for our sin, the substitute for the punishment we deserve.

Lamb of God, a beautiful name! But there's one more paradox: Jesus the capital "L" Lamb becomes the shepherd for those of us who are His lowercase "l" lambs. Defenseless creatures that we are, we need the Good Shepherd to survive. And He comes to us as God's Lamb.

Lamb of God

You were ransomed . . . with the precious blood of Christ,
like that of a lamb without blemish or spot.

1 PETER 1:18–19

1. Your only Son, no sin to hide, but You have sent Him from Your side, to walk up-on this guilt-y sod, and to become the Lamb of God.
2. *Your gift of love, they cru-ci-fied, they laughed and scorned Him as He died, the hum-ble King they named a fraud and sac-ri-ficed the Lamb of God.*
3. I was so lost, I should have died, but You have brought me to Your side, to be led by Your staff and rod, and to be called a lamb of God.

O Lamb of God, sweet Lamb of God, I love the ho-ly Lamb of God! O wash me in His pre-cious blood, my Je-sus Christ the Lamb of God.

TEXT AND TUNE: Twila Paris

LAMB OF GOD

Savior Jesus! What a Friend for Sinners!

TEXT: J. Wilbur Chapman

b. June 17, 1859, Richmond, Indiana
d. December 25, 1918, New York, New York

J. Wilbur Chapman was a Presbyterian minister in Ohio, Indiana, New York, and Pennsylvania. However, he primarily served as an evangelist, traveling from town to town preaching the gospel. He ministered with D. L. Moody at the World's Fair. He trained the famous Billy Sunday in tent evangelism campaigns. He founded the Winona Lake Bible Conference in Indiana, the Montreat Conference Center in North Carolina, and the Stony Brook Conference Center on Long Island, New York. Chapman also wrote three hymns. This one is the only one that remains in use. Its text clearly reflects his passion for evangelism as he describes the many ways in which Jesus can be seen and known.

TUNE: Rowland Hugh Prichard

b. January 14, 1811, Graienyn, North Wales
d. January 25, 1887, Holywell, North Wales

Rowland Prichard wrote HYFRYDOL before he was twenty years old. It was to be included in a handbook he wrote for a Lutheran hymnal called *The Singers' Friend.* The word *hyfrydol* is Welsh for "cheerful."

Chapman chose this tune even before he wrote the words of the hymn. It is used with numerous other hymn texts, including "Come, Thou Long-Expected Jesus" and "Love Divine, All Loves Excelling."

As you sing this hymn . . . think of your friends. Have they ever disappointed or hurt you? Or have you disappointed or hurt them? Friends are a wonderful gift from God, but at some point, they will all fail us, and we will fail them.

But what if God chooses you as a friend? Can He fail you? No, because He is perfect. When the God of Creation in the person of Jesus Christ becomes our "friend," He does not just become our "pal." Nor does He choose to be our friend because we deserve it or because He needs us. Instead, God Almighty reaches down in compassion so that He might do good to us. We need Him for all our needs—most of all, our need of rescue from eternal death. John 15:13 says, "Greater love has no one than this, that someone lay down his life for his friends."

How do we make Jesus our friend? The final stanza answers: We receive Him. We ask for the forgiveness that He alone can give. How do we act as a friend to Him? We obey and love Him with heart, mind, soul, and strength. Jesus again: "You are My friends if you do what I command you" (John 15:14). If you are His friend, sing the chorus of Hallelujahs with joy. He is with you to the end!

Jesus! What a Friend for Sinners!

67

The Son of Man . . . "a friend of tax collectors and sinners!"

MATTHEW 11:19

1. Je - sus! what___ a Friend for sin - ners! Je - sus! lov - er
2. *Je - sus! what___ a strength in weak - ness! Let me hide my -*
3. Je - sus! what___ a help in sor - row! While the bil - lows
4. *Je - sus! what___ a guide and keep - er! While the tem - pest*
5. Je - sus! I___ do now re - ceive_ Him, more than all in

of___ my soul; friends may fail___ me, foes as -
self___ in Him; tempt - ed, tried,___ and some - times
o'er___ me roll, e - ven when___ my heart is
still___ is high, storms a - bout___ me, night o'er -
Him___ I find; He hath grant - ed me for -

sail___ me, He, my Sav - ior, makes_ me whole.
fail - ing, He, my strength, my vic - tory wins.
break - ing, He, my com - fort, helps_ my soul.
takes___ me, He, my pi - lot, hears_ my cry.
give - ness, I am His, and He___ is mine.

Hal - le - lu - jah! what a Sav - ior! Hal - le - lu - jah!

What_ a Friend! Sav - ing, help - ing, keep - ing,

lov - ing, He is with_ me to the end.

TEXT: J. Wilbur Chapman

HYFRYDOL

TUNE: Rowland Hugh Prichard

TEXT: Anna B. Warner | b. August 31, 1820, Long Island, New York
d. January 22, 1915, Highland Falls, New York

Anna Warner's family lived in New York City, where her father was a wealthy law-yer. After the economic depression of 1837, her family had to leave their home in New York for their house up the Hudson River. As teenagers, Anna and her sister Susan wrote poetry and stories for children to assist their family in this time of financial difficulty. They published 106 collections in all. One contained a story called "Say and Seal," which describes a dying little boy, Johnny Fox. In the story, Johnny's Sunday school teacher comforts him by singing, "Jesus loves me, this I know, for the Bible tells me so."

The house on the Hudson sat across from West Point Military Academy, and Anna often went there to teach Bible classes to the Army cadets. This hymn was well-known to the future officers in her classes. She was, in fact, so loved and respected by the sol-diers that, upon her death, she was granted a full military funeral and buried on the Academy grounds.

TUNE: William B. Bradbury | b. October 6, 1816, York, Maine
d. January 7, 1868, Montclair, New Jersey
(for more on Bradbury, see No. 60 and 72)

In 1862, two years after Anna wrote these words, Bradbury discovered them, wrote the tune, and added the chorus.

As you sing this hymn . . . you may find it easy to sing at least the first verse by memory since it is often the first hymn that children learn. Indeed, it is one of the first truths that we should hear. The Scripture on which it is based is often one of the first Scriptures that we memorize: "For God so loved the world, that He gave His only Son, that whoever believes in Him should not perish but have eternal life" (John 3:16). What eternal love is this?! That the Father and Son would plan before the creation of the world to send the Son on a rescue mission to save sinners like us! Jesus didn't have to leave his Father's side. But both He and the Father love us, so He came to earth to live a perfect life, die on the cross for sin, and rise again so that all who repent and believe might have their sins forgiven and be with God forever.

The first stanza and the very last phrase of the chorus declare something very, very important. Someday, someone may challenge your belief and trust in God's love say-ing, "How do you know God loves you?" Your answer should quickly come from this hymn: "The Bible tells me so!"

Jesus Loves Me

68

I have loved you with an everlasting love; therefore
I have continued my faithfulness to you.

JEREMIAH 31:3

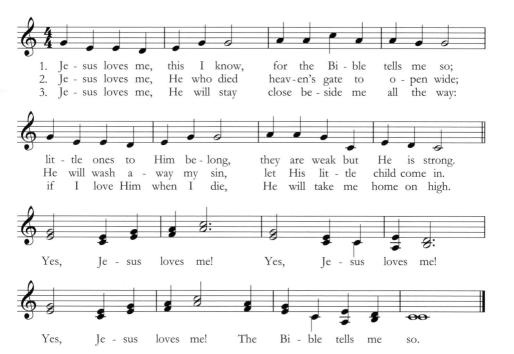

1. Je - sus loves me, this I know, for the Bi - ble tells me so;
2. Je - sus loves me, He who died heav - en's gate to o - pen wide;
3. Je - sus loves me, He will stay close be - side me all the way:

lit - tle ones to Him be - long, they are weak but He is strong.
He will wash a - way my sin, let His lit - tle child come in.
if I love Him when I die, He will take me home on high.

Yes, Je - sus loves me! Yes, Je - sus loves me!

Yes, Je - sus loves me! The Bi - ble tells me so.

TEXT: Anna B. Warner
TUNE: William B. Bradbury

JESUS LOVES ME

| TEXT: Samuel Trevor Francis | b. November 19, 1834, Cheshunt, Hertfordshire, England |
| | d. December 28, 1925, Worthing, Sussex, England |

As a child, Samuel Trevor Francis loved writing poetry so much that he made a book of his own poems. He also loved music and became a member of a church choir when he was nine. As a teenager, however, Francis lived his life far from God. Walking home one night, he began praying for God to have mercy on him. As he crossed the Thames River, he looked down at the rolling, dark water and was tempted to jump in and end his life. The question came to his mind, "Do you believe in the Lord Jesus Christ?" to which he responded, "I do believe." At that point, he says, he turned and put his whole trust in Christ. He became a successful businessman but spent most of his remaining seventy-three years traveling the world to preach and share his written hymns. He wrote the words to this hymn in 1890, when he was fifty-six years old. Indeed God's love had triumphed over his earlier despair.

| TUNE: Thomas John Williams | b. 1869, Ynysmeudwy, Swansea Valley, Glamorganshire, Wales |
| | d. April 23, 1944, Llanelli, Dyfed, Wales |

Thomas John Williams, a Welsh composer and organist, attended a church called Ebenezer (stone of help), after which he named this tune EBENEZER. It is also sometimes called TON-Y-BOTEL ("tune in a bottle") because an English folk singer once said that it must have washed up on the shores of Wales in a bottle! The triplets within the melodic rhythm and the rising and falling melody create a sense of rolling ocean waters.

As you sing this hymn . . . think of standing on a beach, looking at the ocean. The water looks like it goes on forever. Or stand on a boat's deck in the middle of an ocean. The sea's vastness, depth, and power are overwhelming. This is the wonderful picture the hymn writer used to help us faintly grasp the extent of God's love.

Our own love is so limited that we cannot easily comprehend God's. Our love is conditional: meet my conditions, and I will love you. God's love is contra-conditional—He loves us contrary to what we do. Our love is limited; His is infinite.

Paul prayed that believers "may have strength to comprehend with all the saints what is the breadth and length and height and depth, and to know the love of Christ that surpasses knowledge, that you may be filled with all the fullness of God" (Eph. 3:18–19). This hymn will help answer that prayer by pointing to God's greatest demonstration of love, dying for His loved ones. Pray like Paul for God to grow your knowledge of how much He loves you.

O the Deep, Deep Love of Jesus! 69

I bow my knees before the Father, . . . that you, being rooted and grounded in love,
may have strength to comprehend with all the saints what is the breadth and length
and height and depth, and to know the love of Christ that surpasses knowledge.

EPHESIANS 3:14, 17–19

1. O the deep, deep love of Jesus! Vast, un-meas-ured,
2. O the deep, deep love of Jesus! Spread His praise from
3. O the deep, deep love of Jesus! Love of ev-'ry

bound-less, free; roll-ing as a might-y o-cean
shore to shore; how He lov-eth, ev-er lov-eth,
love the best: 'tis an o-cean vast of bless-ing,

in its full-ness o-ver me. Un-der-neath me,
chang-eth nev-er, nev-er-more; how He watch-es
'tis a ha-ven sweet of rest. O the deep, deep

all a-round me, is the cur-rent of Thy love;
o'er His loved ones, died to call them all His own;
love of Je-sus! 'Tis a heav'n of heav'ns to me;

lead-ing on-ward, lead-ing home-ward,
how for them He in-ter-ced-eth,
and it lifts me up to glo-ry,

to Thy glo-rious rest a-bove.
watch-eth o'er them from the throne.
for it lifts me up to Thee.

TEXT: Samuel Trevor Francis
TUNE: Thomas John Williams

EBENEZER (OR TON-Y-BOTEL)

161

TEXT: William Rees | b. November 8, 1802, Denbighshire, Wales
d. November 8, 1883, Chester, England

When a city, region, or country experiences many people becoming Christians in a short span of time, it is called a "revival." Such a revival occurred in Wales, United Kingdom, in 1904. This hymn played a role, said one news report:

> Just after eleven o'clock on a Wednesday evening in 1904, a solo voice rang out with the hymn "Here is love vast as the ocean." . . . A thousand people were in Ebenezer Baptist Church, Abertillery at the time, leaning over the galleries, packing every pew and squeezing into every spare corner. They'd been here for more than four hours, in a service of intense emotion.
>
> Meetings like it were taking place across Wales night after night, with fervent prayer and passionate singing—and similar disregard for the clock. . . . it was reckoned that in little over a year a hundred thousand people had made a new commitment to Jesus Christ.
>
> . . . whole communities changed . . . sparks from their awakening were soon to ignite fires in more than a dozen other countries. And the hymn that soloist struck up spontaneously about "love vast as the ocean" was heard so often that it became known as "the love song of the revival."[50]

William Rees, who wrote the poem in Welsh, was a self-educated farmer, pastor, and prolific Welsh poet. William Edwards, a Welsh theologian and New Testament Greek scholar, translated Rees's poem from Welsh to English.

TUNE: Robert Lowry | b. March 12, 1826, Philadelphia, Pennsylvania
d. November 25, 1899, Plainfield, New Jersey
(for more on Lowry, see No. 73)

This tune was not written until 1876 by American hymn writer Robert Lowry, and he called it CYMRAEG (Welsh). After his death it was linked with "Here Is Love" so it is not known why he called it what he did, nor for what hymn it was initially intended. But the name changed to HERE IS LOVE.

As you sing this hymn . . . picture an ocean. Of course, our eyes cannot see the beginning or end of an ocean. But imagine that ocean filled with God's love. Neither can we see where God's love begins or ends! It is greater than the ocean. It comes from heaven, not like rain but like mighty rivers—incessantly. Over 100,000 people in Wales were drawn to that ocean, to that flood of love. What about you? Do you have a picture of God's love for you? We can see God's love most clearly in that place where the "Prince of Life, our Ransom, shed for us His precious blood." If you belong to Christ, let this hymn be a flood of joy and thanksgiving in your heart and spirit. "See what kind of love the Father has given to us" (1 John 3:1).

Here Is Love

In this is love, not that we have loved God but that He loved us and sent His
Son to be the propitiation for our sins.

I JOHN 4:10

1. Here is love, vast as the o - cean, lov - ing kind - ness as the flood.
2. *On the mount of cru - ci - fix - ion, foun - tains o - pened deep and wide;*

When the Prince of Life, our Ran - som, shed for us His pre - cious blood.
through the flood - gates of God's mer - cy flowed a vast and gra - cious tide.

Who His love will not re - mem - ber? Who can cease to sing His praise?
Grace and love like might - y riv - ers, poured in - ces - sant from a - bove,

He can nev - er be for - got - ten throughout heav'n's e - ter - nal days.
and heav'n's peace and per - fect jus - tice kissed a guilt - y world in love.

TEXT: William Rees
TUNE: Robert Lowry

HERE IS LOVE

Our Hope   O God, Our Help in Ages Past

TEXT: Isaac Watts

b. July 17, 1674, Southampton, England
d. November 25, 1748, London, England
(for more on Watts, see No. 19, 24, 46, and 52)

Isaac Watts wrote this paraphrase of Psalm 90 for his 1719 collection, *Psalms of David Imitated in the Language of the New Testament*. At the time, the Church of England was persecuting "non-conformist" Christians like Watts who worshipped in congregations outside the state-sponsored church. Perhaps these events influenced this text.

This psalm and hymn ask us to behold the God who is timeless, the great I Am for whom days and years are the same. It promises that the same God who has worked in the past and will work in the future is the God who works now, bringing comfort and hope. The hymn has often been sung in times of great significance and change. For example, the British Broadcasting Company aired it on the radio when Britain entered World War II and again years later at the funeral of Winston Churchill, Britain's famed prime minister throughout that war. It is appropriate at funerals and weddings, anniversaries, and memorial occasions.

TUNE: William Croft

baptized: December 10, 1678, Warwickshire, England
d. August 14, 1727, London, England

As a child, William Croft sang as a chorister at the Chapel Royal, where he would later serve as organist, composer, and Master of the Children. Croft received a doctorate from Oxford University and was known as the foremost church musician of his day. He is buried at Westminster Abbey. His tune St. Anne is named for the church in London where he served.

As you sing this hymn . . . remember. Remember who God is. Remember how the Bible testifies to what He has done in the past. Remind yourself of His promises for the future. Israel had a problem remembering. God delivered them from slavery in Egypt, yet they continued to complain. God, weary of their murmuring, passed judgment on them in the wilderness (see Num. 14). Moses wrote Psalm 90 in response.

What about your life? If you are a Christian, can you remember how God made you His own child? Can you remember prayers He has answered and blessings He has given? Have there been times of danger when you know He protected you? Take hope that the God who worked in your past will work in your future.

We only think of time as past, present, and future. That is earth time. But the last phrase of the hymn anticipates another kind of time: eternal home time. One day, remarkably, we will rest in God Himself as our eternal home.

O God, Our Help in Ages Past

Lord, You have been our dwelling place in all generations.

PSALM 90:1

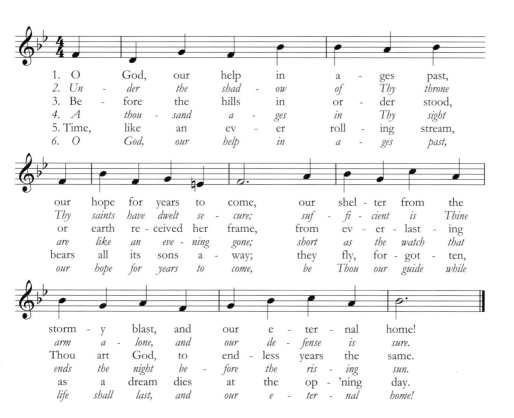

1. O God, our help in a - ges past,
2. *Un - der the shad - ow of Thy throne*
3. Be - fore the hills in or - der stood,
4. *A thou - sand a - ges in Thy sight*
5. Time, like an ev - er roll - ing stream,
6. *O God, our help in a - ges past,*

our hope for years to come, our shel - ter from the
Thy saints have dwelt se - cure; suf - fi - cient is Thine
or earth re - ceived her frame, from ev - er - last - ing
are like an eve - ning gone; short as the watch that
bears all its sons a - way; they fly, for - got - ten,
our hope for years to come, be Thou our guide while

storm - y blast, and our e - ter - nal home!
arm a - lone, and our de - fense is sure.
Thou art God, to end - less years the same.
ends the night be - fore the ris - ing sun.
as a dream dies at the op - 'ning day.
life shall last, and our e - ter - nal home!

TEXT: Isaac Watts
TUNE: William Croft

ST. ANNE

Our Hope The Solid Rock

TEXT: Edward Mote ‖ b. January 21, 1797, London, England
‖ d. November 13, 1874, Horsham, Sussex, England

As a child, Edward Mote did not know there was a God. His parents owned a pub and would not allow a Bible in their home. His Sunday mornings were spent in the streets. However, he heard the gospel as a teenager and became a Christian. Later, he became a successful cabinetmaker and then set that work aside to become a pastor. His own words tell how this hymn was birthed:

> "One morning it came into my mind . . . to write a hymn on the 'Gracious Experience of a Christian.' As I went up to Holborn I had the chorus: *On Christ the solid Rock I stand / All other ground is sinking sand.* In the day, I had four verses complete and wrote them off.
>
> "On the Sabbath following, I met brother King . . . who informed me that his wife was very ill, and asked me to call and see her. . . . He said that it was his usual custom to sing a hymn, read a portion, and engage in prayer before he went to meeting. . . . I said, "I have some verses in my pocket; if he liked, we would sing them." We did, and his wife enjoyed them so much. . . .
>
> "I went home, and by the fireside composed the last two verses. . . . As these verses so met the dying woman's case, my attention to them was the more arrested."[51]

TUNE: William B. Bradbury ‖ b. October 6, 1816, York, Maine
‖ d. January 7, 1868, Montclair, New Jersey
‖ (for more on Bradbury, see No. 60 and 68)

William Bradbury wrote the tune SOLID ROCK specifically for this poem. Therefore, the music "comments" on the text. The first four notes for "My hope is built" sharply rise in an octave sequence in order to picture building a building. The notes of the refrain that accompany "On Christ the solid" are repeated notes, to suggest we are standing on a platform. The notes that accompany "Rock I stand" take a step up, as if stepping onto a higher level. When we sing "all other ground is sinking sand" twice, the melody descends, conveying the idea of sinking. Such word-painting can help us feel the meaning and emotion of the text.

As you sing this hymn . . . picture in your mind a huge rock that withstands wind, rain, ocean waves, and storms. Or look up on the Internet Haystack Rock, which is on the Oregon coast. This single rock is 235 feet tall and one of the world's most well-known monoliths (single stones). Although buffeted by waves and changing tides for eons, Haystack Rock stands immovable, unchanging, and firmly secure. Yet, even more steadfast is the work of Christ. Our salvation does not depend upon our constant faithfulness but upon His.

The Solid Rock

The rain fell, and the floods came, and the winds blew and beat on that house, but it did not fall, because it had been founded on the rock.

MATTHEW 7:25

1. My hope is built on noth-ing less than Je-sus' blood and right-eous-ness;
2. *When dark - ness veils His love - ly face, I rest on His un - chang - ing grace;*
3. His oath, His cov - e - nant, His blood sup - port me in the whelm-ing flood;
4. *When He shall come with trum - pet sound, O may I then in Him be found,*

I dare not trust the sweet-est frame, but whol-ly lean on Je - sus' name.
in ev - ery high and storm - y gale my an-chor holds with - in the veil.
when all a-round my soul gives way, He still is all my hope and stay.
dressed in His right - eous - ness a - lone, fault - less to stand be - fore the throne.

On Christ the sol - id Rock I stand; all oth - er ground is

sink - ing sand; all oth - er ground is sink - ing sand.

TEXT: Edward Mote
TUNE: William B. Bradbury

SOLID ROCK

Our Hope Shall We Gather at the River?

TEXT AND TUNE: Robert Lowry

b. March 12, 1826, Philadelphia, Pennsylvania
d. November 25, 1899, Plainfield, New Jersey
(for more on Lowry, see No. 70)

Robert Lowry started writing hymns when he was a child. He had both an exceptional imagination and a rich vocabulary that enabled him to describe the vivid pictures that came to his mind so that the same thoughts could inspire others. Although God used this ability in his preaching, Lowry realized that he could reach more people with his hymns. "Shall We Gather at the River?" is his most well-known hymn, and some consider it a genuine American folk song. Classical American composers Charles Ives and Aaron Copeland both created arrangements for it.

Lowry himself provides us with an account of how God used his biblically informed imagination to write this song:

> One afternoon in July, 1864, when I was pastor at Hanson Place
> Baptist Church, Brooklyn, the weather was oppressively hot, and I was
> lying on a lounge in a state of physical exhaustion. . . . My imagination
> began to take itself wings. Visions of the future passed before me with
> startling vividness. The imagery of the apocalypse took the form of a
> tableau. Brightest of all were the throne, the heavenly river, and the
> gathering of the saints. . . . I began to wonder why the hymn writers
> had said so much about the "river of death" and so little about the "pure
> water of life, clear as crystal, proceeding out of the throne of God and
> the Lamb." As I mused, the words began to construct themselves. They
> came first as a question of Christian inquiry, "Shall we gather?" Then
> they broke in chorus, "Yes, we'll gather." On this question and answer
> the hymn developed itself. The music came with the hymn.[52]

The tune, HANSON PLACE, comes from the church name.

As you sing this hymn . . . you might think that heaven is a long way off for you. You have no idea what lies between now and your life ahead. But this hymn can help you anticipate the glories of heaven and the gathering of all the saints. Read Revelation 22:1–5, which inspired this hymn, and meditate on the apostle John's description of heaven, which God revealed to him. It should make your "happy heart quiver" in anticipation to see that river, the Tree of Life, and the Lord God, who replaces the sun. You will want to shout "Yes!" as you sing the answer to the question, "Shall we gather at the river?"

William O. Douglas, the longest-serving justice on the U.S. Supreme Court, requested this song, which he had learned as a child, be sung at his funeral service. What hymn are you learning right now that you would want people celebrating your life to sing?

Shall We Gather at the River?

73

Then the angel showed me the river of the water of life, bright as crystal,
flowing from the throne of God and of the Lamb . . . on either side
of the river, the tree of life with its twelve kinds of fruit.

REVELATION 22:1–2

1. Shall we gath-er at the riv - er, where bright an-gel feet have
2. *Ere we reach the shin-ing riv - er, lay we ev' - ry bur - den*
3. Soon we'll reach the shin-ing riv - er, soon our pil-grim-age will

trod,_____ with its crys - tal tide for - ev - er
down;_____ grace our spir - its will de - liv - er,
cease;_____ soon our hap - py hearts will quiv - er

flow - ing by the____ throne of____ God?
and pro - vide a____ robe and____ crown.
with the mel - o - dy of____ peace.

Yes, we'll gath-er at the riv - er, the beau-ti-ful, the beau-ti-ful____

riv - er, gath-er with the saints__ at the riv - er,

that flows by the throne of____ God.

TEXT AND TUNE: Robert Lowry   HANSON PLACE

Children of the Heavenly Father

TEXT: Carolina Berg || b. October 3, 1832, Fröderyd, Sweden
d. 1903, Stockholm, Sweden

Carolina Berg has been called the "Fanny Crosby of Sweden," and her hymn "Children of the Heavenly Father" is one of the most loved of all Swedish hymns. Lina, as she was called, was the daughter of a pastor. As a child she was never physically strong and preferred playing in her father's study to playing outside. At one point she contracted a mysterious illness that left her legs paralyzed. The doctor said her case was hopeless and that she would never walk. Yet one Sunday while her family was at church, Lina prayed, and when her family returned home, they found her dressed and walking around the house! Her love for God and faith in Him was greatly encouraged by this miracle, and she began writing down her thoughts in poetry. At age sixteen she published her first book of poems. Ten years later tragedy again came to Lina when she and her father were crossing Lake Vättern. The boat lurched, throwing her father overboard, and he drowned before her eyes.

TUNE: Oscar Ahnfelt || b. May 21, 1813, Gullarp, Skåne, Sweden
d. October 22, 1882, Karlshamn, Blekinge, Sweden

TRYGGARE KAN INGEN VARA is Swedish for "safer no one can be." It was written by Oscar Ahnfelt, known as the "Swedish troubadour." He lived in Sweden at the same time as Miss Berg and wrote the melodies for all of her hymns. He traveled throughout the country singing and playing them on his ten-string guitar, even though the state church opposed such "Pietist" hymns. The authorities eventually ordered Ahnfelt to sing them before King Karl XV, who, upon hearing them, said that Ahnfelt could sing them anywhere. Carolina Berg said of the singer that he "has sung my songs into the hearts of the people."[53] The songs were made even more popular by the famous Swedish singer Jenny Lind, when she toured America.

As you sing this hymn . . . it will be obvious to you that, in spite of the sadness and tragedy in her life, Berg found amazing comfort in her heavenly Father. She had seen her earthly father drown. How could she sing "neither life nor death shall ever from the Lord His children sever"? Only because she understood the eternal love of God for His children. She knew that our experiences in this life, both good and bad, are part of His loving plan. If we belong to Him, He has one goal in every circumstance, even in tragedy: "to preserve us pure and holy." May this hymn's profound faith and truth sink deep in your heart and become your cry and song during whatever sadness God may permit in your future.

Children of the Heavenly Father

74

See what kind of love the Father has given to us,
that we should be called children of God; and so we are.

1 JOHN 3:1

1. Chil - dren of the heav'n - ly Fa - ther safe - ly
in His bo - som gath - er; nest - ling bird nor star in
heav - en such a ref - uge e'er was giv - en.

2. God His own doth tend and nour - ish, in His
ho - ly courts they flour - ish; from all e - vil things He
spares them, in His might - y arms He bears them.

3. Nei - ther life nor death shall ev - er from the
Lord His chil - dren sev - er; un - to them His grace He
show - eth, and their sor - rows all He know - eth.

4. Praise the Lord in joy - ful num - bers, your Pro -
tec - tor nev - er slum - bers; at the will of your De -
fend - er ev - 'ry foe - man must sur - ren - der.

5. Though He giv - eth or He tak - eth, God His
chil - dren ne'er for - sak - eth; His the lov - ing pur - pose
sole - ly to pre - serve them pure and ho - ly.

TEXT: Carolina Sandell Berg
TUNE: Oscar Ahnfelt, trans. Ernest W. Olson

TRYGGARE KAN INGEN VARA

Protector   The Church's One Foundation

TEXT: Samuel J. Stone	b. April 25, 1839, Whitmore, Staffordshire, England
	d. November 19, 1900, Charterhouse, Somerset, England

Samuel Stone was a pastor to poor people who lived in the neighborhood of England's Windsor Castle, a residence of the royal family outside of London. Among the theologians of his day, he was one who clung to orthodox beliefs while others began to stray. He was known to vigorously defend what he believed, even if it meant a fight.

Concerned that people were reciting the Apostles' Creed without knowing what it meant, Stone wrote a collection of twelve hymns, each focusing on a section of the creed. This hymn comes from that series and is by far the most well-known. Hymnologist Erik Routley counted this hymn as one of the dozen greatest hymns in the English language.[54]

TUNE: Samuel Sebastian Wesley	b. August 14, 1810, London, England
	d. April 19, 1876, Gloucester, England

Samuel Wesley wrote this tune for another hymn called "Jerusalem the Golden," so Wesley's wife suggested he name the tune AURELIA, from the Latin word for golden, *aureus*. Wesley was the grandson of the legendary hymn writer Charles Wesley. He began his musical career as a choir boy in the Chapel Royal and St. Paul's Cathedral and became a well-known theater organist and conductor.

As you sing this hymn . . . you will learn that the church is not a Sunday event. This church is not a building. The church is a people. It's a people you will find scattered around the world and throughout history. It is all those who have ever been or will be saved by grace alone through faith alone.

Jesus Christ is the foundation of the church. He left heaven, says stanza 1, to seek her out as a bride. Then He paid for her with His own blood. He is her one Lord, says stanza 2. And the church everywhere is united in this one name, one faith, one birth, one food, one hope.

Unfortunately, the church sometimes argues, sometimes splits, sometimes is even deceived by false teachers. These are the schisms and heresies, toil and tumult, mentioned in stanzas 3 and 4. Wonderfully, God promises a coming victory and rest, even a "peace forevermore." One day she will enjoy the communion of God, the Three in One. One cannot help but conclude the hymn's last stanza with a prayer for the grace to finally dwell on high with God and all His church.

The Church's One Foundation

75

For no one can lay a foundation other than that which is laid,
which is Jesus Christ.

I CORINTHIANS 3:II

1. The Church's one foun - da - tion is Je - sus Christ, her Lord;
2. *E - lect from ev - ery na - tion, yet one o'er all the earth,*
3. Though with a scorn-ful won - der we see her sore op - pressed,
4. *'Mid toil and trib - u - la - tion, and tu - mult of her war,*
5. Yet she on earth hath un - ion with God, the Three in One,

she is His new cre - a - tion, by wa - ter and the Word:
her char - ter of sal - va - tion; one Lord, one faith, one birth;
by schi-sms rent a - sun - der, by her - e - sies dis - tressed:
she waits the con - sum - ma - tion of peace for - ev - er - more,
and mys - tic sweet com - mun - ion with those whose rest is won:

from heaven He came and sought her to be His ho - ly bride;
one ho - ly name she bless - es, par - takes one ho - ly food,
yet saints their watch are keep - ing, their cry goes up, "How long?"
till with the vi - sion glo - rious her long - ing eyes are blest,
O hap - py ones and ho - ly! Lord, give us grace that we,

with His own blood He bought her, and for her life He died.
and to one hope she press - es with ev - ery grace en - dued.
and soon the night of weep - ing shall be the morn of song.
and the great Church vic - to - rious shall be the Church at rest.
like them, the meek and low - ly, on high may dwell with Thee.

TEXT: Samuel J. Stone
TUNE: Samuel S. Wesley

AURELIA

TEXT: Frances Ridley Havergal ‖ b. December 14, 1836, Astley, Worcestershire, England
d. June 3, 1879, Caswell Bay, Swansea, Wales
(for more on Havergal, see No. 113)

Frances, or Fanny, Havergal was the youngest daughter of her family during Britain's Victorian period. She was a happy and very bright child, and by the age of three, could be found under the table reading favorite books. Her father, a pastor and hymn writer, called her "Little Quicksilver." Although she was not strong physically, Havergal began writing poetry and memorizing Scripture by the age of seven. She could quote from the Psalms, Isaiah, the Minor Prophets, and the New Testament. She learned Hebrew, Greek, and several other languages. And she loved music!

Her mother became ill when Frances was only eleven, and she told her daughter to pray that God would prepare her for all He had in store for her. Frances herself became quite ill a few years later with a condition that lasted nine years. It was during this time that she wrote "Like a River Glorious." When Havergal's doctor told her at the age of forty-two that she would not live much longer, she told him that was too good to be true![55] She died shortly after that.

TUNE: James Mountain ‖ b. July 16, 1844, Leeds, Yorkshire, England
d. June 27, 1933, Tunbridge Wells, Kent, England

James Mountain wrote the melody he called WYE VALLEY specifically for this hymn. The Wye Valley is a beautiful stretch of land on the border between England and Wales. The tune was first published in *Hymns for Consecration and Faith* in 1876.

As you sing this hymn . . . can you remember ever standing on the banks of a large, wide river? That much water moving is powerful, but not rough and noisy like the ocean. It is quiet, yet unrelenting and unstoppable, embracing everything in its path. So is God at work. He is overpowering, but peaceful.

Notice that while the first stanza talks about God's peace, stanzas 2 and 3 introduce foes, traitors, worry, care, and trials. This is where God's peace differs from anything the world has to offer. Only God makes peace possible among hardships as we are "stayed," or fixed in trust, "upon Jehovah." There are two Bible verses about peace that every Christian should memorize: "You keep him in perfect peace whose mind is stayed on You, because he trusts in You" (Isa. 26:3); and, "Peace I leave with you; My peace I give to you. Not as the world gives do I give to you. Let not your hearts be troubled, neither let them be afraid" (John 14:27).

Like a River Glorious

76

I will extend peace to her like a river . . .
As one whom his mother comforts, so I will comfort you.

ISAIAH 66:12–13

1. Like a riv - er glo - rious is God's per - fect peace,
2. *Hid - den in the hol - low of His bless - ed hand,*
3. Ev - 'ry joy or tri - al fall - eth from a - bove,

o - ver all vic - to - rious in its bright in - crease;
nev - er foe can fol - low, nev - er trai - tor stand;
traced up - on our di - al by the Sun of Love.

per - fect, yet it flow - eth full - er ev - 'ry day,
not a surge of wor - ry, not a shade of care,
We may trust Him ful - ly all for us to do;

per - fect yet it grow - eth deep - er all the way.
not a blast of hur - ry, touch the spir - it there.
they who trust Him whol - ly find Him whol - ly true.

Stayed up - on Je - ho - vah, hearts are ful - ly blest,

find - ing, as He prom - ised, per - fect peace and rest.

TEXT: Frances R. Havergal
TUNE: James Mountain

WYE VALLEY

Bless the Lord, O my soul, and all that is within me,
bless His holy name!
Bless the Lord, O my soul, and forget not all His benefits,
who forgives all your iniquity,
who heals all your diseases,
who redeems your life from the pit,
who crowns you with steadfast love and mercy,
who satisfies you with good so that
your youth is renewed like the eagle's.

PSALM 103:1–5

We Respond

PRAISE
THANKSGIVING
CONFESSION
PETITION
TESTIMONY
COMMITMENT

TEXT: William Kethe ‖ b. 1561
d. June 6, 1594, Dorsetshire, England

Written over 400 years ago and printed in the first English Psalter, this hymn is the oldest English hymn text that we sing. Other hymns with earlier dates are translations of German, Latin, or Greek texts.

William Kethe, a Scotsman, was a minister in the Church of England. During the reign of Queen Mary (1553–1558), persecution of Protestants was so severe that public singing ceased almost entirely. Protestants fled England to escape persecution. Kethe fled to Germany where he was greatly influenced by John Calvin and by the forms of worship in the Reformed movement. When he later returned to Scotland, he and his friends, impressed with the *Scottish Psalter*, created the *Genevan Psalter*. "All People That on Earth Do Dwell" is a poetic or metrical setting of Psalm 100 and is sung today exactly as it was over 400 years ago. Other than Psalm 23, it is the most sung of all the Psalms.

TUNE: Louis Bourgeois ‖ b. ca. 1510, Paris, France
d. 1561, Paris, France

OLD HUNDREDTH is obviously named for Psalm 100. As a devoted follower of John Calvin and the Reformed Reformation Movement in Switzerland, Bourgeois was commissioned to write tunes for many new metrical psalms being written at that time. The *Genevan Psalter* became the hymn book used by the Pilgrims in America.

There is another text well known to us that often uses this tune. Do you know what it is? Hint: it was written by Thomas Ken.

As you sing this hymn . . . you are declaring that the reason God created us is to praise Him. This was the heart of the psalmist David. "The chief end of man is to glorify God" is the foundational creed of the Westminster Confession. Erik Routley proposes that there is no greater witness to the world than the Christian life of praise. Have you made this your purpose in life? By learning this hymn and all the hymns of this hymnal, you are creating a bank account of words from which to draw for praise and thanksgiving as you live out your life before God.

Why should you do this, stanza 4 asks? Because God is good, His mercy is sure, and His truth always stands. Stanza 5 is also known as the Doxology and is often sung by itself in many churches as a declaration of praise to the Trinity.

All People That on Earth Do Dwell 77

Make a joyful noise to the LORD, all the earth! Serve the LORD with gladness!
Come into His presence with singing!

PSALM 100:1–2

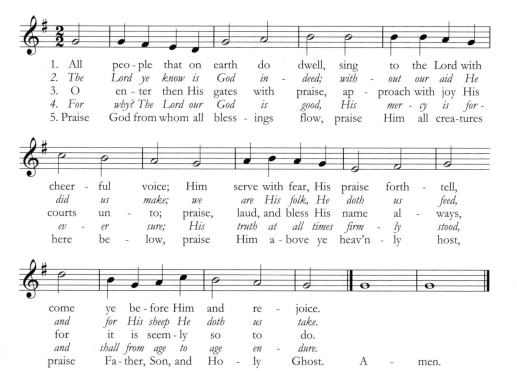

1. All peo-ple that on earth do dwell, sing to the Lord with
2. The Lord ye know is God in - deed; with - out our aid He
3. O en - ter then His gates with praise, ap - proach with joy His
4. For why? The Lord our God is good, His mer - cy is for -
5. Praise God from whom all bless - ings flow, praise Him all crea-tures

cheer - ful voice; Him serve with fear, His praise forth - tell,
did us make; we are His folk, He doth us feed,
courts un - to; praise, laud, and bless His name al - ways,
ev - er sure; His truth at all times firm - ly stood,
here be - low, praise Him a - bove ye heav'n - ly host,

come ye be - fore Him and re - joice.
and for His sheep He doth us take.
for it is seem - ly so to do.
and shall from age to age en - dure.
praise Fa - ther, Son, and Ho - ly Ghost. A - men.

TEXT: Psalm 100, William Kethe   OLD HUNDREDTH
TUNE: Louis Bourgeois in *Genevan Psalter*

TEXT: St. Francis of Assisi ‖ b. ca. 1182, Assisi, Italy
d. October 3, 1226, Assisi, Italy

In the late twelfth century, Giovanni Francesco Bernardone was born into a wealthy, highly educated Italian family. He became a soldier and lived a self-indulgent life. However, spending a year as a prisoner of war and falling into serious illness caused Francis to turn to God. He renounced his privileged life and devoted himself as a monk to serve the poor. He also took good care of animals and would eventually be called "the patron saint of animals." Francis knew from Scripture that God created all creatures to praise Him. Since he worked in Assisi, Italy, Francis is now known as St. Francis of Assisi.

St. Francis wrote this hymn near the end of his life when he was almost blind and was suffering intense pain. It may be the oldest religious poem in the Italian language and is also known as "Canticle of the Sun." Around 1899, William Draper translated it into English for an English children's worship festival.

TUNE: *Geistliche Kirchengesange*, Cologne, 1623, ‖
arr. Ralph Vaughan Williams, 1906, Gloucestershire, England ‖

Lasst Uns Erfreuen literally means "let us delight," and in the early 1620s it was a popular tune for an Easter hymn in the German Catholic church. Three hundred years later the famous British composer Ralph (pronounced "Rafe") Vaughan Williams arranged the tune for the *English Hymnal*, where it was combined with the St. Francis lyrics.

As you sing this hymn . . . you join all creation in singing praise to God. The psalmist tells us that the rivers clap their hands, the hills sing for joy, and the skies declare His handiwork (Ps. 98:8; 19:1). Jesus even says that if people failed to praise Him, "the very stones would cry out" (Luke 19:40). When you listen to the flowing water of a brook or a waterfall, do you ever think of it as a song to God? Have you ever considered that fire and the burning sun are images that reflect the fearsome power of God?

The fourth stanza of this hymn reminds us that praising the God of creation will enable us to be more caring and forgiving of others and will help us to trust God in difficult times. The last stanza summarizes creation's praise in a great doxology, words of praise to the Trinity—Father, Son, and Holy Spirit. This tune can be used to sing the traditional Doxology as well: "Praise God from whom all blessings flow." Try performing this hymn antiphonally. One group (I) sings the first phrase, another (II) the second phrase, and so forth. All join together on the final "Alleluia!"

All Creatures of Our God and King 78

All Your works shall give thanks to You, O LORD,
and all Your saints shall bless You!

PSALM 145:10

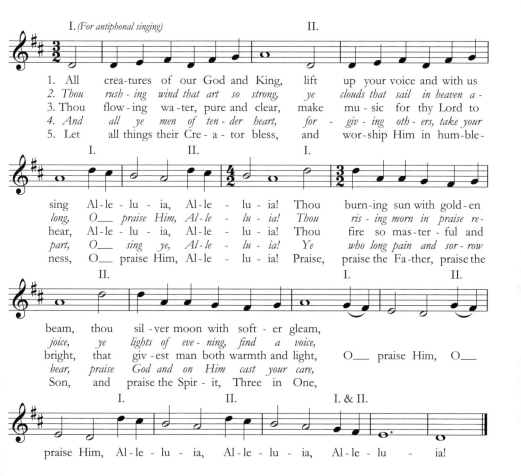

I. *(For antiphonal singing)*   II.

1. All   crea-tures of our God and King,   lift   up your voice and with us
2. Thou   rush-ing   wind that art so strong,   ye   clouds that sail in heaven a-
3. Thou   flow-ing   wa-ter, pure and clear,   make   mu-sic for thy Lord to
4. And   all ye   men of ten-der heart,   for - giv-ing oth-ers, take your
5. Let   all things their Cre-a-tor bless,   and   wor-ship Him in hum-ble-

sing Al-le-lu-ia, Al-le-lu-ia! Thou   burn-ing sun with gold-en
long, O__ praise Him, Al-le-lu-ia! Thou   ris-ing morn in praise re-
hear, Al-le-lu-ia, Al-le-lu-ia! Thou   fire so mas-ter-ful and
part, O__ sing ye, Al-le-lu-ia! Ye   who long pain and sor-row
ness, O__ praise Him, Al-le-lu-ia! Praise, praise the Fa-ther, praise the

beam, thou sil-ver moon with soft-er gleam,
joice, ye   lights of eve-ning, find a voice,
bright, that giv-est man both warmth and light, O__ praise Him, O__
bear, praise God and on Him cast your care,
Son,   and   praise the Spir-it, Three in One,

praise Him, Al-le-lu-ia, Al-le-lu-ia, Al-le-lu-ia!

TEXT: St. Francis of Assisi
TUNE: *Geistliche Kirchengesange,* 1623

LASST UNS ERFREUEN

Praise   O Worship the King

TEXT: Robert Grant ‖ b. 1779, Bengal, India
d. July 9, 1838, Bombay, India

O ne day Robert Grant was reading Psalm 104, which offers a magnificent portrayal of God's heavenly majesty. He could not help but compare this King to his earthly monarch, the king of England. Grant was well acquainted with power and privilege. His father was the chairman of the East India Company and later a Member of Parliament. But the greatest legacy he left his son was his strong Christian commitment, which helped the younger Grant discern the contrast between earthly power and the true King of heaven. Grant's meditation on Psalm 104 inspired him to write this hymn. English hymnist Routley calls it one of the six finest hymns in the English language because of its beauty and grace.[56]

Grant was a graduate of Cambridge University, a lawyer, and a Member of Parliament. In 1832, he became judge advocate general, and in 1834, he was knighted (which is why there is a "Sir" in front of his name). He then returned to India, where he had grown up, and became the governor of Bombay. Someone named a medical school for him, which remains there today.

TUNE: Joseph Martin Kraus ‖ b. June 20, 1756, Miltenberg am Main, Germany
d. December 15, 1792, Stockholm, Sweden

T he tune LYONS, named for the French city, has long been regarded as written by Johann Michael Haydn, brother of Franz Joseph Haydn. A recent study shows that it was most likely written by a German composer living in Sweden, Joseph Martin Kraus. It is a much loved and powerful melody. Note the rise in lines one, two, and four, which creates the effect of ascending to a throne. Line three steps upward more slowly and carefully, as if to punctuate the stately attributes of the King.

As you sing this hymn . . . you not only describe our glorious King, but you also respond to His greatness by calling others to worship, tell, and sing of His glory: "O worship the King, all glorious above, O gratefully sing His power and His love." He is the inimitable God who both rides in "chariots of wrath" and comes with "bountiful care." Stanza 4 reminds us that we are frail children made of dust. Yet still, He is our Maker, Defender, Redeemer, and Friend. This great and glorious God lowers Himself to have a relationship with us!

As you learn this hymn, read Psalm 104. You might even imagine Sir Robert Grant sitting and meditating upon it. We continue the praise that he began almost 200 years ago.

O Worship the King

O LORD my God, You are very great!
You are clothed with splendor and majesty.

PSALM 104:1

1. O   wor - ship   the   King,   all   glo - rious   a - bove,
2. O   tell   of   His   might,   O   sing   of   His   grace,
3. Thy   boun - ti - ful   care   what   tongue   can   re - cite?
4. *Frail   chil - dren   of   dust,   and   fee - ble   as   frail,*

O   grate - ful - ly   sing   His   power_ and   His   love;
Whose   robe   is   the   light,   whose   can - o - py   space.
It   breathes   in   the   air,   it   shines_ in   the   light;
in   Thee   do   we   trust,   nor   find___ Thee   to   fail;

our   Shield   and   De - fend - er,   the   An - cient   of   Days,
His   char - iots   of   wrath   the   deep   thun - der   clouds   form,
it   streams from   the   hills,   it   de - scends   to   the   plain,
Thy   mer - cies   how   ten - der,   how   firm   to   the   end,

pa - vil - ioned   in   splen - dor   and   gird - ed   with   praise.
and   dark   is   His   path   on   the   wings_ of   the   storm.
and   sweet - ly   dis - tills   in   the   dew_ and   the   rain.
our   Ma - ker,   De - fend - er,   Re - deem - er   and   Friend.

TEXT: Robert Grant
TUNE: Joseph Martin Kraus

LYONS

Praise Come, Christians, Join to Sing

TEXT: Christian H. Bateman ‖ b. August 9, 1813, Wyke, Scotland
d. July 27, 1889, Carlisle, England

Christian Bateman was an English hymn writer whose ministry was not confined to one denomination. He began his ministerial career as an ordained minister in the Moravian Church of Scotland. Later, he transferred his ordination, a very unusual action, to the Congregational Church. Later still, he was ordained into the Church of England when he was in his fifties. Perhaps this broad experience of the church gave him the ability to write numerous hymns that crossed denominational lines.

In 1853, while a Congregationalist, he wrote a Sunday school song, "Come, Children, Join to Sing." He published it along with others he had written in a children's hymnal entitled *The Sacred Song Book*. It was very popular in Scotland and sold more than six million copies. Over time the hymn's name was changed to "Come, Christians, Join to Sing" because adults enjoyed it as well. It is the repeated "Alleluia!" (praise God) and "Amen" (so be it!) at the end of each phrase that makes this a text that children love to sing.

TUNE: Traditional Spanish melody, ‖
arr. David Evans, 1927

The tune, MADRID, is a traditional Spanish melody. Philadelphia music publisher Benjamin Carr first put it with Bateman's words. David Evans, an Oxford scholar, music professor, and organist, arranged it in 1927 into the form we now know.

As you sing this hymn . . . you are singing an invitation! With the same enthusiasm you might use to invite friends to come and join you in a game, invite other people to sing with "loud praise," with total joy and abandon! You are telling each other why you are so joyful: He, the almighty God, is our "guide and friend" and "to us He'll condescend." What does it mean to condescend? The word means to come down to a lower level. That is what Jesus did when He came to earth. He condescends when He listens from the great throne of heaven to our poor human praise. He condescends when He reaches into our lives to save and to help us. Yet we know He does so gladly. He is not a distant King, but one who walks among us. How can we not rejoice and sing about that?

In the last stanza, we remind ourselves that this joyful song will not end here on earth but will continue in heaven . . . forever and ever!

Come, Christians, Join to Sing

80

Oh come, let us sing to the LORD; . . . Let us come into His presence with
thanksgiving; let us make a joyful noise to Him with songs of praise!

PSALM 95:1–2

1. Come, Chris-tians, join to sing / Al - le - lu - ia! / A - men!
2. *Come, lift your hearts on high, / Al - le - lu - ia! / A - men!*
3. Praise, yet our Christ a - gain, / Al - le - lu - ia! / A - men!

loud praise to Christ our King; / Al - le - lu - ia! / A - men!
let prais - es fill the sky; / Al - le - lu - ia! / A - men!
life shall not end the strain; / Al - le - lu - ia! / A - men!

Let all, with heart and voice, / be - fore His throne re - joice;
He is our Guide and Friend; / to us He'll con - de - scend;
On heav-en's bliss - ful shore, / His good-ness we'll a - dore,

3rd vs. only

praise is His gra-cious choice. / Al - le - lu - ia! / A - men!
His love shall nev - er end, / Al - le - lu - ia! / A - men!
sing - ing for - ev - er - more, / "Al - le - lu - ia! / A - men!"

TEXT: Christian H. Bateman
TUNE: Traditional Spanish melody,
arr. David Evans

MADRID

Praise to the Lord, the Almighty

TEXT: Joachim Neander ‖ b. 1650, Bremen, Germany
d. May 31, 1680, Bremen, Germany

Joachim Neander's father, grandfather, great-grandfather, and great-great-grand-father were all pastors. They were also all named Joachim Neander! Yet, as a teenager Neander rebelled and chose friends who were a bad influence. One evening, when he was twenty years old, he and his friends attended a church service for the purpose of making fun of the new pastor. Providentially, the words spoken that night made such an impression on Neander that he stayed afterward to pray. He later came to faith in Christ through that same pastor, and they remained friends their whole lives. Sadly, Neander died of tuberculosis at the young age of thirty. Yet it was while he was ill that he wrote "Praise to the Lord, the Almighty."

A favorite place of Neander's was a valley on the Rhine River. The beauty of the valley inspired his poetry. In the mid-nineteenth century, the cement industry started to quarry the limestone, and the narrow ravine became a wide valley, which was then named the Neander Valley. A cave in which he sat to write was called "Neander's Cave" (in German, *Neanderthal*). The "Neanderthal Man" was found there in the summer of 1856, giving Joachim the distinction of being the only pastor with what some consider an evolutionary fossil named after him!

TUNE: *Erneuerten Gesangbuch,* 1665 ‖

Neander chose a tune from a book of songs called *Erneuerten Gesangbuch of 1665* and adapted it for his text. The tune, LOBE DEN HERREN, or "Praise to the Lord," was used by J. S. Bach in his Cantatas 57 and 137.

As you sing this hymn . . . you are declaring your priorities. People think they set their priorities by deciding what is most important and then doing it. But someone once said, in order to determine what you truly consider most important, simply look at what you do! *That* is your priority.

We were created in God's image to praise and glorify Him. The Westminster Catechism reminds us, "The chief end of man is to glorify God and enjoy Him for-ever." This is the priority that God has set for our lives and why church services typically begin with hymns and prayers of praise. Praising God forces us to take our eyes off of ourselves. We need to "ponder anew" all the ways He "shelters and sustains us." In unity, we do it together: "All ye who hear," . . . "all that hath life and breath," . . . "join me in glad adoration!"

Praise to the Lord, the Almighty

81

O LORD God of hosts, who is mighty as You are, O LORD,
with Your faithfulness all around You?

PSALM 89:8

1. Praise to the Lord, the Al - might-y, the King of cre - a - tion!
2. *Praise to the Lord, who o'er all things so won - drous - ly reign - eth,*
3. Praise to the Lord, who doth pros-per thy work and de - fend thee,
4. *Praise to the Lord! O let all that is in me a - dore Him!*

O my soul, praise Him, for He is thy health and sal - va - tion!
shel - ters thee un - der His wings, yea, so gen - tly sus - tain - eth!
sure - ly His good -ness and mer - cy here dai - ly at - tend thee.
All that hath life and breath, come now with prais - es be - fore Him!

All ye who hear, now to His tem - ple draw near;
Hast thou not seen how thy de - sires e'er have been
Pon - der a - new what the Al - might - y can do,
Let the A - men sound from His peo - ple a - gain:

join me in glad ad - o - ra - tion!
grant - ed in what He or - dain - eth?
if with His love He be - friend thee.
glad - ly for - ev - er a - dore Him.

TEXT: Joachim Neander, trans. Catherine Winkworth
TUNE: *Erneuerten Gesangbuch, 1665*

LOBE DEN HERREN

Joyful, Joyful, We Adore Thee

TEXT: Henry Van Dyke || b. 1852, Germantown, Pennsylvania
d. April 10, 1933, Princeton, New Jersey

Although Henry Van Dyke was born into the home of a Presbyterian minister, he was hardly a model child. His father once said of him and his brother, "Paul was born good, but Henry was saved by grace."[57] Henry graduated from Princeton Seminary and became the pastor of The Brick Presbyterian Church in New York City, where he gained national recognition as a preacher. He is also a well-known American writer and poet, best known for his Christmas story, "The Other Wise Man," published in 1896.

Dr. Van Dyke wrote this hymn while visiting Williams College in 1907. During the visit, he arrived at breakfast one morning, laid the words of the poem in front of the president of the college, and said, "Here is a hymn for you. Your mountains [the Berkshires] were my inspiration. It must be sung to the music of Beethoven's 'Hymn to Joy.'"[58] The hymn was published in 1911, accompanied by more words of instruction: the hymn was to be sung "by people who know the thought of the age, and are not afraid that any truth of science will destroy their religion or that any revolution on earth will overthrow the Kingdom of Heaven."

TUNE: Ludwig van Beethoven || b. December 16, 1770, Bonn, Germany
d. March 26, 1827, Vienna, Austria

ODE TO JOY is one of the best known and beloved melodies in all classical music. Beethoven composed it for the fourth movement of his great and final Ninth Symphony, also called the Choral Symphony because it uses a choir. Beethoven's text is a poem about joy by the German poet von Schiller. Beethoven composed and conducted this symphony after he had become totally deaf.

As you sing this hymn . . . consider what makes you joyful. This hymn points to the wonders of nature which cause joy. But more importantly, it points to the joy found in love—love from God and other people, particularly the love which comes through forgiveness: "Thou art giving and forgiving." Is there a difference between happiness and joy? Yes, joy runs deeper and comes from God. It can be present even when sin and sadness rob us of temporary happiness.

Notice, too, the third line of this melody. It is almost like a little laugh or giggle as it turns up and down with an eighth-note motif that is repeated two times. It is almost impossible to sing without smiling!

Joyful, Joyful, We Adore Thee

82

Then our mouth was filled with laughter,
and our tongue with shouts of joy.

PSALM 126:2

1. Joy - ful, joy - ful, we a - dore Thee, God of glo - ry, Lord of love;
2. *All Thy works with joy sur - round Thee, earth and heaven re - flect Thy rays,*
3. Thou art giv - ing and for - giv - ing, ev - er bless - ing ev - er blest,

hearts un - fold like flowers be - fore Thee, open - ing to the sun a - bove.
stars and an - gels sing a - round Thee, cen - ter of un - bro - ken praise.
well - spring of the joy of liv - ing, o - cean depth of hap - py rest!

Melt the clouds of sin and sad - ness, drive the dark of doubt a - way;
Field and for - est, vale and moun - tain, flow - ery mead - ow, flash - ing sea,
Thou our Fa - ther, Christ our Broth - er, all who live in love are Thine;

giv - er of im - mor - tal glad - ness, fill us with the light of day!
chant - ing bird and flow - ing foun - tain call us to re - joice in Thee.
teach us how to love each oth - er, lift us to the joy di - vine.

TEXT: Henry Van Dyke
ODE TO JOY
TUNE: Ludwig van Beethoven

TEXT: Walter Chalmers Smith, 1867	b. December 5, 1824, Aberdeen, Scotland
	d. September 19, 1908, Scotland

L ike so many of our hymn writers, Walter Smith was a pastor, scholar, and author. In 1867, he published his own hymnal, *Hymns of Christ and the Christian Life*, but only this one jewel survives. Hymn historian Erik Routley describes the text as "a fine, simple hymn full of plump polysyllables and very popular with young people."[59] You know what a syllable is. And "poly" means "many." Not only do the words in this hymn contain many syllables, but also, they are "plump." They are stuffed with meaning, just like words describing God should be! You will find eight such words in the first stanza alone. How many others can you find? Of course, it is impossible to truly describe God, but hymns like this one give us better words to use.

TUNE: Traditional Welsh hymn melody

S T. DENIO is the name of a French patron saint. The tune is based on a traditional Welsh ballad adapted for a Welsh hymn melody before it was attached to this hymn. The tune is perfect for a text that speaks of the greatness and power of God. Listen to the descending triads that begin lines one, two, and four. The three-note chords reinforce the polysyllable words, with the accented syllable falling on the strongest beat of the measure. Sing it: "Im-MOR-tal, in-VIS-i-ble." Do you hear and feel the strength in it?

As you sing this hymn . . . think about the greatest source of light you know, the sun. We cannot look directly upon the sun because its brightness would damage our eyes. This hymn reminds us that we cannot look directly upon God either, so great is His glory and so vile is our sin. Think of how God told Moses that he cannot look directly upon His face (see Ex. 33:18–23), or how the mighty seraphim cover their eyes before God's throne (see Isa. 6:2). So this hymn recalls, "Thine angels adore thee, all veiling their sight." And His inaccessible light is hid from our eyes, it says. God is utterly glorious!

This story began on that awful day when Adam and Eve sinned in the Garden, and so God removed Himself from human sight. God's justice soars high like mountains, and His holy light will destroy all sin. But this story will end on that amazing day when the veil is removed from our eyes because all vile things are removed from our hearts. We will once again see God, the Bible promises (1 John 3:1–3). In fact, we will no longer need the sun because God Himself will light all things (Rev. 21:23). Can you imagine? How the anticipation of that day heartens our praises now!

Immortal, Invisible, God Only Wise 83

To the King of the ages, immortal, invisible, the only God,
be honor and glory forever and ever. Amen.

I TIMOTHY 1:17

1. Im - mor - tal, in - vis - i - ble, God on - ly wise,
2. Un - rest - ing, un - hast - ing and si - lent as light,
3. Great Fa - ther of glo - ry, pure Fa - ther of light,

in light in - ac - ces - si - ble hid from our eyes,
nor want - ing, nor wast - ing, Thou rul - est in might;
Thine an - gels a - dore Thee, all veil - ing their sight;

most bless - ed, most glo - rious, the An - cient of Days,
Thy jus - tice like moun - tains high soar - ing a - bove
all praise we would ren - der; O help us to see

al - might - y, vic - to - rious, Thy great name we praise.
Thy clouds which are foun - tains of good - ness and love.
'tis on - ly the splen - dor of light hid - eth Thee.

TEXT: Walter Chalmers Smith
TUNE: Traditional Welsh hymn melody

JOANNA (OR ST. DENIO)

TEXT: Michael Perry   b. 1942, Beckenham, Kent, England
d. 1996, Tonbridge, Kent, England

Michael Perry was a pastor and one of Britain's leading hymn writers of the twentieth century. A contemporary publisher who carries almost 200 of Perry's works calls him "one of England's bright and shining stars."[60] Sadly, his life was cut short at the age of fifty-four by an inoperable brain tumor.

Perry was the editor and director of Jubilate Hymns, a British group of talented poets and hymn writers founded in the early 1960s. Seven other composers in this hymnal were part of this group. Their stated purpose was "to meet the challenge of a new generation in the UK, a generation which wished to extend its singing beyond the foursquare ways of metrical hymnody."[61] Perry's hymn text provides an excellent example of their goal. Each verse consists of three groups of paired rhyming couplets. However, the unusual meter of 13.13.13.13.13.13 "hides" the fact that it is a rhyming poem. "Meter" is simply how many syllables are in each line. In this hymn, each line has thirteen syllables.

TUNE: Gustav Holst   b. September 21, 1874, Cheltenham, England
d. May 25, 1934, London, England

Perry chose an elegant tune that lifts his text to greatness. Famed classical composer Gustav Holst adapted this tune in 1921 for an English patriotic poem, "I Vow to Thee, My Country." He took it from the movement "Jupiter" in his well-known orchestral suite, *The Planets*, and named it THAXTED after the English village where he lived most of his life. It is stately, majestic, even imperial. It is these qualities that make it appropriate for use as a wedding processional.

As you sing this hymn . . . you may be surprised that it has only two stanzas. That is very unusual. Perhaps it says all that needs to be said! Stanza 1 helps us to consider the wonder of a God whose love and greatness are beyond words. Stanza 2 helps us to respond in love, service, trust, adoration, and the sacrifice of praise. The two verses present a simple yet complete summary of our life with God. He is revealed and we respond.

Why is praise called a sacrifice? Hebrews 13:15 says, "Through Him then let us continually offer up a sacrifice of praise to God, that is, the fruit of lips that acknowledge His name." To sacrifice means to surrender or give up something we want to keep. In our sinful condition, we want all praise. But the Christian heart knows that Jesus went to the cross to "bear the reproach" we deserved (Heb. 13:13), and now wants to give Christ all praise. When we have problems, we may not want to praise God, but rather to complain. But praise that comes in such a time is a sweet-smelling aroma to God. It is a sacrifice offered up to Him.

O God Beyond All Praising

*You have multiplied, O LORD my God, Your wondrous deeds and Your
thoughts toward us; none can compare with You! I will proclaim and tell of
them, yet they are more than can be told.*

PSALM 40:5

1. O God be-yond all prais-ing, we wor-ship You to - day
2. Then hear, O gra-cious Sav - ior, ac - cept the love we bring,

and sing the love a - maz - ing that songs can-not re - pay;
that we who know Your fa - vor may serve You as our King;

for we can on - ly won - der at ev - ery gift You send,
and wheth - er our to - mor - rows be filled with good or ill,

at bless-ings with - out num - ber and mer-cies with - out end;
we'll tri - umph through our sor - rows and rise to bless You still:

we lift our hearts be - fore You and wait up - on Your Word,
to mar - vel at Your beau - ty and glo - ry in Your ways,

we hon - or and a - dore You, our great and might - y Lord.
and make a joy - ful du - ty our sac - ri - fice of praise.

TEXT: Michael Perry
TUNE: From Gustav Holst's *The Planets*, 1918

THAXTED

Praise, My Soul, the King of Heaven

	b. June 1, 1793, Ednam, Scotland
TEXT: Henry Lyte	d. November 20, 1847, Nice, France
	(for more on Lyte, see No. 104)

Henry Lyte became an orphan at a young age. In spite of poverty and poor health, he was able to attend Trinity College in Dublin, Ireland. He originally wanted to become a doctor, but following the death of a close friend, he chose to become a minister. Lyte pastored a small seashore parish, All Saints Church, in Devonshire, England. He also wrote for his congregation a collection of 300 hymns called *The Spirit of the Psalms*, which were versifications, or paraphrases, of the Psalms. In them he sought "the spirit" of each psalm. This hymn became one of the most often sung hymns in England. Although Lyte was not well-known during his lifetime, he is well remembered and respected for two great hymns, "Praise, My Soul, the King of Heaven" and "Abide with Me."

	b. March 21, 1875, Lincolnshire, England
TUNE: Mark Andrews	d. December 10, 1939, Montclair, New Jersey

Mark Andrews studied music at Westminster Abbey in London but came to the United States in 1902. He was an organist, choir director, and active composer in Montclair, New Jersey. Queen Elizabeth II chose this hymn text for her wedding in 1947, and it was set to a tune Andrews had written in 1930, called ANDREWS, rather than the original tune, LAUDA ANIMA, written in 1869. Interestingly, the Queen's wedding day occurred exactly one hundred years after the death of Henry Lyte.

As you sing this hymn . . . you are given wonderful words from Psalm 103 with which to praise and thank God. Although there are infinite reasons for praising God, we often resort to the same few, limited expressions. Psalm 103 provides a wealth of reasons to praise Him, and this song condenses these for us. Twenty-two verses in the psalm are paraphrased in just five stanzas. Stanza 1 covers the first five verses of Psalm 103 in four words: "ransomed, healed, restored, forgiven." The "people in distress" of stanza 2 refers to the "people of Israel" in verse 7 of the psalm. Stanza 2 also praises God for being "slow to chide, swift to bless," drawing from verses 8–12 of the psalm. In stanza 3, we rejoice that God cares for us as a Father, as verses 13 and 14 of the psalm emphasize. In stanza 4 we sing of God's unchanging and everlasting nature, like verses 15–18 of the psalm highlight. Stanza 5 condenses verses 20–22 and has us join with the angels and all creation to praise Him.

The word "bless" is repeated throughout the psalm. Here we express it as "Alleluia" and repeat it with each joyous discovery of God's nature.

Praise, My Soul, the King of Heaven   85

Bless the LORD, O my soul,
and forget not all His benefits.

PSALM 103:2

1. Praise, my soul, the King of heav - en,
2. *Praise Him for His grace and fa - vor*
3. Fa - ther - like, He tends and spares us;
4. *Frail as sum - mer's flow'r we flour - ish,*
5. An - gels help us to a - dore Him,

to His feet your trib - ute bring;
to all peo - ple in dis - tress.
well our fee - ble frame He knows.
Blows the wind and it is gone;
you be - hold Him face to face.

ran - somed, healed, re - stored, for - giv - en,
Praise Him, still the same for - ev - er,
In His hands He gen - tly bears us,
But while mor - tals rise and pe - rish,
Sun and moon bow down be - fore Him;

ev - er - more His prais - es sing.
slow to chide and swift to bless.
res - cues us from all our foes.
God en - dures un - chang - ing on.
all who dwell in time and space.

Al - le - lu - ia! Al - le - lu - ia!

Praise the ev - er - last - ing King!
Glo - rious in His faith - ful - ness!
Wide - ly as His mer - cy flows.
Praise the high e - ter - nal One.
Praise with us the God of grace.

TEXT: Henry F. Lyte, paraphrase of Psalm 103   ANDREWS
TUNE: Mark Andrews

	b. December 18, 1707, Epworth, England
TEXT: Charles Wesley	d. March 29, 1788, London, England
	(for more on Wesley, see No. 2, 4, 31, 37, 41, 63, and 103)

This is a hymn about conversion. For years Charles Wesley was a minister who believed he was a Christian. But it was not until he entered into a personal relationship with Christ that he was truly converted. Instrumental to Wesley's conversion—and to his brother, John's—were the Christian Moravians, an early Protestant group that began in Bohemia (the current Czech Republic). One of the church's leaders, Peter Böhler, once said to Charles, "Had I a thousand tongues, I would praise Christ Jesus with all of them!"[62]

On May 21, 1739, the first anniversary of his own conversion, Charles wrote this hymn text. He called it "For the Anniversary Day of One's Conversion." It originally began, "Glory to God, and praise and love," and then continued on for eighteen verses, which musicologist Erik Routley described as an "astonishing outpouring . . . of high spirits and joy."[63] What we use today as the lead stanza, which begins with "O, for a thousand tongues to sing," was originally verse seven. John Wesley placed it first when he published his 1779 *Collection of Hymns for the Use of the People Called Methodists*.

| | b. May 4, 1784, Weissenfels, Germany |
| TUNE: Carl Gotthelf Gläser | d. April 16, 1829, Barmen, Germany |

Carl Gläser was a German music teacher and composer. He wrote the tune AZMON, which is commonly used with this text in America. (Another tune is more common in England.) Azmon is a location near the southern border of Israel that is mentioned twice in the Bible. The name means "strength in numbers," which seems appropriate for a song about a thousand singing tongues!

As you sing this hymn . . . can you sing of your conversion? This hymn joyfully thanks God for the changes He has made and is making in the life of a believer. Routley encourages us to consider what's involved in Christian conversion: God moves us from darkness to light, blindness to sight, sadness to joy, fear to confidence, and death to life!

The Bible says that if we are in Christ, we are new creations (2 Cor. 5:17). That means we participate in His resurrection power. We learn that our sorrows are not ultimate. Our bad habits will not have the last word. Our sin will not overcome us. Instead, we become more and more like Jesus, and we discover, little by little, the joy and freedom of Christ's resurrection. One day we will know such joy and freedom fully. Are even a thousand tongues sufficient to praise God for such great promises?!

O for a Thousand Tongues to Sing 86

Then my tongue shall tell of Your righteousness
and of Your praise all the day long.

PSALM 35:28

1. O for a thou - sand tongues to sing my
2. *Je - sus! the name that charms our fears, that*
3. He breaks the power of can - celed sin, He
4. *He speaks, and lis - tening to His voice, new*
5. My gra - cious Mas - ter and my God, as -

great Re - deem - er's praise, the glo - ries of my
bids our sor - rows cease, 'tis mu - sic in the
sets the pris - oner free; His blood can make the
life the dead re - ceive; the mourn - ful bro - ken
sist me to pro - claim, to spread through all the

God and King, the___ tri - umphs of His grace.
sin - ner's ears, 'tis___ life and health and peace.
foul - est clean; His___ blood a - vailed for me.
hearts re - joice; the___ hum - ble poor be - lieve.
earth a - broad the___ hon - ors of Thy name.

TEXT: Charles Wesley
TUNE: Carl G. Gläser, arr. Lowell Mason

AZMON

| TEXT: E. Margaret Clarkson | b. June 8, 1915, Melville, Saskatchewan, Canada |
| | d. March 17, 2008, Shepherd Lodge, Toronto, Canada |

Margaret Clarkson was born into an unhappy home; her parents divorced when she was twelve. Her first words were, "My head hurts."[64] She suffered throughout life with migraine headaches and arthritis, even being homebound for a time at the age of three. She described her childhood as filled with "tension, fear, insecurity, and isolation." Growing up, she was involved in her church but even there felt no connection with others. She passed sermon time looking through the hymnal, which introduced her to "such people as John Bunyan, John and Charles Wesley, Martin Luther, William Cowper, Isaac Watts, Fanny Crosby." Through this, she said she began to see the church as "one continuous, living stream of the grace of God." Clarkson taught and wrote for years, eventually retiring because of the pain that never really went away. In 1972, she wrote her well-known book, *Grace Grows Best in Winter*. She had learned early in life that during "long hours of solitude and weakness, repeating hymns and Scriptures . . . could help . . . withstand the ravages of pain." In all, she wrote seventeen books that were translated into seven languages.

In 1946, Margaret was asked by the head of InterVarsity Christian Fellowship to write a hymn to "link together the widely scattered groups that made up the young student movement."[65] Although she had written other songs, she called "We Come, O Christ, to You" her "first real hymn."[66] There is no hint of her own issues in the text.

TUNE: John Darwall	b. January 13, 1731, Haughton, Staffordshire, England
	d. December 18, 1789, Walsall, West Midlands, England
	(for more on Darwall, see No. 41)

Darwall is the perfect strong melody for the declarative words that begin each stanza. Also, the last musical phrase of each stanza, an ascending scale of an octave plus one note, reflects what the text says about aspiring toward knowing God, doing His will, and being in His presence.

As you sing this hymn . . . you are uniting with other believers to worship Christ to declare who He is. Creed-like, each stanza draws from John 14:6. What did Jesus mean when He called Himself "the way, and the truth, and the life"? And how should these truths change our lives? Stanzas 2 to 4 provide the answer. Stanza 5 then begins with the only appropriate response: "We worship You, Lord Christ, our Savior and our King; to You our youth and strength adoringly, we bring." This hymn offers an ideal prayer for any youth worship gathering or a Christian school graduation. It would provide a fitting testimony and prayer for a Christian wedding. Or one can just read it with a group of Christian friends.

We Come, O Christ, to You

Jesus said to him, "I am the way, and the truth, and the life."

JOHN 14:6

1. We come, O Christ, to You, true Son of God and man;
   by whom all things con - sist in whom all life be - gan:
   in You a - lone we live and move, and have our be - ing in Your love.

2. *You are the Way to God, Your blood our ran - som paid;*
   in You we face our Judge and Mak - er un - a - fraid;
   be - fore the throne ab - solved we stand: Your love has met Your law's de - mand.

3. You are the liv - ing Truth, all wis - dom dwells in You,
   the source of ev - ery skill, the one e - ter - nal TRUE!
   O great I AM! in You we rest, sure an - swer to our ev - ery quest.

4. *You on - ly are true Life, to know You is to live*
   the more a - bun - dant life that earth can nev - er give.
   O ris - en Lord! we live in You: in us each day Your life re - new!

5. We wor - ship You, Lord Christ, our Sav - ior and our King;
   to You our youth and strength a - dor - ing - ly we bring:
   so fill our hearts that all may view Your life in us, and turn to You!

TEXT: E. Margaret Clarkson
TUNE: John Darwall

DARWALL

Praise the Lord! O Heavens, Adore Him

TEXT: Anonymous, stanzas 1 and 2;   ‖   b. January 31, 1798, Falmouth, Cornwall
Edward Osler, stanza 3   ‖   d. March 7, 1863, Truro, Cornwall

Although the author of stanzas 1 and 2 is anonymous, the hymn is certainly based on Psalm 148. It was first published in a 1796 English hymnal called *The Foundling Hospital Collection*. Later, Dr. Edward Osler added the third verse. Osler was a doctor who served at Guy's Hospital in London. He also excelled in the literary field, writing several books, poems, and hymns.

TUNE: Franz Joseph Haydn   ‖   b. March 31, 1732, Rohrau, Austria
   ‖   d. May 31, 1809, Vienna, Austria

Multiple tunes are used for this text, but AUSTRIAN HYMN was chosen for this hymnal because it so well reflects the joy and strength of the text. The famous composer Franz Joseph Haydn adapted the tune from a Croatian folk melody he knew as a child. Haydn was the court musician for the Hapsburg dynasty which at the time ruled most of Europe. He wrote over one hundred symphonies, twenty-two operas, four oratorios, sixteen masses, and a great number of chamber music works. He has been called the "Father of the Symphony" and the "Father of the String Quartet." Haydn's music is characterized by joy. He once said, "When I think of the Divine Being, my heart is so full of joy that the notes fly off as from a spindle."[67]

As you sing this hymn . . . you join the cosmic chorus of sun, moon, stars, and all creation in giving praise to God. Don't think for a minute that if humans fail to worship God, no praise will ascend to heaven. According to Psalm 148, all that God has created, from angels to animals, from mountains to morning mist, proclaims the wonders of the Creator. Even the laws of nature like gravity and the orbit of planets, observes stanza 1, are a declaration of praise.

If stanza 1 offers the story of creation, stanza 2 recounts the story of redemption. God's greatest act was to buy back for Himself a creation marred by sin. Since He is gracious, He gives His people victory over sin and death. In His redemption is our greatest song of praise.

The final and newer stanza summarizes this call to worship for young and old alike. It speaks of bending the knee, pointing to the right heart posture or attitude for worship. It's not finally just inanimate creation that should praise God; we must. And so we borrow from the Lord's Prayer in the hymn's last line, "So on earth Your will be done."

Praise the Lord! O Heavens, Adore Him 88

Praise the LORD from the heavens; praise Him in the heights!

PSALM 148:1

1. Praise the Lord! O heav'ns, a - dore Him; praise Him, an - gels, in the height.
2. *Praise the Lord for He is glo - rious; ne - ver shall His pro - mise fail.*
3. Wor - ship, ho - nor, glo - ry, bless - ing, Lord, we of - fer un - to Thee.

Sun and moon re - joice be - fore Him; praise Him all you stars of light.
God has made His saints vic - to - rious; sin and death shall not pre - vail.
Young and old, Your praise ex - press - ing, in glad ho - mage bend the knee.

Praise the Lord! for He has spo - ken, worlds His migh - ty voice o - beyed.
Praise the God of our sal - va - tion! Hosts on high His pow'r pro - claim,
All the saints in heav'n a - dore You; we would bow be - fore Your throne.

Law which nev - er can be bro - ken for their guid - ance He has made.
Heav'n and earth and all cre - a - tion laud and mag - ni - fy His name.
As Your an - gels serve be - fore You, so on earth Your will be done.

TEXT: v. 1–2 Anonymous, v. 3 Edward Osler   AUSTRIAN HYMN
TUNE: Franz Joseph Haydn

When Morning Gilds the Skies

Katholisches Gesangbuch, Wurzburg ‖

The author of this hymn is unknown, but it first appeared in a German Catholic hymnal titled *Katholisches Gesangbuch*, which was published in 1828. The text is based on Psalm 113:3: "From the rising of the sun to its setting, the name of the LORD is to be praised!" Certainly, this hymn was written by someone who understood the importance of praising God at all times and in all circumstances. In 1854, a Catholic priest named Edward Caswall translated the German text into English.

TUNE: Sir Joseph Barnby ‖ b. August 12, 1838, York, England
d. January 28, 1896, Westminster, London, England

The tune LAUDES DOMINI was written by Joseph Barnby and published in *Hymns Ancient and Modern* (London, 1868). *Laudes Domini* is Latin for "the praises of the Lord." Barnby's father was a musician, and Joseph entered the choir of Yorkminster at age seven. He became an organist and choirmaster at age twelve, spending his lifetime as a teacher, composer, and conductor, including at the famed Westminster Abbey. He was knighted in 1892 for his outstanding musical contributions.

People often slow down or *ritard* as they sing at the end of stanzas. But that is not necessary here. The last phrase, "May Jesus Christ be praised!" doubles the length of time each word is sung, moving from quarter notes to half notes. The slowing tempo is built in, which emphasizes these exultant words.

As you sing this hymn . . . consider the many times in which you are encouraged to sing the words, "may Jesus Christ be praised." But how often do we pout instead of praise? How often do we complain or feel sorry for ourselves instead of honoring God with a heart of gratitude? Our version of this hymn has four stanzas, but the original English version had twenty-eight stanzas. Here are a few of those lines:

> *When you begin the day, O never fail to say, May Jesus Christ be praised!*
> *And at your work rejoice, to sing with heart and voice, May Jesus Christ be praised!*
> *Be this at meals your grace, in every time and place, May Jesus Christ be praised!*
> *Be this when day is past, of all your thoughts the last, May Jesus Christ be praised!*

Are there not countless times to praise Christ? What lines might you write?

> *When I have a challenging test and want to do my best, May Jesus Christ be praised!*
> *When I fail to win a race, and feel my own disgrace, May Jesus Christ be praised!*
> *When friendships come and go, my heart is filled with woe, May Jesus Christ be praised!*
> *I say in every day, and feel in every way, May Jesus Christ be praised!*

When Morning Gilds the Skies

From the rising of the sun to its setting,
the name of the LORD is to be praised!

PSALM 113:3

1. When morn-ing gilds the skies,____ my heart a - wak - ing cries,
2. *Does sad - ness fill my mind?____ A sol - ace here I find,*
3. The night be-comes as day,____ when from the heart we say,
4. *Be this, while life is mine,____ my can - ti - cle di - vine,*

may Je - sus Christ be praised! A - like at work and prayer
may Je - sus Christ be praised! Or fades my earth - ly bliss?
may Je - sus Christ be praised! The powers of dark-ness fear
may Je - sus Christ be praised! Be this th'e - ter - nal song

to Je - sus I re - pair, may Je - sus Christ be praised!
My com - fort still is this, may Je - sus Christ be praised!
when this sweet chant they hear, may Je - sus Christ be praised!
through all the a - ges long, may Je - sus Christ be praised!

TEXT: *Katholisches Gesangbuch,* Wurzburg, 1828,
trans. Edward Caswall
TUNE: Joseph Barnby

LAUDES DOMINI

TEXT: Fanny J. Crosby	b. March 24, 1820, Putnam County, New York
	d. February 12, 1915, Bridgeport, Connecticut
	(for more on Crosby, see No. 106)

At six weeks of age, Fanny Crosby was left blind by the misapplication of hot cloths to her infant eyes. At the age of eighty-five, she stated that she had never once resented the incompetent doctor who had made that mistake.[68] She believed in God's love and sovereignty over her life. She trusted in His purposes: "One of the earliest resolves that I formed in my young heart was to leave all care to yesterday and to believe that the morning would bring forth its own peculiar joy."[69]

Throughout her childhood, her grandmother became her eyes and taught her. Her blindness led her to practice memorization so that by age ten she had memorized the first four books of the Old Testament and the four Gospels completely. At fifteen, she began attending the School for the Blind in New York City, where she attended for seven years, then taught there for eleven. In 1843, she appeared before the United States Senate, being the first woman to do so in order to provide testimony for the education of the blind. She was the friend of several presidents and, during her life, was one of the most well-known women in the United States.

"To God Be the Glory" first became known and loved in England during a D. L. Moody crusade. Evangelist Billy Graham discovered it at his 1952 London crusade. He then introduced it to America, where it became as popular as it had been in England.

TUNE: William H. Doane	b. February 3, 1832, Preston, Connecticut
	d. December 23, 1915, Rhode Island

William Doane was an inventor and successful businessman. He was the president of a company that manufactured woodworking machinery. Music, however, was his avocation, and in 1875, he received a doctorate in music from Denison University. He composed over 2,000 hymn tunes, including many for Fanny Crosby, like this one.

As you sing this hymn . . . there should be a transfer in your mind and heart from *your* glory to *God's* glory. As humans, we like to take all of the attention or praise that comes to us. But to God alone belongs all the praise and fame for what He did through Christ. The first two stanzas declare that salvation is God's greatest act of love, that the blood of Christ purchased it, and that His pardon is available to all. In response to that good news, the refrain sings, "Praise the Lord!" The final stanza is a reminder that regarding heaven, we are all blind. But what wonder it will be "when Jesus we see."

To God Be the Glory

Ascribe to the LORD the glory due His name.

PSALM 29:2

1. To God be the glo - ry, great things He hath done,
2. O per - fect re - demp - tion, the pur - chase of blood,
3. Great things He hath taught us, great things He hath done,

so loved He the world that He gave us His Son,
to ev - ery be - liev - er the prom - ise of God;
and great our re - joic - ing through Je - sus the Son;

who yield - ed His life an a - tone - ment for sin,
the vil - est of - fend - er who tru - ly be - lieves,
but pur - er, and high - er and great - er will be

and o - pened the life - gate that all may go in.
that mo - ment from Je - sus a par - don re - ceives.
our won - der, our trans - port, when Je - sus we see.

Praise the Lord, praise the Lord, let the earth hear His voice!

Praise the Lord, praise the Lord, let the peo - ple re - joice!

O come to the Fa - ther through Je - sus the Son,

and give Him the glo - ry, great things He hath done.

TEXT: Fanny J. Crosby
TUNE: William H. Doane

TO GOD BE THE GLORY

TEXT: *Münster Gesangbuch*, 1677 ‖

In 1662, this anonymous text first appeared in manuscript form, but in 1677, the Roman Catholic Jesuits in Germany published it in a hymnbook under the title *Schönster Herr Jesu*, which means "most beautiful Lord Jesus." We don't know who translated the words from German into English, except for the fourth verse. Joseph A. Seiss, a Lutheran pastor in Philadelphia, entered it into a Lutheran Sunday school book in 1873. He titled the hymn "Beautiful Savior," a name often still used.

TUNE: Silesian folk song ‖

The origin of this tune name is also unknown. One legend is that it was sung by twelfth-century German crusaders to Palestine, so the name CRUSADER'S HYMN is sometimes used. But it is believed to be from Silesia, a region of Europe that is now Poland. It was there that a German man, Heinrich von Fallerslebein, heard it sung by a group of Silesian peasants. He wrote it down and put it into his folk song collection, *Schlesische Volkslieder*, Leipzig, in 1842, under the title SCHÖNSTER HERR JESU.

As you sing this hymn . . . you are addressing Jesus, our Savior. Many hymns are written to God the Father, or to the entire Godhead, but this is to Jesus alone.

On the surface, the hymn sounds as if it is commending His physical appearance as fair by comparing Him to the beauties of nature. Yet Isaiah clearly said that Messiah would not be physically attractive: "He had no form or majesty that we should look at Him, and no beauty that we should desire Him" (Isa. 53:2). After that, the Bible says nothing more. We do not know if He was tall or short or anything about His appearance. We do know that people were quickly drawn to Him. Little children crawled up in His lap without fear. How, then, is He beautiful?

Looks are very important to us, and we want our heroes to be good-looking. But Jesus is beautiful because of who He is. He is the kindest, most compassionate, bravest, and strongest man who has ever lived. He is also the humblest man who has ever lived because He endured the worst humiliation, bearing the sin and shame of the world. Yet Jesus is 100 percent sinless. He did not simply create beauty. He *is* beauty. He is its source and essence. So we sing "glory, honor, praise, adoration, now and forevermore be Thine."

Fairest Lord Jesus

*You are the most handsome of the sons of men; grace is poured upon
Your lips; therefore God has blessed You forever.*

PSALM 45:2

1. Fair - est Lord Je - sus, Rul - er of all na - ture,
2. Fair are the mead - ows, fair___ are the wood - lands,
3. Fair is the sun - shine, fair___ is the moon - light,
4. Beau - ti - ful Sav - ior! Lord___ of the na - tions!

Son of___ God and___ Son of Man!
robed in the bloom - ing___ garb of spring:
and all the twink - ling,___ star - ry host:
Son of___ God and___ Son of Man!

Thee will I cher - ish, Thee will I
Je - sus is fair - er, Je - sus is
Je - sus shines bright - er, Je - sus shines
Glo - ry and hon - or, praise, ad - o -

hon - or, Thou, my soul's glo - ry, joy, and crown.
pur - er, Who makes the woe - ful heart to sing.
pur - er than all the an - gels heav'n can boast.
ra - tion, now and for - ev - er - more be Thine.

TEXT: *Münster Gesangbuch*
TUNE: Silesian folk song *Schlesische Volkslieder*, Leipzig

CRUSADER'S HYMN

Thanksgiving Now Thank We All Our God

TEXT: Martin Rinkart || b. April 23, 1586, Eilenburg, Saxony, Germany
d. December 8, 1649, Eilenburg, Saxony, Germany

There is hardly a more respected hymn writer than Martin Rinkart. His hymn "Now Thank We All Our God" is sung and loved by people today, four hundred years after he lived, because of how he endured great hardship. Rinkart was a Lutheran minister in the town of his birth during the Thirty Years' War. Since Eilenburg was a walled city, it was an important haven for refugees seeking protection from the Swedish Army. Consequently, the city became vastly overcrowded, suffering both famine and plague. The strain imposed on the city's pastors by so many needy people either led to their deaths or caused them to flee the city. Pastor Rinkart alone survived and stayed. For a period of time, he performed as many as fifty funerals a day and cared for the many ill. One year he buried 4,500 people, many of whom were his own family and friends. Twice, he took great risks in attempts to mediate peace with the enemy. Rinkart lived for less than a year after the war's end in 1649.

It is not easy to translate the poetry of hymns from one language to another. One prolific hymn translator was Catherine Winkworth. Born in London in 1827, she spent one year in Dresden, Germany, which evoked her interest in hymnody. In 1854, she translated and published a volume of German hymns, calling it *Lyra Germanica*. More volumes followed in 1858, 1863, and 1869.

TUNE: Johann Crüger || b. April 9, 1598, Grossbreisen, Germany
d. February 23, 1662, Berlin, Germany

Johann Crüger was a German composer of the early Baroque period known for his hymn tunes. Since the words *"Nun danket alle Gott"* are the first line of Rinkart's hymn, the Crüger tune is called NUN DANKET.

As you sing this hymn . . . try to imagine what it must have been like to perform fifty funerals a day and bury 4,500 people in one year. It is hard to relate to how sad that would be, and Rinkart's sorrow emerges at one point in the second stanza: "guide us when perplexed and free us from all ills." However, he spends most of the hymn expressing thanks: "Thank you, God. You have done wondrous things!" It is astounding that someone could write such a hymn in these circumstances. Sometimes we can barely say "thank you, God" when it's raining outside!

How different we would be if we trusted God's love in good times and bad, giving thanks always: *"Rejoice always . . .* give thanks in all circumstances; for this is the will of God in Christ Jesus for you" (1 Thess. 5:16, 18, emphasis added).

Now Thank We All Our God

And now we thank You, our God,
and praise Your glorious name.

I CHRONICLES 29:13

1. Now thank we all our God with heart and hands and voic - es,_____ who won - drous things hath done, who from our moth - ers' arms, hath blessed us on our way with count - less gifts of love, and still is ours to - day.

2. *O may this boun - teous God through all our life be near us,_____ with ev - er - joy - ful hearts and bless - ed peace to cheer us;_____ and keep us in His grace, and guide us when per - plexed, and free us from all ills in this world and the next.*

3. All praise and thanks to God the Fa - ther now be giv - en,_____ the Son, and Him who reigns with them in high - est heav - en, the one e - ter - nal God, whom earth and heav'n a - dore; for thus it was, is now, and shall be ev - er - more.

TEXT: Martin Rinkart, trans. Catherine Winkworth

NUN DANKET

TUNE: Johann Crüger

TEXT: Henry Alford ‖ b. October 7, 1810, Bloomsbury, England
d. January 12, 1871, Canterbury, England

Henry Alford was a minister's son (actually, the fifth consecutive generation of ministers) and a precocious student. Before he was ten, he had written several Latin odes, a history of the Jewish people, and a series of homiletic outlines. After graduating from Trinity College, Cambridge, he entered the Anglican ministry and rose quickly from one position to another until he became the Dean of Canterbury. He was well known as a Greek scholar who spent twenty years writing his four-volume edition of the *Greek Testament*. He was musically gifted as well and wrote several books of hymns. A devout man, it is said that at the end of every day and every meal, he would stand and thank God for His loving care and gifts.

TUNE: George J. Elvey ‖ b. March 27, 1816, Canterbury, England
d. December 9, 1893, Windlesham, Surrey, England
(for more on Elvey, see No. 43)

The tune ST. GEORGE'S WINDSOR is taken from the name of a church in Windsor, England, where George Elvey was organist when he composed this tune. Elvey's family loved music, and he began his musical career as a singer in the boys' choir at Canterbury Cathedral. He later attended the Royal Academy of Music, where he became "master of the boys." He died in 1893 and is buried at St. George's.

As you sing this hymn . . . realize that it is about a way of life with which you are probably unfamiliar. We seldom think of harvest time today. Food is as close as the refrigerator or the grocery store. This hymn takes us back to a day when a good harvest in the fall meant being able to eat the following year. Communities held celebrations when the long months of planting, tending, and harvesting resulted in full barns and silos. People rejoiced over their labor and the sight of grain safely stored before winter. Our Thanksgiving time has lost some meaning because we don't have these literal reminders of God's provision.

However, this hymn has another meaning that does relate to us. Only the first stanza speaks of an earthly harvest, and it is an allegory to teach us about God gathering His people into His Kingdom. We are His harvest. When harvest time comes, the weeds are thrown out and the wheat is kept. So, too, when Christ comes again, He will preserve His people but judge all those who have rejected Him. Jesus tells us this will happen at the end of history (Matt. 13:24–43). As Christians, we do not want simply to be wheat, but an excellent and pleasing harvest: "Lord of harvest, grant that we, wholesome grain and pure may be."

Come, Ye Thankful People, Come   93

*The harvest is the end of the age,
and the reapers are angels.*

MATTHEW 13:39

1. Come, ye thank-ful peo-ple, come, raise the song of har-vest home:
2. *All the world is God's own field, fruit un-to His praise to yield;*
3. For the Lord our God shall come, and shall take His har-vest home;
4. *E-ven so, Lord, quick-ly come to Thy fi-nal har-vest home;*

all is safe-ly gath-ered in, ere the win-ter storms be-gin;
wheat and tares to-geth-er sown, un-to joy or sor-row grown:
from His field shall in that day all of-fens-es purge a-way;
gath-er Thou Thy peo-ple in, free from sor-row, free from sin;

God, our Mak-er doth pro-vide for our wants to be sup-plied:
first the blade, and then the ear, then the full corn shall ap-pear:
give His an-gels charge at last in the fire the tares to cast,
there for-ev-er pu-ri-fied, in Thy pres-ence to a-bide:

come to God's own tem-ple, come, raise the song of har-vest home.
Lord of har-vest, grant that we whole-some grain and pure may be.
but the fruit-ful ears to store in His gar-ner ev-er-more.
come, with all Thine an-gels, come, raise the glo-rious har-vest home.

TEXT: Henry Alford   ST. GEORGE'S WINDSOR
TUNE: George J. Elvey

TEXT: Folliott S. Pierpont   ‖   b. October 7, 1835, Bath, England
‖   d. March 10, 1917, Newport, England

Folliott Pierpont was born in a beautiful part of England, the city of Bath. The Avon River runs through the rolling hills where warm springs come from the ground, making it a popular vacation and health resort. Pierpont left his home to attend Cambridge University, but walking the hills upon his return at age twenty-nine, he wrote this poem. It was not simply a sonnet about nature but a comprehensive song of adoration to be used for the communion services in his Anglican church. Therefore, each stanza ended with the words, "Christ, our God, to Thee we raise this our sacrifice of praise." The song spread to America, where it has become a traditional Thanksgiving hymn. Here, the final phrase evolved to "Lord of all, to Thee we raise this our hymn of grateful praise."

TUNE: Conrad Kocher,   ‖   b. December 16, 1786, Ditzingen, Württemberg, Germany
adapt. William H. Monk, 1861   ‖   d. March 12, 1872, Stuttgart, Germany

The tune Dɪx is named for William Chatterton Dix, the poet of the Christmas carol, "As with Gladness Men of Old." It was composed, however, by Conrad Kocher for his 1838 collection of German hymns. Another musician, William H. Monk, adapted the melody for the Dix Christmas carol, although Dix himself did not like the match. Other tunes have been used with "For the Beauty of the Earth," but Dɪx is the most widely used today.

As you sing this hymn . . . you are obeying and loving God by enumerating your praises to Him. He loves to hear it, and you were created to praise Him! The words remind us not only of things we see, but also of intangible beauties we often take for granted. They include the joy of human love, the guidance of parents and family, the unfolding of time ("the wonder of each hour"), and the church. The last verse culminates with the best gift: "For Thyself, best gift divine to our race so freely given."

Do you often begin your prayers of thanks with only the easy and obvious things? "We thank you for this day, and for our food, and our family. . . . " Have you ever thought of the combined blessing of all our senses? In stanza 3, Pierpont speaks of "mystic harmony" to describe how our sight and hearing join together to enjoy God's gifts! Do you ever thank God for touch, or smell, or taste? Consider how much of a loss it would be to lose one of these senses.

As you sing this hymn, thank God for the wonder of your senses. But never forget to give thanks for the greatest gift, God's Son and our Savior, Jesus.

For the Beauty of the Earth

94

Every good gift and every perfect gift is from above,
coming down from the Father of lights, with whom there is no
variation or shadow due to change.

JAMES 1:17

1. For the— beau - ty of the earth, for the glo - ry of the skies,
2. *For the— beau - ty of each hour of the day and of the night,*
3. For the— joy of ear and eye, for the heart and mind's de - light,
4. *For the— joy of hu - man love, bro - ther, sis - ter, par - ent, child,*
5. For the—Church that ev - er - more lift - eth ho - ly hands a - bove,
6. *For Thy - self, best gift di - vine, to the world so free - ly giv'n;*

for the— love which from our birth o - ver and a - round us lies,
hill and— vale, and tree, and flower, sun and moon and stars of light,
for the— mys - tic har - mo - ny link - ing sense to sound and sight,
friends on— earth and friends a - bove, for all gen - tle thoughts and mild,
off - 'ring— up on ev - ery shore her pure sa - cri - fice of love,
for that— great, great love of Thine, peace on earth and joy in heav'n,

Lord of all, to Thee we raise this our hymn of grate - ful praise.

TEXT: Folliott S. Pierpont

TUNE: Conrad Kocher, adapt. William H. Monk

DIX

Thanksgiving   For the Fruit of All Creation

TEXT: Fred Pratt Green   ‖   b. September 2, 1903, Roby, Lancashire, England
d. October 22, 2000, Norwich, England

Reverend Green was a Methodist minister and one of the foremost hymn writers of the twentieth century. Although some called him the Charles Wesley of the time, he strongly rejected that label, saying, "We are all dwarfs alongside Wesley and Watts!"[70] He did, however, author over 300 hymns during his career as a Methodist clergyman in Great Britain. Green desired to be an architect, but first spent four years working with his father in the leather business. It was during that time he discovered that he loved writing. He did not begin to write hymns until his forties after he had already published four books of poetry. The popularity of his hymns spread, and when royalties began to come during his retirement, he used the money not to enrich himself but to establish a trust that helped others write hymns and study hymnology. He is remembered as a wise, gentle man with a quick wit and ready sense of humor.

TUNE: Traditional Welsh melody   ‖

Although Green originally wrote his text for the tune EAST ACLAM, American music publishers have employed AR HYD Y NOS, a tune familiar to most ears despite its unfamiliar name. It is the wonderful lullaby "All Through the Night," an ancient Welsh folk song, first notated in 1784.

As you sing this hymn . . . you are singing about far more than a list of things for which to be thankful. Although the first stanza does provide a list of many things, how often have you thanked God that things grow twenty-four hours a day—while we are sleeping (including children)? In stanza 2 we are reminded of our responsibility to care for others as God has cared for us. The final stanza affirms the reason for our gratefulness: the spiritual harvest of the Holy Spirit and His gifts which are ours only because God saw us in our unfortunate state and stooped to rescue us. This should continually "astound" and "confound" us!

As you sing this Thanksgiving hymn, you may wonder why you sing about helping your neighbor in the middle stanza—what does that have to do with being thankful? Do you remember what Jesus said is the greatest commandment? He said the first is to love God with all your heart and the second is to love your neighbor as yourself. He said that the second is as important as the first, and that all of the Law and the Prophets depend on these two commandments (Matt. 22:37–40). The gospel has horizontal implications. If we are sincerely thankful to God, we best prove our gratitude through obedience. Genuinely thankful people will love their neighbors as themselves.

For the Fruit of All Creation

95

At the works of Your hands I sing for joy.

PSALM 92:4

1. For the fruit of all cre - a - tion, thanks be to God.
2. *In the just re - ward of la - bor, God's will is done.*
3. For the har - vests of the Spir - it, thanks be to God.

For His gifts to ev - ery na - tion, thanks be to God.
In the help we give our neigh - bor, God's will is done.
For the good we all in - her - it, thanks be to God.

For the plow - ing, sow - ing, reap - ing, si - lent growth while we are sleep - ing,
In our world - wide task of car - ing for the hun - gry and de - spair - ing,
For the won - ders that a-stound us, for the truths that still con-found us,

fu - ture needs in earth's safe-keep - ing, thanks be to God.
in the har - vests we are shar - ing, God's will is done.
most of all that love has found us, thanks be to God.

TEXT: Fred Pratt Green
TUNE: Welsh melody, 18th c.

AR HYD Y NOS

TEXT: Katherine K. Davis ‖ b. June 25, 1892, St. Joseph, Missouri
d. April 20, 1980, Littleton, Massachusetts

Katherine had her first piano lesson when she was six years old. At fifteen, she wrote her first song, called "Shadow March." She loved playing from the score of the opera *Madame Butterfly*, which had been a gift from her father. Katherine attended Wellesley College in Massachusetts and the New England Conservatory of Music. She returned to Wellesley to teach but spent most of her career at the Concord Academy in Concord, Massachusetts, and at the Shady Hill School for Girls in Philadelphia, Pennsylvania. Believing there was not enough music for girls' choruses to perform, she composed many of her 600 pieces of music for women's voices. Perhaps her most famous composition is "The Little Drummer Boy," made famous by the Trapp Family Singers of *Sound of Music* fame.

TUNE: Traditional Welsh melody ‖

ASH GROVE, the Welsh folk tune that Miss Davis used for this text, is found in harp books as early as the seventeenth century. The Welsh text is a sad ballad about a lover of the country whom a bow hunter accidentally shoots.

Students of music theory will notice the chord progression is a sevenfold repetition of tonic-subdominant-dominant chords (I, IV, V). Rather than sounding stilted and repetitious, the melody of running eighth notes above this repeated chord sequence creates the very picture of nature's contradictions of predictability and randomness.

As you sing this hymn . . . you are discovering and affirming God's revelation of Himself to His creation. He did not simply create us and then leave us on earth to fare the best we can. Instead, He protects, stays, guides, and leads. We have a banner of love over us and light before us until the future time when all shadows and darkness are gone.

The universe is similarly guided. The orbits of stars and planets are so precise that scientists can predict their movements and send a spacecraft hundreds of thousands of miles to meet them. The immensity of space is such that it takes centuries for light from distant galaxies to arrive at our earth. It has been said, "An unbelieving astronomer must be mad."

The great difference between humans and the rest of creation is that we sometimes reject God's direction and light. We do not stay in the "orbits" He has designed for us. As you sing this hymn, recognize that you are uniting with all of creation in a timeless song of thanksgiving and commit yourself anew to following His lead and direction as your wise and loving Creator.

Let All Things Now Living

96

Let everything that has breath praise the LORD!

PSALM 150:6

TEXT: Katherine K. Davis
TUNE: Traditional Welsh melody

ASH GROVE

Confession   I Lay My Sins on Jesus

TEXT: Horatius Bonar ‖ b. December 19, 1808, Edinburgh, Scotland
d. July 31, 1889, Edinburgh, Scotland

Since the children in his church could become noisy and restless, Pastor Horatius Bonar wrote a hymn "in a desire to provide something which children could sing and appreciate in divine worship."[71] Dr. Bonar wrote many of his hymns for the children, yet "they are so spiritually profound they will always satisfy the most mature Christian mind, despite their simplicity."[72] This hymn is only one of almost 600 written in his lifetime, approximately 100 in common use in Britain and the United States. Bonar became known as "the prince of Scottish hymn writers."[73] At a memorial following his death, his friend, the Reverend Lundie, said,

> His hymns were written in very varied circumstances, sometimes timed by the tinkling brook that babbled near him; sometimes attuned to the ordered tramp of the ocean, whose crested waves broke on the beach by which he wandered; sometimes set to the rude music of the railway train that hurried him to the scene of duty; sometimes measured by the silent rhythm of the midnight stars that shone above him.[74]

TUNE: Anonymous ‖

This anonymous tune first appeared in *The Sunday-Scholars Tune Book*, published in London. It is named CALCUTTA, simply from an association with Reginald Heber, author of "Holy, Holy, Holy," who was the Anglican bishop of Calcutta, India, when he died. It was at one time believed to have been written by him.

As you sing this hymn . . . stop and wonder at the fact that Jesus is both utterly unique and that we are called to be like Him. He is utterly unique, the first stanza says, because He alone can bear our sin, remove the accursed load, and wash the stain of guilt away. Since God is good and just, He cannot leave sin unpunished. That means either we must pay the penalty for our sin, or a substitute must pay. Jesus is that substitute if only we would repent of our sins and "lay them" on Jesus by putting our trust in Him.

Jesus is unique, the only one who can remove sin, and He calls us to live obediently like Him. So the last stanza calls us to be strong, loving, lowly, and mild like Him. Of course, we can only be like Him by resting on Him and trusting Him.

Have you ever been disappointed and frustrated by your sin? Ask Jesus to forgive your sin, and then follow after Him. He will release you from your guilt and sorrow.

I Lay My Sins on Jesus

97

The LORD has laid on Him the iniquity of us all.

ISAIAH 53:6

1. I___ lay my sins on Je - sus, the spot - less Lamb of God;
2. *I___ lay my needs on Je - sus; all full - ness dwells in Him;*
3. I___ long to be like Je - sus, meek, lov - ing, low - ly, mild;

He___ bears them all and frees us from the ac - curs - ed load.
He___ heals all my dis - eas - es, my soul He does re - deem.
I___ long to be like Je - sus, the Fa - ther's ho - ly Child.

I bring my guilt to Je - sus, to wash my___ crim - son___ stains
I lay my griefs on Je - sus, my bur - dens___ and my___ cares;
I long to be with Je - sus, a - mid the___ heav'n - ly___ throng,

clean in His blood most pre - cious, till not a spot re - mains.
He___ from them all re - leas - es; He all my sor - rows shares.
to___ sing with saints His prais - es, to learn the an - gels' song.

TEXT: Horatius Bonar
TUNE: Anonymous

CALCUTTA

Confession   Come, Thou Fount of Every Blessing

TEXT: Robert Robinson   ‖   b. September 27, 1735, Norfolk, England
d. June 9, 1790, Birmingham, England

Robert Robinson's father died when he was eight years old. His mother had difficulty raising him, so she sent him to London and apprenticed him to a barber.
There he spent more time with wayward friends than he did learning his trade. But one
evening Robinson and his friends attended an evangelistic service of the great preacher
George Whitefield. God began working on Robinson's heart that night, and three years
later, he became a Christian. In time, he became a minister.

Robinson wrote "Come, Thou Fount" for his congregation to sing as a prayer on
Pentecost Sunday. He understood from experience the power of sin. Even Christians
are "prone to wander" from God. So it was appropriate that churches would again
invite the Holy Spirit to work in their lives on the Sunday when they historically celebrate the coming of the Holy Spirit as described in Acts 2. The reference to "flaming
tongues" is found in Acts 2:3.

TUNE: Unknown   ‖

Nettleton is attributed to two different men. One is John Wyeth, who included
this hymn in a book of folk tunes in 1813, called *Repository of Sacred Music*. The
other is Asahel Nettleton, an evangelist of that time. Some even think that a friend of
Mr. Nettleton's wrote the tune and named it after him.

As you sing this hymn . . . you are like the person who invites the piano tuner knocking
on the door to come inside and tune your piano. You are asking the Holy Spirit to tune
your heart to God's praises. God's great mercy deserves songs of praise. But sadly, our
sinful hearts wander from God's "melody." We need the Holy Spirit as a "fetter," or
restraint, to bind our hearts to God. He seals us for "the courts above."

The name *Ebenezer* in stanza 2 refers to 1 Samuel 7:12's stone of remembrance. The
prophet Samuel marked the place where Israel defeated the Philistines with this stone
he called "Ebenezer," which means "the Lord helped us." As you sing "Here I raise my
Ebenezer," think of a time and place when God helped you. At home? Or church? Or a
summer camp? Think most of all of how He sent His Son to die on the cross for sinners
like us, and for all of this give praise to Him in song.

Come, Thou Fount of Every Blessing 98

Samuel . . . called its name Ebenezer; for he said,
"Till now the LORD has helped us."

I SAMUEL 7:12

1. Come, thou fount of ev-'ry bless-ing, tune my heart to sing Thy grace;
2. Here I raise my Eb-en - e - zer; hith-er by Thy help I'm come;
3. O to grace how great a debt - or dail-y I'm con-strained to be;

streams of mer - cy, ne - ver ceas - ing, call for songs of loud-est praise.
and I hope, by Thy good plea - sure, safe-ly to ar - rive at home.
let Thy grace now, like a fet - ter, bind my wan-d'ring heart to Thee.

Teach me_ some me - lo-dious son - net, sung by_ flam-ing tongues a - bove;
Je - sus_ sought me when a stran-ger, wan-d'ring from the fold of God:
Prone to_ wan-der, Lord, I feel_ it, prone to_ leave the God I love:

praise the mount! I'm fixed up - on it, mount of God's re - deem-ing love.
He, to res - cue me from dan - ger, in - ter-posed His pre - cious blood.
here's my heart, O take and seal it, seal it for Thy courts a - bove.

TEXT: Robert Robinson
TUNE: Unknown

NETTLETON

Petition   Speak, O Lord

TEXT: Stuart Townend   ‖   b. June 1, 1963, West Yorkshire, England
(for more on Townend, see No. 12, 26, 34, 62, and 65)

As Townend and the Gettys collaborated on this hymn, they wanted to offer a song to pray before hearing a sermon at church. Keith Getty states that "we worship a God who has spoken—who is not silent. From God the Father, speaking the world into creation, to speaking through His Living word in Christ, to speaking by His Spirit through the written word."[75] Therefore, we can expect God to speak to us!

TUNE: Keith Getty   ‖   b. December 16, 1974, Lisburn, Northern Ireland
(for more on Getty, see No. 12, 34, 62, and 65)

You may find a lesson in how this melody is shaped. Every time "Speak, O Lord" is sung, it is to a repeated three-note *motif* (a short musical idea) of 1–5–3 in the scale. That motif is used three times for each stanza, and its repetition begins to stick in your mind. It emphasizes the importance of our repeated prayers and of our plea to God.

Composers sometimes call little motifs like this a melody hook. They hook in your mind in such a way that they're also humorously referred to as "brain worms"! You cannot get them out of your head. With this prayer that is good! May these words hook in our minds so that we always seek God's truth and direction for living our lives.

As you sing this hymn . . . you may wonder, "How do I know God is speaking to me? I can't literally hear Him as did Samuel." But remember that we have something Samuel did not have: the completed Bible. In it God has revealed all the truth that we need to know. You have many people at church, home, and maybe at school who will teach and explain the truths found in the Bible. But you have to listen! Although it is bad to ignore what your parents or teachers or any other authorities say, how much worse it is to ignore God. Therefore, this hymn is your prayer and your commitment not only to hear God speak but also to obey what He says. It is your plea "to grasp the heights of Your plan for us." It is your commitment to "stand on Your promises and . . . walk as You walk with us." Please see Proverbs 2:1–5 to read a very important word of encouragement for all children of God on listening to God speak.

It is not just before a sermon that we need to pray, "Speak, O Lord." In our personal devotional lives or in family worship, parents should pray that God would speak. At the beginning of the school year, Christian teachers should pray that God would use His Word to speak to their students. There is no moment in our lives when it is not important to listen for God's truth. This hymn provides a wonderful song of prayer for a bride and groom in their wedding ceremony as they begin lives together.

Speak, O Lord

99

And the LORD came and stood, calling as at other times, "Samuel! Samuel!"
And Samuel said, "Speak, for Your servant hears."

I SAMUEL 3:10

1. Speak, O Lord, as we come to You to re-ceive the food of Your
2. *Teach us, Lord, full o-be-di-ence, ho-ly re-ver-ence, true hu-*
3. Speak, O Lord, and re-new our minds; help us grasp the heights of Your

Ho-ly Word. Take Your truth, plant it deep in us;
mil-i-ty; test our thoughts and our at-ti-tudes
plans for us. Truths un-changed from the dawn of time

shape and fash-ion us in Your like-ness.
in the ra-di-ance of Your pur-i-ty.
that will ech-o down through e-ter-ni-ty.

That the light of Christ might be seen to-day in our
Cause our faith to rise; cause our eyes to see Your ma-
And by grace we'll stand on Your pro-mi-ses, and by

acts of love and our deeds of__ faith. Speak, O Lord, and ful-
jes-tic love and auth-o-ri-ty. Words of pow'r that can
faith we'll walk as You walk with__ us. Speak, O Lord, till Your

fill in us all Your pur-po-ses for Your glo-ry.
ne-ver fail, let their truth pre-vail ov-er un-be-lief.
Church is built and the earth is filled with Your glo-ry.

TEXT: Stuart Townend
TUNE: Keith Getty

TEXT: Augustus M. Toplady ‖ b. November 4, 1740, Farnham, Surrey, England
d. August 11, 1778, Kensington, Middlesex, England

Augustus Toplady was a well-educated scholar and priest in the Anglican Church. In later years he developed strong theological convictions about the Reformed doctrines of John Calvin. At the age of thirty-five and only three years before his death, he left the Anglicans to begin preaching in a French Calvinist church.

Toplady was once caught in a terrible storm in a rocky terrain. Taking shelter in a deep crevice in the middle of a high limestone rock, he wrote the words to this hymn, "Rock of Ages." He later included it in a hymnal he created called *Psalms and Hymns* (1776). Interestingly, instead of his own name he used a pseudonym, *Minimus,* which means being of the smallest size. We can only speculate as to why he chose it.

Toward the end of life, Toplady became very ill from what was called consumption. A doctor said that his pulse was beating weaker every day. Toplady replied with a smile, "Why, that is a good sign that my death is fast approaching; and, blessed be God, I can add that my heart beats stronger and stronger every day for glory."[76]

TUNE: Thomas Hastings ‖ b. October 15, 1784, Washington, Connecticut
d. May 15, 1872, New York, New York

Thomas Hastings was a farm boy who walked six miles to school even in winter. He was known as a hard and diligent worker who worked until three days before he died. A music teacher, Hastings wrote over 1,000 hymn tunes and 600 texts. He named this tune TOPLADY after the hymn writer.

As you sing this hymn . . . perhaps you can imagine needing shelter from a big storm. You would surely welcome the sight of a huge rock with space underneath. The word "rock" in the Bible refers to God or His words. This hymn, in fact, merges the image of two different rocks. First is the rock in Exodus 33:22, where God hid Moses in its cleft. Second is the rock of Exodus 17:6. Moses struck this rock and water came out of it, pointing us, says the hymn, to Jesus' blood spilled for us. The storm from which we need hiding is the wrath of God against our sin. Nothing we do will protect us from this storm. We can work hard, go to church, even weep for our sin, but such works will not wash away the guilt. They leave us as naked before a violent storm. Only clinging to the cross of Jesus Christ will dress us in Christ's own righteousness and protect us from this storm of God's wrath. In the Rock of Christ, the rock for all ages (eras), we find refuge and covering. When death comes, we need not fear it. We can confidently face God's judgment throne because the Rock of Ages has covered us.

Rock of Ages, Cleft for Me

100

Oh come, let us sing to the LORD;
let us make a joyful noise to the rock of our salvation!

PSALM 95:1

1. Rock of A - ges, cleft for me, let me
2. *Not the la - bors of my hands can ful -*
3. Noth - ing in my hand I bring, sim - ply
4. *While I draw this fleet - ing breath, when my*

hide my - self in Thee; let the wa - ter and the
fill Thy law's de - mands; could my zeal no res - pite
to Thy cross I cling; na - ked, come to Thee for
eyes shall close in death, when I soar to worlds un -

blood, from Thy wound - ed side which flowed, be of
know, could my tears for - ev - er flow, all for
dress, help - less, look to Thee for grace; foul, I
known, see Thee on Thy judg - ment throne, Rock of

sin the dou - ble cure, save from wrath and make me pure.
sin could not a - tone; Thou must save and Thou a - lone.
to the foun - tain fly, wash me, Sav - ior, or I die!
A - ges, cleft for me, let me hide my - self in Thee.

TEXT: Augustus M. Toplady
TUNE: Thomas Hastings

TOPLADY

Petition   Guide Me, O Thou Great Jehovah

TEXT: William Williams ‖ b. February 11, 1717, Pantycelyn, Wales
d. January 11, 1791, Pantycelyn, Wales

William Williams lived in Wales at the time of a spiritual revival known as the "Great Awakening." Williams graduated from medical school with plans to become a doctor. But when he heard a sermon by Howell Harris, he accepted Christ as his Savior, and for forty-three years, traveled about Wales preaching. Both Harris and Williams are now remembered for the evangelism that took place in Wales at that time. Williams is said to have traveled 95,000 miles by foot or on horseback. He spoke to crowds of more than 10,000. Once he spoke to 80,000! This, of course, was well before the days of microphones, and he spoke outdoors. But he said that God gave him the ability to speak loudly enough so that most of the crowd could hear him.

Williams is remembered today more for his hymn writing. He was called the "sweet singer of Wales."[77] He wrote 800 hymns (he was also called the "Watts of Wales"),[78] and in 1745, he published a collection called *Alleluia*. In that book is his hymn, "Strength to Pass through the Wilderness," which at some point was renamed "Guide Me, O Thou Great Jehovah."

TUNE: John Hughes ‖ b. November 22, 1873, Dowlais, Wales
d. May 14, 1932, Pontypridd, Wales

Cwm Rhondda is the Welsh name for the Rhondda Valley. John Hughes wrote the tune in 1907 and named it after the valley to commemorate a musical festival held there. The people of Wales are known for their powerful and enthusiastic singing, and this tune is one of their favorites. It is their "unofficial national anthem," and you may often hear this tune sung at Welsh soccer games.

As you sing this hymn . . . look for all the references to ancient Israel passing through the wilderness. Williams uses a literary device called "typology" in which aspects of Israel's journey are treated as *types* of things that reoccur in our journey through life if we are Christians. Just like Israel, Christians are pilgrims in a strange land, too weak to pass through on our own. Just as Israel was given water, so God provides us a crystal fountain of refreshment and healing. Just as Israel had the fire and cloudy pillar to lead them by night and day, we need clear direction. Just as Israel crossed the Jordan River into the Promised Land, we find ourselves anxiously on the "verge of Jordan," approaching death, waiting to cross into heaven. For those of us who belong to Him, God promises the "death of death" and "hell's destruction" and the eternal safety of heaven where "songs of praises, I will ever give to Thee!"

Guide Me, O Thou Great Jehovah 101

This is God, our God forever and ever.
He will guide us forever.

PSALM 48:14

1. Guide me, O Thou great Je - hov - ah, pil - grim through this bar - ren land;
2. *O - pen now the crys - tal_ foun - tain, whence the heal - ing stream doth flow;*
3. When I tread the verge of_ Jor - dan, bid my anx - ious fears sub - side;

I am weak, but Thou art_ might - y; hold me with Thy_
*let the fire and cloud - y_ pil - lar lead me all my_*
Death of death, and hell's_ de - struc - tion, land me safe on_

pow'r ful hand; Bread of heav - en, Bread of heav - en,
jour - ney through. Strong De - liv - 'rer, strong De - liv - 'rer,
Ca - naan's side; songs of prais - es, songs of prais - es

feed me till I want no more, feed me till_ I_ want no more.
be Thou still my strength and shield, be Thou still_ my_ strength and shield.
I will ev - er give to Thee, I will ev - er_ give to Thee.

TEXT: William Williams
TUNE: John Hughes

CWM RHONDDA

Petition We Gather Together

TEXT: Netherlands folk hymn ‖

At the end of the sixteenth century, the Dutch people prayed for freedom from Spanish rule. Among other harsh decrees, the Spanish king had denied them the freedom to gather for worship. In 1597, the Spaniards were defeated, and a cry of victory can be heard in the hymn someone wrote for the occasion, "We Gather Together." Most sources list the author as anonymous, but some credit a Dutch poet named Adrianus Valerius with authorship. The title points to the very thing the Christians had been denied. Stanza 1's line, "The wicked oppressing now cease from distressing," refers directly to former Spanish oppressors. And stanza 3's prayer, "Let thy congregation escape tribulation," expresses the Dutch church's hope for the future.

The Dutch text was translated to English in 1894, almost 300 years later, by Theodore Baker, an American musicologist. Michael Hawn, professor of sacred music at Southern Methodist University, notes that it gained popularity in America first in World War I, and even more during World War II. For Americans, the "wicked oppressors" were Nazi Germany and Imperial Japan.[79] Through the years it has become a tradition to sing this hymn at Thanksgiving time to express gratitude to God for His protection throughout history and each year.

TUNE: *Nederlandtsch Gedenckclank,* ‖ b. April 10, 1838, Vienna, Austria
1626, arr. Edward Kremser ‖ d. November 27, 1914, Vienna, Austria

Edward Kremser, a Viennese choirmaster and composer, gained esteem as a collector of traditional Viennese songs. He discovered and revised this tune taken from the Dutch collection listed above 250 years after it was written. We now call the tune KREMSER after him.

As you sing this hymn . . . think about all the times in a single week that you gather with Christians to learn about God and worship Him. Then think about people worldwide today who are praying for the freedom to gather as Christians, just as the Dutch did in the sixteenth century. There are many Christians persecuted throughout our world.

Psalm 32:8 and Romans 8:31, listed under the hymn title, point to God's precious promise to protect His children. Although sometimes He may permit us to suffer for a time, He is sure to guard our souls and give us strength in the tribulations. This hymn helps us to give thanks even in the midst of such trials.

We Gather Together

I will instruct you and teach you in the way you should go;
I will counsel you with My eye upon you. . . .
If God is for us, who can be against us?

PSALM 32:8, ROMANS 8:31

1. We gath - er to - geth - er to ask the Lord's bless - ing;
2. *Be - side us to guide us, our God with us join - ing,*
3. We all do ex - tol Thee, Thou lead - er tri - um - phant,

He chas - tens and has - tens His will to make known;
or - dain - ing, main - tain - ing His king - dom di - vine;
and pray that Thou still our de - fend - er wilt be.

the wick - ed op - press - ing now cease___ from dis - tress - ing:
so from the be - gin - ning the fight___ we were win - ning:
Let Thy con - gre - ga - tion en - dure thro' trib - u - la - tion:

sing prais - es to His name; He for - gets not His own.
Thou, Lord, wast at our side:___ all glo - ry be Thine!
Thy name be ev - er praised!___ O Lord, make us free!

TEXT: Netherlands folk hymn
TUNE: *Nederlandtsch Gedenckclank,* arr. Edward Kremser

KREMSER

TEXT: Charles Wesley	b. December 18, 1707, Epworth, England
	d. March 29, 1788, London, England
	(for more on Wesley, see No. 2, 4, 31, 37, 41, 63, and 86)

This hymn has been referred to as "the finest heart-hymn in the English language."[80] Many hymns remind us that God is *transcendent*, beyond our understanding. This hymn, however, points us to God's *immanence*, meaning He is present with us and protects us. Written a year after his conversion, it is one of Charles Wesley's most famous hymns. It was first published in 1740, under the title, "In Time of Prayer and Temptation." No one knows what specific circumstances in Wesley's life prompted him to write about life's storms in this hymn.

| TUNE: Joseph Parry | b. May 21, 1841, Merthyr Tydfil, Wales |
| | d. February 17, 1903, Cambridge, England |

The tune ABERYSTWYTH was chosen for this hymnal because the D minor key seems to match the storms of life and the power of sin we can experience. Yet in the middle (the third phrase), it moves briefly into F major as a sign of hope and assurance. Parry wrote the tune ABERYSTWYTH, named after a town in Wales. When he was thirteen, he became an ironworker when his family moved to America. He later returned to Wales, however, and studied at the Royal Academy of Music and Cambridge University before becoming a professor of music at the University of Wales. He wrote operas, oratorios, cantatas, piano pieces, and hymn tunes.

As you sing this hymn . . . you might recall a time when you felt afraid during a storm. Perhaps it was the crashing thunder or fierce wind, or maybe you were far away from shelter. While storms can be frightening, we know that God is able to protect us. There are greater storms, though, that occur in our hearts and minds. They can cause truly great sorrow, hurt, and anger. These are the storms of which this text speaks.

God's presence in our lives is found in the person of Jesus Christ, and this hymn will give you words to use when you need to call on Him. Jesus is the "lover" of our souls. He is a "fountain," "healer," "wing," and "pilot." He is also the Creator to whom we cry based on His limitless love, authority, and power (see stanza 3). Of course, seeing Him makes us mindful of our sin and spiritual poverty. So we can call upon His grace (see stanza 4), perhaps the most precious word in the Christian vocabulary. This hymn expresses the gospel: God graciously and lovingly sent His Son for sinful and needy souls like us to pay the penalty for sin on the cross. He died, was buried, and rose again. When we recognize our sinfulness and need of Him, we "fly" to Him to be saved, loved, and protected.

Jesus, Lover of My Soul

Who shall separate us from the love of Christ? Shall tribulation, or distress, or persecution, or famine, or nakedness, or danger, or sword? . . . No, in all these things we are more than conquerors through Him who loved us.

ROMANS 8:35, 37

1. Je - sus,_ lov - er of my soul, let me to Thy bo - som fly,
2. *Oth - er_ ref - uge have I none, hangs my help - less soul_ on Thee;*
3. Thou, O_ Christ, art all I want; more than all in Thee I find:
4. *Plen - teous_ grace_ with Thee is found, grace to cov - er all_ my sin;*

while the_ near - er wa - ters roll, while the_ tem - pest still is high:
leave, ah!_ leave_ me not a - lone, still sup - port and com - fort me!
raise the_ fall - en, cheer the faint, heal the_ sick, and lead the blind.
let the_ heal - ing streams a - bound; make and_ keep me pure with - in:

hide me, O my Sav - ior,_ hide, till the storm of life is_ past;
All my trust on Thee is_ stayed, all my help from Thee I_ bring;
Just and ho - ly is Thy_name; I am all un - righ - teous-ness;
Thou of life the foun - tain_ art, free - ly let me take of_ Thee;

safe in - to the ha - ven guide, O re - ceive my soul at last!
cov - er my de - fense - less head with the_ shad - ow of Thy wing.
false and full of sin I am, Thou art_ full_ of truth and grace.
spring Thou up with - in my heart, rise to_ all_ e - ter - ni - ty.

TEXT: Charles Wesley
TUNE: Joseph Parry

ABERYSTWYTH

	b. June 1, 1793, Ednam, Scotland
TEXT: Henry Francis Lyte	d. November 20, 1847, Nice, France
	(for more on Lyte, see No. 85)

Henry Lyte spent his adult life as the minister to a humble congregation of fishermen and sailors in the small seaport village of Brixham, which is in southwest England. He was frail of health, yet he worked relentlessly. In September 1847, at the age of fifty-four, Lyte decided he must travel to Italy to live in a warmer climate. He preached his last sermon to his beloved congregation. He walked to the seashore to watch the sunset. He returned home, locked himself in his study, and after one hour, came out and handed a relative the text of "Abide with Me." The following week he left for Italy but made it only to Nice, France, where he died two months later. His last words were, "Peace! Joy!"[81] Many believe that Lyte wrote this poem about the end of life because he felt that he was in the evening of his own. Though unknown in his life, he became renowned to tens of thousands after his death because of the power of this hymn. It was a favorite of King George V and was sung at the weddings of both King George VI and his daughter, Queen Elizabeth. It was also sung at the funeral of Mother Teresa.

	b. March 16, 1823, London, England
TUNE: William H. Monk	d. March 1, 1889, London, England

When William Monk wrote the tune EVENTIDE, he was the editor of a significant and historic hymnal called *Hymns Ancient and Modern* (1861). According to his wife, he wrote it one evening while the two watched the sunset during a season of great sorrow for them.

As you sing this hymn . . . notice it begins and ends with a word that is not common today: *abide*. To abide is to continue, to stay, to wait, or to live with. Jesus promised to do just that as He urged us to remain in Him: "Abide in Me, and I in you. As the branch cannot bear fruit by itself, unless it abides in the vine, neither can you, unless you abide in Me" (John 15:4). When we abide in Christ, we can endure failing friends (stanza 1), constant change (stanza 2), the devil's attacks (stanza 3), or the coming of death (stanza 4). Amanda Leeman, mother to one of this hymnal's authors, quoted from this hymn as her final words on earth, even though severe dementia had robbed all memory. A few minutes before dying, she suddenly opened her eyes and said, "Change and decay in all around I see. Oh, Thou who changest not, abide with me." What will be your final words when that day arrives in your life?

Abide with Me

By this we know that He abides in us,
by the Spirit whom He has given us.

1 JOHN 3:24

1. A - bide with me: fast falls the e - ven - tide;
2. *Swift to its close ebbs out life's lit - tle day;*
3. I need Thy pres - ence ev - ery pass - ing hour;
4. *I fear no foe, with Thee at hand to bless;*
5. Hold Thou Thy cross be - fore my clos - ing eyes;

the dark - ness deep - ens; Lord, with me a - bide:
earth's joys grow dim, its glo - ries pass a - way;
what but Thy grace can foil the tempt - er's pow'r?
ills have no weight, and tears no bit - ter - ness.
shine through the gloom, and point me to the skies:

when oth - er help - ers fail, and com - forts flee,
change and de - cay in all a - round I see;
Who like Thy - self my guide and stay can be?
Where is death's sting? Where, grave, thy vic - to - ry?
heav'n's morn - ing breaks, and earth's vain shad - ows flee:

help of the help - less, O a - bide with me.
O Thou who chang - est not, a - bide with me.
Through cloud and sun - shine, O a - bide with me.
I tri - umph still, if Thou a - bide with me.
in life, in death, O Lord, a - bide with me.

TEXT: Henry F. Lyte   EVENTIDE
TUNE: William H. Monk

All Praise to Thee, My God, This Night

TEXT: Thomas Ken ‖ b. July, 1637, Little Berkhamsted, England
d. March 19, 1711, Longleat, Wiltshire, England

Thomas Ken was orphaned at an early age and raised by his sister Ann. Her husband was a famous fisherman, and fishing with his brother-in-law was a favorite childhood pastime of Ken's. He attended Winchester College, a prestigious boys' school, followed by Oxford University. He then became a clergyman and returned to Winchester to teach. Here, Ken wrote three hymns for his students to pray daily, alone in their rooms. There was a morning hymn, an evening hymn, and one for midnight, should they awaken. It is the evening hymn that remains to this day. The final stanza, "The Doxology," is perhaps the most familiar song in the English language and is used as a liturgical response.

Ken served as a chaplain for two kings, Charles II and James II. He was imprisoned in the Tower of London for a time and eventually lost his position as bishop for refusing to swear allegiance to William and Mary. He was never afraid to stand for what was right, even if it meant standing alone. It was said of Ken, "He came as near to the ideal of Christian perfection as human weakness permits."[82]

TUNE: Thomas Tallis ‖ b. 1505
d. December 3, 1585, Greenwich, England

The TALLIS CANON ("round") is named after Thomas Tallis, considered one of the best early English composers. He was a court musician for Henry VIII, Edward VI, Queen Mary, and Queen Elizabeth I. While these were stormy times in the church, Thomas was able to avoid the controversies that raged around him.

As you sing this hymn . . . memorize it to sing at bedtime. Are you ever fearful of night and darkness? You are not alone. Parents have sung and prayed with their children at night throughout history. Perhaps you know the poem "Now I Lay Me Down to Sleep." This hymn is a poem and a prayer to sing each night. Augustine said that our minds are more developed into a flame by holy words when they are sung than when they are not.[83]

Adults have cares at night as well. Small worries of the day grow large in the dark and loneliness of the night. Even King David sought peaceful sleep, as seen in the verse under the title. This hymn teaches that such peace is found first in praise. Peace comes when we know that God Almighty watches over and protects us. Peace comes in repentance and knowing we are forgiven and have forgiven others. Peace comes when fearful and fretful thoughts are replaced by heavenly ones. Sing this hymn tonight as you go to sleep!

All Praise to Thee, My God, This Night   105

In peace I will both lie down and sleep;
for You alone, O LORD, make me dwell in safety.

PSALM 4:8

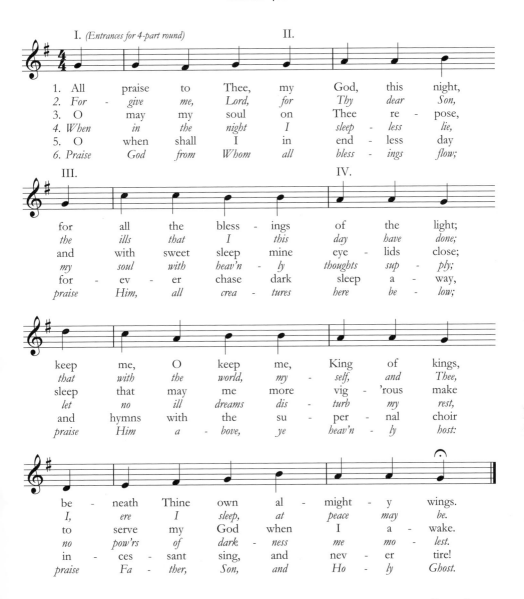

I. *(Entrances for 4-part round)*   II.

1. All praise to Thee, my God, this night,
2. For - give me, Lord, for Thy dear Son,
3. O may my soul on Thee re - pose,
4. When in the night I sleep - less lie,
5. O when shall I in end - less day
6. Praise God from Whom all bless - ings flow;

III.   IV.

for all the bless - ings of the light;
the ills that I this day have done;
and with sweet sleep mine eye - lids close;
my soul with heav'n - ly thoughts sup - ply;
for - ev - er chase dark sleep a - way,
praise Him, all crea - tures here be - low;

keep me, O keep me, King of kings,
that with the world, my - self, and Thee,
sleep that may me more vig - 'rous make
let no ill dreams dis - turb my rest,
and hymns with the su - per - nal choir
praise Him a - bove, ye heav'n - ly host:

be - neath Thine own al - might - y wings.
I, ere I sleep, at peace may be.
to serve my God when I a - wake.
no pow'rs of dark - ness me mo - lest,
in - ces - sant sing, and nev - er tire!
praise Fa - ther, Son, and Ho - ly Ghost.

TEXT: Thomas Ken
TUNE: Thomas Tallis

TALLIS CANON

TEXT: Fanny J. Crosby	b. March 24, 1820, Putnam County, New York
	d. February 12, 1915, Bridgeport, Connecticut
	(for more on Crosby, see No. 90)

Although Fanny Crosby, who was blind from infancy, lived in a very poor district of Brooklyn, New York, she had been befriended by a wealthy woman named Phoebe Knapp. Knapp lived in a mansion which had a music room filled with a collection of fine musical instruments. One day, while Fanny was visiting, Phoebe took her into the music room to play a tune she had just written. Fanny listened to her friend play, clapped her hands, and cried, "Why, that says 'Blessed Assurance!'"[84] At that moment she began to write the hymn.

Throughout her lifetime Fanny authored over 8,000 hymns. They were different than the older English and German hymns because they offered first-person testimonies of life as a Christian, and they were paired with joyous, warm, singable melodies. Some of the more familiar ones remaining in hymnals today include "To God Be the Glory," "Safe in the Arms of Jesus," "Pass Me Not, O Gentle Savior," "Jesus, Keep Me Near the Cross," "I Am Thine, O Lord," "All the Way My Savior Leads Me," "Praise Him, Praise Him," "Saved by Grace," and "Rescue the Perishing." Fanny's songs became well known across the country and around the world when the evangelist D. L. Moody, together with his song leader, Ira Sankey, used many of them in their national crusades.

| TUNE: Phoebe P. Knapp | b. March 9, 1839, New York, New York |
| | d. July 10, 1908, Poland, Maine |

Phoebe was raised in a home of Methodist evangelists. She married Joseph Knapp, who was the founder and second president of the Metropolitan Life Insurance Company. When he died, Phoebe gave away much of their great wealth, although she kept a large pipe organ in her apartment! She wrote over 500 hymn tunes. This tune, named ASSURANCE, is by far her most well-known.

As you sing this hymn . . . you are making Fanny Crosby's testimony your testimony. Start by asking yourself, Is it true? Do you have the assurance that Jesus is your Savior? Are you "blessed," or favored, with this confidence? If you are a Christian, God means to assure you through His Word that you are an "Heir of salvation, purchase of God, born of His Spirit, washed in His blood." Like Fanny, don't use physical eyes but rather spiritual eyes to be "Watching and waiting, looking above." If the answers to these questions are yes, then declare with joy and thanksgiving what God has done: "This is my story, this is my song, praising my Savior all the day long."

Blessed Assurance

Let us draw near with a true heart in full assurance of faith. . . .
Through Him then let us continually offer up a sacrifice of praise to God,
that is, the fruit of lips that acknowledge His name.

HEBREWS 10:22; 13:15

1. Bless-ed as - sur - ance, Je - sus is mine!___ O what a
2. *Per - fect sub - mis - sion, per - fect de - light,___ vis - ions of*
3. Per - fect sub - mis - sion, all is at rest,___ I in my

fore - taste of glo-ry di - vine!___ Heir of sal - va - tion, pur-chase of
rap - ture now burst on my sight;___ an - gels de - scend - ing, bring from a -
Sav - ior am hap-py and blest;___ watch-ing and wait - ing, look-ing a -

God,___ born of His Spir - it, washed in His blood.___
bove___ ech - oes of mer - cy, whis-pers of love.___
bove,___ filled with His good - ness, lost in His love.___

This is my sto - ry, this is my song, prais-ing my

Sav - ior all the day long: this is my sto - ry, this is my

song, prais-ing my Sav - ior all the day long.

TEXT: Fanny J. Crosby
TUNE: Phoebe P. Knapp

ASSURANCE

TEXT: John Newton;   b. July 24, 1725, London, England
John P. Rees, stanza 5   d. December 21, 1807, London, England

For this story, we begin at the end. John Newton, before he died, wrote these words for his tombstone:

> John Newton, clerk, once an infidel and Libertine, a servant of slavers
> in Africa, was, by the rich mercy of our Lord and Savior Jesus Christ,
> preserved, restored, pardoned, and appointed to preach the faith he had
> long labored to destroy.[85]

It is not surprising that this was the same man who wrote about an "amazing grace" that "saved a wretch." One of the world's most beloved hymns, "Amazing Grace," is John Newton's personal testimony. He originally titled it "Faith's Review and Expectation."

Newton's godly mother died when he was six years old. An unloving stepmother and absent sailor father made his childhood very unhappy. He apprenticed with his father as a sailor at age eleven, leading to a career as a sailor and slave trader. One night in a horrible storm at sea, Newton prayed for rescue when he was sure of death. This led to a rejection of his sinful life and his becoming a Christian. Not only did he spend the rest of his life as a pastor, but he was an ally with William Wilberforce in the crusade that ended slavery in Great Britain.

TUNE: *Virginia Harmony*, 1831,
adapt. Edwin Excell, 1909

Scholars are not certain what tune Newton's church in Olney used, but NEW BRITAIN, the tune so familiar today, is an American tune that did not appear in print until 1829 nor linked to this text until 1835. In 1909 Edwin Excell selected the stanzas and arranged the tune as we sing it today. It was a part of the shaped-note *Southern Harmony* tradition and is in a pentatonic scale. Therefore, it can be sung in canon or round.

As you sing this hymn . . . meditate upon the amazing grace God has shown for sinners by sending His Son to pay the penalty for sin of all who would repent of their sin and put their trust in Him. Interestingly, this hymn has become quite popular among non-Christians! It has been recorded by popular artists who show no evidence of believing the gospel. You hear it at private funerals and at memorials of a public nature, such as the 9/11 memorial service, sung by people who have never personally received God's saving grace. Why is this? Likely, they do not understand the word "saved." They take it to mean being saved from sadness or difficulty. But that is not what Newton meant! He is speaking of the grace of salvation through faith in Christ: "For by grace you have been saved through faith. And this is not your own doing; it is the gift of God" (Eph. 2:8). That is truly "amazing"!

Amazing Grace! How Sweet the Sound 107

Who am I, O Lord God, and what is my house,
that You have brought me thus far?

I CHRONICLES 17:16

1. A - maz - ing grace! how sweet the sound
2. 'Twas grace that taught my heart to fear,
3. The Lord has pro - mised good to me,
4. Through man - y dan - gers, toils, and snares,
5. When we've been there ten thou - sand years,

that saved a wretch like me!
and grace my fears re - lieved;
His Word my hope se - cures;
I have al - read - y come;
bright shin - ing as the sun,

I once was lost, but now am found,
how pre - cious did that grace ap - pear,
He will my shield and por - tion be
'tis grace has brought me safe thus far,
we've no less days to sing God's praise

was blind but now I see.
the hour I first be - lieved.
as long as life en - dures.
and grace will lead me home.
than when we'd first be - gun.

TEXT: John Newton
TUNE: Virginia Harmony

NEW BRITAIN

239

TEXT: Horatio G. Spafford ‖ b. October 20, 1828, North Troy, New York
d. October 16, 1888, Jerusalem, Israel

Mr. and Mrs. Horatio Spafford lived in Chicago, Illinois, with their four children. The great Chicago fire of 1871 destroyed much of the city and with it much of the Spafford fortune. Two years later, they were preparing to sail to England on the luxurious *S. S. Ville du Havre*, but at the last minute Mr. Spafford was delayed for business. He sent his wife ahead with their daughters, Maggie, Tanetta, Annie, and Bessie. At 2:00 a.m., November 22, 1873, another vessel rammed the ship and it went down into the sea. The lives of the four Spafford girls were lost, along with 222 others. Mrs. Spafford cabled her husband upon reaching Wales: "Saved alone what shall I do."[86] In December, Mr. Spafford sailed to meet his wife, and the captain pointed out to him the place where the *Ville du Havre* had gone down. After a sleepless night, he wrote the poem to the now-famous hymn, "It Is Well with My Soul."

Years later, the Spaffords moved to Israel and established an American colony where they did charitable work, especially caring for children. There remains today in Jerusalem the "Spafford Children's Center," which serves children of all nationalities.

TUNE: Philip P. Bliss ‖ b. July 9, 1838, Clearfield County, Pennsylvania
d. December 29, 1876, Ashtabula, Ohio

A songwriter friend of the Spaffords, Philip Bliss, offered to write a melody for this poem. In 1876, he introduced it to over a thousand pastors meeting in Chicago. Bliss named the tune VILLE DU HAVRE after the ship. Ironically, only a month later, Mr. and Mrs. Bliss were taking a train from New York to Chicago, having left their two children with their grandmother. A few hours into the journey, a bridge in Ohio gave way, plunging the entire train into the water below. Both of the Blisses perished.

As you sing this hymn . . . remember the great difference between Christians and non-Christians. Amidst life's tragedies, those without Christ have no assurance that a good God rules and that He will make all things right. They have no guarantees about an unknown future. And they bear guilt over wrongs committed. But the apostle Paul promises Christ's people a peace beyond understanding, a peace that guards our hearts and minds because our sins are forgiven, and our future is sure (Phil. 4:7). The sorrows that we encounter on earth can be met with the same kind of hope in God found by these grieving parents.

When asked, "How are you?" we often answer, "I am well, thank you." But knowing God in Christ, we can confront life's greatest sorrows and also sing, "It is well with my soul."

It Is Well with My Soul

And the peace of God, which surpasses all understanding,
will guard your hearts and your minds in Christ Jesus.

PHILIPPIANS 4:7

1. When peace, like a riv - er, at - tend - eth my way, when
2. Though Sa - tan should buf - fet, though tri - als should come, let
3. My sin, O the bliss of this glo - ri - ous thought: my
4. O Lord, haste the day when the faith__ shall be sight, the

sor - rows like sea bil-lows roll, what - ev - er my lot, Thou hast
this blest as - sur - ance con - trol: that Christ has re - gard - ed my
sin, not in part, but the whole is nailed to the cross and I
clouds be rolled back as a scroll, the trump shall re - sound and the

taught me to say, "It is well, it is well with my soul."____
help - less es - tate, and has shed His own blood for my soul.____
bear it no more, praise the Lord, praise the Lord, O my soul!____
Lord shall de - scend: "E - ven so," it is well with my soul.____

It is well_____ with my soul;_____

It is well with my

soul; it is well, it is well with my soul.

TEXT: Horatio G. Spafford
TUNE: Philip P. Bliss

VILLE DU HAVRE

My Faith Has Found a Resting Place

<table>
<tr><td>TEXT: Eliza Hewitt</td><td>b. June 28, 1851, Philadelphia, Pennsylvania
d. April 24, 1920, Philadelphia, Pennsylvania</td></tr>
</table>

This poem is signed *Lidie H. Edmunds*. However, no one knows exactly who that was! Most believe it was Eliza Hewitt, a hymn writer who used Lidie as a pseudonym. A pseudonym is a "fake name" that writers used so that a hymnal would not contain too many hymns from one author. Fanny Crosby, for instance, used over 200 different names.

Hewitt wrote and published over seventy hymns. She was a schoolteacher who had to retire early because of spinal problems and was an invalid for the rest of her life. Eliza then turned to hymn writing and Sunday school work. She was superintendent at the Northern Home for Friendless Children and later at Calvin Presbyterian Church, both located in Philadelphia, where she spent her entire life.

TUNE: Norwegian folk melody

The melody LANDÅS comes from the name of a town in Norway. When first published, the tune was listed as a Norwegian melody attributed to André E. M. Grétry (1741–1813). But it has never been found in any of Grétry's music, so the true origin is conjecture. Whoever wrote it, the tune was later adapted to fit this poem by William Kirkpatrick (1838–1921), another Pennsylvanian who wrote almost 100 hymn tunes.

As you sing this hymn . . . consider the hymn's original title, "No Other Plea," based on the words from the chorus. A plea is what you hear in a courtroom when, at the beginning of a trial, the judge says to the defendant, "How do you plead?" One day, we will all face the courtroom of God's judgment, and when He asks us how we plead, we will only be able to say, "Guilty" (Rom. 3:23). We were born guilty (Ps. 51:5). However, the "good news," or gospel, is that Jesus died for the guilt of all who repent and put their trust in Him. He also gives to them His own righteousness! That way, when God says, "How do you plead?" we can say, "I plead the righteousness of Christ!" It brings to mind another court term that attorneys use after they have given their full arguments for defending the accused: "The defense rests." After we plead Christ, we will hear our Defender, Jesus, declare, "The defense rests." Then we will sing, "It is enough that Jesus died, and that He died for me."

If you are trusting in Christ, let the truths of this hymn erase your guilt, doubts, and fears. Lean on His Word. Trust the Great Defender. No more argument is needed. You are innocent and free. Hallelujah!

My Faith Has Found a Resting Place   109

While we were still weak, at the right time
Christ died for the ungodly.

ROMANS 5:6

1. My faith has found a rest-ing place, not in de-vice nor creed;
2. E - nough for me that Je - sus saves, this ends my fear and doubt;
3. My heart is lean - ing on the Word, the writ-ten Word of God,
4. My Great Phy - si - cian heals the sick, the lost He came to save;

I trust the ev - er - liv-ing One, His wounds for me shall plead.
a sin-ful soul, I come to Him, He'll nev - er cast me out.
sal - va-tion by my Sav-ior's name, sal - va - tion through His blood.
for me His pre - cious blood He shed, for me His life He gave.

I need no oth - er ar - gu - ment, I need no oth - er plea,___

it is e-nough that Je-sus died, and that He died for me.

TEXT: Lidie H. Edmunds   LANDAS
TUNE: André Grétry, arr. William J. Kirkpatrick

TEXT: Charitie Lees Bancroft ‖ b. June 21, 1841, Bloomfield, Ireland
d. June 20, 1923, Oakland, California

Little is known about Charitie Lees Bancroft, except that she was the fourth child of a minister's family, born near Dublin, Ireland. She wrote many poems, some of which were placed in a collection called "Within the Veil" (1867). This is a biblical reference to the Holy of Holies in ancient Israel's temple, which was closed off by a veil.

The Holy of Holies is where Israel's high priest would go once a year to advocate on behalf of a sinful people before a holy God. God gave Israel this high priest to teach the whole world that everyone needs such an advocate. We have all sinned, and God, because He is holy, must punish that sin. Who will advocate on our behalf? The good news is, Israel's high priest also points the world to another priest and advocate, and this hymn tells us His name. Mrs. Bancroft, when she first wrote this song, entitled it "The Advocate." It is about Jesus Christ, the Great High Priest, who is an advocate to God for everyone who repents and believes.

TUNE: Vikki Cook ‖ b. July 26, 1960, Glendora, California

Have you ever looked for buried treasure? The text of this hymn is a "treasure" that was buried in the distant past and found in recent years by Vikki Cook. She wrote this tune for this older text in 1997. Mrs. Cook has cowritten numerous songs with her husband, Steve Cook, and is part of the Sovereign Grace Music team of composers. Directing school choirs and teaching piano and voice lessons are her other music endeavors.

As you sing this hymn . . . realize it is only true for those who recognize their sin and their need for an advocate before a good and holy God. It is a hymn that belongs to everyone who trusts the good news of Jesus' death and resurrection for sin and follows Him as Lord. These people can know that their names are now engraved on His hands: "Behold, I have engraved you on the palms of My hands; your walls are continually before Me" (Isa. 49:16). He is their advocate, and they can stand before God's throne with boldness and confidence. Is that you? If so, rejoice!

The word "thence" is an old English word that means "from that place." From that place, from the throne of God, no one can condemn us, not even Satan. As you sing, visualize standing before God without guilt or fear, not because you are so good, but because Jesus Christ is so good, and He has paid the penalty on your behalf. Behold Him with *spiritual eyes*—the perfect Lamb of God who has purchased a people from every tribe, tongue, and nation. Sing these words today with joy and gratitude.

Before the Throne of God Above

For we do not have a high priest who is unable to sympathize with our weaknesses. . . . Let us then with confidence draw near to the throne of grace, that we may receive mercy and find grace to help in time of need.

HEBREWS 4:15–16

1. Be - fore the throne of God a - bove, I have a strong and per - fect plea,
2. *When Sa - tan tempts me to des - pair and tells me of the guilt with - in,*
3. Be - hold Him there, the ri - sen Lamb, my per - fect spot - less right - eous - ness,

a great High Priest whose name is Love, who ev - er lives and pleads for me.
up - ward I look and see Him there, who made an end of all my sin.
the great un - change - a - ble I AM, the King of Glo - ry and of Grace.

My name is gra - ven on His hands. My name is writ - ten on His heart.
Be - cause the sin - less Sav - ior died, my sin - ful soul is count - ed free.
One with Him - self, I can - not die. My soul is pur - chased by His blood.

I know that while in heav'n He stands no tongue can
For God, the Just, is sat - is - fied to look on
My life is hid with Christ on high, with Christ my

bid me thence de - part, no tongue can bid me thence de - part.
Him and par - don me, to look on Him and par - don me.
Sav - ior and my God, with Christ my Sav - ior and my God.

TEXT: Charitie Lees Bancroft
TUNE: Vikki Cook

HOUSTON

TEXT AND TUNE: Kathleen Thomerson ‖ b. 1934, Tennessee

B orn in Tennessee, Kathleen Thomerson was raised in Mississippi, California, and Texas. She studied music at the Universities of Colorado and Texas, at the Flemish Royal Conservatory in Antwerp, and in Paris. She has served most recently as organist and music director at Mt. Olive Lutheran Church in Austin, Texas.

In the summer of 1966, a heat wave at her home in St. Louis sent Thomerson to seek the air-conditioned comfort of her mother's house in Houston, Texas. This hymn came to her as she thought about visiting her "brothers and sisters in Christ at the Episcopal Church of the Redeemer in Houston." That is why the tune is called HOUSTON. She intended it as a prayer and meditation on Scripture. Twelve separate passages from the Bible inspired it, the primary text being Ephesians 5:8: "For at one time you were darkness, but now you are light in the Lord. Walk as children of light."

As you sing this hymn . . . ask yourself what it means to walk as a child of the light. People don't usually think of themselves as children of darkness, as in the science-fiction movie *Star Wars*, where characters purposely refer to themselves as belonging to "the dark side." But, in fact, anyone who is not living in the light of the knowledge of God belongs to the dark side. God and God's truth are light. So a child of the light is someone who knows God and lives by His truth.

Have you ever been in a deep cave with a flashlight? Suppose your light suddenly went out, and you had to find your way out by feeling along the cave walls. That could become frightening, especially if any length of time passed. And how joyfully you would greet even the faintest glow of light as you moved toward the cave's entrance. You would want to be a child of the light.

Philosophers have used the darkness of caves to speak about human ignorance. But the Bible talks about darkness as both ignorance and our willful sin and rebellion. Leaving the darkness begins with repentance, turning away from our sin and trusting in Christ. It means looking to Jesus, the "clear Sun of Righteousness." It is His righteousness that leads us to the Father.

The final stanza holds out the hope of light as nothing more than the hope of seeing Jesus return. True Christians grow tired of the darkness of this world and long for Him to come back. What joy that will be to see the "Lamb [who] is the light in the city of God."

Until that day, we pray that Jesus would shine in our hearts. When He does shine out, those around us may discover the joy of knowing the Light of the World.

I Want to Walk as a Child of the Light 111

The sun shall be no more your light by day, nor for brightness
shall the moon give you light; but the LORD will be your everlasting
light, and your God will be your glory.

ISAIAH 60:19

TEXT AND TUNE: Kathleen Thomerson

TEXT: Ancient Irish hymn,
attributed to Dallan Forgaill, 8th c. ‖

This text dates back to eighth-century Ireland. But the Irish story of Christianity dates back to several hundred years before that, when the Irish kidnaped a sixteen-year-old named Patrick from his home in Scotland. While meditating on the Christian lessons of his youth, Patrick, whom we often call St. Patrick, gave his life to the Lord Jesus when he was a slave in Ireland. Eventually, he escaped and returned home to Scotland. Later, however, he believed that God wanted him to return to Ireland as a missionary. Many tried to kill him, but Patrick persisted in serving God, starting about 200 churches and baptizing 100,000 converts. Christianity in Ireland had begun, out of which this text of devotion and faith was written.

Mary E. Byrne, a scholarly woman in Dublin, Ireland, translated the Irish words into English in 1905. It was versified, or made into poetry, by Eleanor Hull, an English woman from Manchester, in 1912.

TUNE: Irish melody ‖

The tune, named SLANE, comes from a medieval Irish folk song about the Hill of Slane, a small village on the left bank of the River Boyne. According to tradition, St. Patrick defied a royal edict at this location on March 26, 433. The edict stipulated that no fire could be lit before High King Logaire of Tara lit one in order to begin the pagan spring festival. Patrick ignored this and lit candles for Easter Eve. Rather than punish Patrick, the king was so impressed with his devotion that he allowed him to continue his missionary work. It is believed the Irish folk song SLANE was written for this occasion.

As you sing this hymn . . . you are singing a prayer. This prayer should be the earnest desire of every true believer—the ability to have spiritual eyesight to see God as He is and to see as God sees. Our spiritual vision is now impaired by living in a sinful world and by our worldly desires. Yet we long to see the goodness of God and the purposes of God, particularly as we walk through life's battles. Notice that the word *Vision* is capitalized in both the first and fifth stanzas. God Himself is Vision, just as God is Love. Christ enables us to see God and to see through the fog of this world.

Now that you know what Christians faced in ancient Ireland, perhaps you can see why this prayer petitions God with words such as *battle shield, sword, dignity, delight, shelter,* and *high tower.* Carefully note each request in every stanza, and make it your own prayer in whatever challenges you face now or in the future. The "High King and Ruler of All" wants to answer your prayer and fulfill your needs.

Be Thou My Vision

We have seen His glory, glory as of the only Son from the Father,
full of grace and truth.

JOHN 1:14

1. Be Thou my__ Vi - sion, O Lord of my heart;
2. *Be Thou my__ Wis - dom, and Thou my true Word;*
3. Be Thou my__ bat - tle shield, sword for my fight;
4. *Rich - es I__ heed not, nor man's emp - ty praise,*
5. High King of__ heav - en, my vic - to - ry won,

naught be all else to me, save that Thou art;
I ev - er with Thee and Thou with me, Lord;
be Thou my dig - ni - ty, Thou my de - light,
Thou mine in - her - i - tance, now and al - ways:
may I reach heav - en's joys, O bright heav'n's Sun!

Thou my__ best__ thought, by day or by night,__
Thou my__ great__ Fa - ther, I Thy true son,__
Thou my__ soul's_ shel - ter, Thou my high tow'r:__
Thou and__ Thou__ on - ly, first in my heart,__
Heart of__ my__ own heart, what - ev - er be - fall,__

wak - ing or sleep - ing, Thy__ pres - ence my light.
Thou in me dwell - ing, and__ I with Thee one.
raise Thou me heav'n- ward, O__ Pow'r of my pow'r.
High King of heav - en, my__ trea - sure Thou art.
still be my Vi - sion, O__ rul - er of all.

TEXT: Ancient Irish hymn, 8th c.

TUNE: Irish folk melody

SLANE

TEXT: Frances R. Havergal

b. December 14, 1836, Astley, Worcestershire, England
d. June 3, 1879, Caswall Bay, Swansea, Wales
(for more on Havergal, see No. 76)

Frances Havergal has been called "a bright but short lived candle in English hymnody."[87] She was a talented singer and pianist and spent much of her brief life writing prose and poetry. In her own words, her primary goal was to be a "personal spiritual benefit upon others." This commitment to others is evident in the story of writing this particular poem, which she called a "consecration hymn":

> I went for a little visit of five days. There were ten persons in the house, some unconverted and long prayed for, some converted but not rejoicing Christians. He gave me the prayer, "Lord, give me all in this house!" And He just did! Before I left the house, everyone had got a blessing. The last night of my visit I was too happy to sleep and passed most of the night in praise and renewal of my own consecration, and these little couplets formed themselves and chimed in my heart one after another, till they finished with, "Ever, ONLY, ALL for Thee!"[88]

After writing the phrase in this hymn, "Take my voice and let me sing only for my King," Havergal decided to give up her career as a concert soloist. And after writing "Take my silver and my gold," she donated her large jewelry collection to mission causes.[89]

TUNE: Henri César Malan

b. July 7, 1787, Geneva, Switzerland
d. May 18, 1864, Vandoeuvres, Switzerland

Henri Malan, a believer in Jesus Christ from childhood, was a pastor and hymn writer. He is most remembered as an originator of the modern hymn movement in the French Reformed Church. He was once removed from ministry in the state church for preaching a sermon on salvation by faith alone in Christ alone, the same doctrine that launched the Protestant Reformation. The name HENDON, taken from a village in England, was assigned to this tune by Lowell Mason, the hymn's first publisher.

As you sing this hymn . . . you are singing a song or prayer of aspiration. To aspire means to hope and work toward something. And in this hymn, you aspire to give your life completely to God. Such words should not be sung lightly. At times you will fail. Some days Satan, who opposes you, will win. When that happens, you must not give up. You confess it to God and thank Him for being patient, understanding, and forgiving. As a Christian, your walk with God will involve a lifetime of saying to Him day after day, "Take my life and let it be consecrated to Thee." He promises to answer this prayer: "for it is God who works in you, both to will and to work for His good pleasure" (Phil. 2:13).

Take My Life and Let It Be Consecrated 113

You were bought with a price. So glorify God in your body.

I CORINTHIANS 6:20

1. Take my life,— and— let it be con - se - cra - ted,— Lord, to— Thee; Take my mo - ments and my days,— let them flow in cease - less— praise,— let them flow in— cease - less praise.
2. *Take my hands,— and— let them move at the im - pulse— of Thy— love. Take my feet, and— let them be— swift and beau - ti - ful— for— Thee,— swift and beau - ti - ful for Thee.*
3. Take my voice,— and— let me sing al - ways on - ly— for my— King. Take my lips, and— let them be— filled with mes - sag - es— from— Thee,— filled with mes - sag - es from Thee.
4. *Take my sil - ver - and my gold; not a mite— would I with - hold. Take my in - tel - lect and use— ev - ery power as— Thou— shalt— choose,— ev - ery power as— Thou shalt choose.*
5. Take my will,— and— make it Thine, it shall be— no— long - er - mine. Take my heart, it— is Thine own,— it shall be Thy roy - al— throne,— it shall be Thy— roy - al throne.
6. *Take my love;— my— God, I pour at Thy feet— its— trea - sure— store. Take my- self, and— I will be— ev - er, on - ly— all— for— Thee,— ev - er, on - ly— all for Thee.*

TEXT: Frances R. Havergal
TUNE: Henri A. César Malan

HENDON

| TEXT: Kate B. Wilkinson | b. August 27, 1859, Woodlands Bank, Cheshire, England |
| | d. December 28, 1928, Kensington, London, England |

L ittle is known about Kate Wilkinson. She was a member of an Anglican church in London and was involved in helping young women on the west side of London. This hymn was first published in an English children's hymnbook called *Golden Bells* in 1925.

In 1968, the president of Wheaton College, Dr. Hudson T. Armerding, included this text in the commencement program, where it has continued to be used every year. He considered it to be particularly important for the young, "who have so much potential." It was also regularly sung at the conclusion of Wheaton College's chapel services.[90]

| TUNE: Arthur Cyril Barham-Gould | b. 1891, England |
| | d. February 14, 1953, Tunbridge Wells, Kent, England |

A rthur Barham-Gould, educated at Cambridge University, became an Anglican priest in 1928, and served at All Souls Church, Holy Trinity Church, and St. Paul's, Onslow Square. He composed the tune ST. LEONARDS for this text while living at St. Leonards-by-the-Sea, England.

As you sing this hymn... you are praying for the "mind of Christ," based on Philippians 2:5–9 and Romans 12:1–2. Each stanza adds to the picture of what this looks like. Such a mind is where the Word dwells richly, where God's peace rules, where Jesus' love fills us. Stanza 5 asks for the perseverance of a runner in "looking only unto Jesus," drawing from Hebrews 12:1–2.

Stanza 6 concludes with a prayer for God's beauty—for His love and character to rest on us as we share the gospel with the lost so that people don't see us but Him. It's a prayer like John the Baptist's: may I decrease so that He would increase (John 3:30).

If you are still in school, your goal is to educate your mind. And what a worthy goal! But as you pursue this, don't neglect the even greater charge of Romans 12:2: "Do not be conformed to this world, but be transformed by the renewal of your mind, that by testing you may discern what is the will of God, what is good and acceptable and perfect."

May the Mind of Christ My Savior 114

Have this mind among yourselves, which is yours in Christ Jesus. . . .
It is God who works in you, both to will and to work for His good pleasure.

PHILIPPIANS 2:5,13

1. May the mind of Christ my Sa - vior live in me from day to day, by His love and power con - trol - ling all I do and say.

2. *May the Word of God dwell rich - ly in my heart from hour to hour, so that all may see I tri - umph on - ly through His power.*

3. May the peace of God my Fa - ther rule my life in ev - ery - thing, that I may be calm to com - fort sick and sor - row - ing.

4. *May the love of Je - sus fill me as the wa - ters fill the sea, Him ex - alt - ing, self a - bas - ing, this is vic - to - ry.*

5. May I run the race be - fore me, strong and brave to face the foe, look - ing on - ly un - to Je - sus as I on - ward go.

6. *May His beau - ty rest up - on me as I seek the lost to win, and may they for - get the chan - nel, see - ing on - ly Him.*

TEXT: Kate B. Wilkinson
TUNE: A. Cyril Barham-Gould

ST. LEONARDS

TEXT AND TUNE: Bob Kauflin ‖ b. January 1, 1955, Somers Point, New Jersey

"O Great God" reflects this entire hymnal by combining ancient and modern. The text is based on a prayer that is hundreds of years old, but it has been adapted and given a modern tune by hymn writer Bob Kauflin. The prayer is found in the exquisite volume, *The Valley of Vision: A Collection of Puritan Prayers and Devotions.* Called "Regeneration," the prayer asks God to occupy and reign supreme in the heart, to lay low every rebel power, and to let no vile passion resist His holy war. Kauflin writes, "I wanted to set that prayer to music because of how often I'm asking God to do whatever He needs to do to make me love and glorify Him more."[91]

Kauflin graduated from Temple University with a degree in piano performance. For over twenty-five years, he arranged music, composed, and sang with the *a cappella* singing group Glad. He has served as a music pastor at churches in South Carolina, Maryland, and Kentucky. Kauflin also directs the music ministry for Sovereign Grace Ministries, which has allowed him to produce a host of professional recordings. Through books, blogs, conferences, and seminars, he equips pastors, musicians, and songwriters in the theology and practice of congregational worship.

As you sing this hymn . . . you are singing words that sum up the purpose of this hymnal, hymns every child should sing. Why are they essential? Because they present the good news of the gospel, they praise God for that gospel, and they teach you how to live in light of the gospel. If you learn all of these hymns by heart, but you do not know God's good news, your learning is ultimately worthless. You have wasted your time! These hymns call for a response. Is Christ your Savior and Lord? "O Great God" can serve as your response.

The hymn begins by naming the One we adore: the great God of highest heaven. And it begins here because of the size of the problem that stanza 1 presents: our hearts are still occupied by rebel powers. Vice, or immoral behavior, remains. God has wonderfully purchased us, but we don't always act like it. What should we do? Stanza 2 answers by recalling how powerfully God has already worked in our lives: As non-Christians, we were blinded by sin. We could not see God's love and truth. But then the Holy Spirit opened our eyes to the gospel and gave us hope and peace. This act of remembering should hearten us to ask for still more in the final stanza: to live depending on His grace, to be kept from evil, to praise Him with every thought and deed, and to glorify Him with our whole lives.

As you sing the hymn, make it your prayer. The great God who worked in your life yesterday will hear and answer you today and tomorrow and forever.

O Great God

115

Search me, O God, and know my heart! Try me and know my thoughts!
And see if there be any grievous way in me, and lead me in the way everlasting!

PSALM 139:23–24

1. O great God of high-est heav'n, Oc-cu-py my low-ly heart;
2. *I was blind-ed by my sin, had no ears to hear Your voice;*
3. Help me now to live a life that's de-pen-dent on Your grace;

Own it all and reign su-preme, Con-quer ev'-ry reb-el pow'r.
Did not know Your love with-in, had no taste for heav-en's joys.
Keep my heart and guard my soul from the e-vils that I face.

Let no vice or sin re-main that re-sists Your ho-ly war,
Then Your Spir-it gave me life, o-pened up Your Word to me;
You are wor-thy to be praised with my ev-'ry thought and deed;

You have loved and pur-chased me, make me Yours for-ev-er more.
Through the gos-pel of Your Son, gave me end-less hope and peace.
O great God of high-est heav'n, glo-ri-fy Your name through me.

TEXT AND TUNE: Bob Kauflin

The Lord works righteousness and justice
for all who are oppressed.
He made known His ways to Moses,
His acts to the people of Israel.
The Lord is merciful and gracious,
slow to anger and abounding in steadfast love.

PSALM 103:6–8

Spirituals

AFRICAN AMERICAN HYMNS FROM THE 19TH AND 20TH CENTURIES

Spirituals are named from the apostle Paul's third designation of three kinds of songs that Christians should sing: psalms, hymns, and *spiritual songs.* (Col. 3:16). The texts often reflect the difficult lives of African Americans, either from slavery, suffering, or racist treatment against them. Although these have sometimes been called *sorrow songs*, they could be called *hopeful songs*, expressing confidence in God. There is a deep soulfulness in the melodies and rhythms that combines with the texts to draw out our emotions and faith. Eileen Guenther says of these songs, "Spirituals affirm a complete trust in God to make right in the next world what was done wrong in this world."[92] In concluding a book of heritage hymns, we believe it is important to add these from the heritage of African American believers. From thousands of spirituals, these five were chosen for their first-person fervent prayers for God's help in times of need. May they become a part of your singing heritage no matter what your ethnicity.

TEXT AND TUNE: Anonymous ‖

As is the case in many spirituals, the author and composer of this spiritual is unknown. However, it is believed that it was created in the 1750s. In *Negro Slave Songs of the United States*, Miles Mark Fisher quotes a story from Hanover, Virginia: "A black slave asked a Presbyterian preacher named William Davies, 'I come to you, sir, that you may tell me good things concerning Jesus Christ and my duty to God, for I am resolved not to live anymore as I have done.'" The slave was telling Davies he wanted to be a Christian.[93]

The tune is written to allow a "call and response" style of singing. A soloist or ensemble can sing the first two phrases, and others echo it back. The soloist sings "in my heart," and the family or gathering echoes it back. All sing both on the last phrase, "Lord, I want to be a Christian." As a prayer it should be sung slow and meditatively. Do your best to hold out the long notes on the word "heart" as this will give this prayer greater emotion and sincerity.

As you sing this hymn . . . what are *you* saying? This may be the prayer of someone who has never considered themselves a Christian, or it may be a Christian who wants to take their commitment to a deeper level and live more like a true believer.

How do you become a Christian in your heart? It is not something you can do for yourself. To become a Christian, you must realize you are a sinner, like the man in the above story. Jesus is the one who came to earth and paid the price for those sins by dying on the cross. You must believe that and ask Jesus to forgive your sin and enter your heart. Read the words of Jesus in John 3:16: "For God so loved the world, that He gave His only Son, that whoever believes in Him should not perish but have eternal life."

A fifth stanza is included in several hymnals from the early 1900s: "I don't want to be like Judas." Judas claimed to be a Christ follower, but his betrayal of Jesus reveals that he was a Christian in name only.

The Holy Spirit then takes up residence in our hearts to help us be more loving, more holy, more like Jesus.

Second Peter 1:5–8 gives a clear outline of what becoming a growing Christian "in the heart" looks like:

> Make every effort to supplement your faith with virtue, and virtue
> with knowledge, and knowledge with self-control, and self-control
> with steadfastness, and steadfastness with godliness, and godliness with
> brotherly affection. For if these qualities are yours and are increasing,
> they keep you from being ineffective or unfruitful in the knowledge of
> our Lord Jesus Christ.

This is how we join the slave in the powerful statement, "I am resolved not to live anymore as I have done."

Lord, I Want to Be a Christian

116

Blessed are those who hunger and thirst for righteousness,
for they shall be satisfied.

MATTHEW 5:6

1. Lord, I want to be a Chris-tian in my heart, in my heart,
2. Lord, I want to be more lov - ing in my heart, in my heart,
3. Lord, I want to be more ho - ly in my heart, in my heart,
4. Lord, I want to be like Je - sus in my heart, in my heart,

Lord, I want to be a Chris-tian in my heart.
Lord, I want to be more lov - ing in my heart.
Lord, I want to be more ho - ly in my heart.
Lord, I want to be like Je - sus in my heart.

In my heart, in my heart,

Lord, I want to be a Chris-tian in my heart.
Lord, I want to be more lov - ing in my heart.
Lord, I want to be more ho - ly in my heart.
Lord, I want to be like Je - sus in my heart.

TEXT AND TUNE: Unknown

Spiritual   There Is a Balm in Gilead

TEXT AND TUNE: Unknown ‖

U pon hearing this song as a child, I thought it said, "there is a bomb in Gilead." When I found the word was "balm," I learned it is a healing agent, an ointment to put on a wound. I also did not know where Gilead is. It turned out that this spiritual is a metaphor for something else.

Gilead is a mountainous area in Israel on the east side of the Jordan River. The balm mentioned in the book of Jeremiah (seen above the music) is found there in the resin of a flowering plant, something like aloe. God is speaking through Jeremiah metaphorically about a substance, when applied, would bring soothing, healing results. Israel would go through suffering and slavery from their exile to Babylon, similar to the African slaves who had been taken from their home country into forced labor in America. An African American theologian named Howard Thurman (1899-1981) said this about the writer of this song: "The slave caught the mood of this spiritual dilemma and with it did an amazing thing. He straightened the question mark in Jeremiah's sentence into an exclamation point: 'There *is* a balm in Gilead!' Here is the note of creative triumph." Jesus is the "Balm in Gilead."[94]

The result of this "creative triumph" is a greatly loved spiritual, appearing in over sixty-five hymnals. Many commentators see it from a New Testament viewpoint. Matthew Henry said of the passage in Jeremiah, "The blood of Christ is the balm in Gilead, His Spirit is the physician there, both sufficient and all-sufficient, so that they [Israel] might have been healed, but would not."[95]

As you sing this hymn . . . notice the healing sought is for the "sin-sick soul," the soul that has never been cleansed by the blood of Jesus. We cannot save ourselves. Notice that the author did not mention his physical pain or abuse. Few of us will ever go through this as did the slaves who sang this song, but because of sin in this world, pain is common to everyone, even for the Christian. It may be physical or emotional. Our feelings are hurt, we feel failure, or an unexpected tragedy enters our life.

When you have an emotional wound, no medicine or Band-Aid will fix it. As the stanzas describe, when you feel unable to talk to someone who is not a Christian, how will you do so? When you feel discouraged and lonely or lacking in wisdom, who will teach you? Sing this hymn as a reminder to yourself that the answer to all these questions is Jesus, the "Balm in Gilead"!

There Is a Balm in Gilead

117

Is there no balm in Gilead? Is there no physician there?...
Go up to Gilead, and take balm, O virgin daughter of Egypt!

JEREMIAH 8:22; 46:11

Refrain
There_ is a balm in Gil-e-ad to make the wound-ed whole,_

Fine
There_ is a balm in Gil-e-ad to heal the sin-sick soul.

1. Some - times I feel dis - cour-aged, and_ think my work's in_ vain,
2. *If you can - not sing like an - gels, if you can - not preach like_ Paul,*
3. Don't_ ev - er feel dis - cour-aged, for_ Je - sus is your friend;

D.C. Refrain
but_ then the Ho - ly Spir - it re - vives my soul a - gain._____
you can tell the love of Je - sus, and say, "He died for all."_____
and_ if you lack for know-ledge He'll ne'er re-fuse to lend._____

TEXT AND TUNE: Unknown

Spiritual   Just a Closer Walk with Thee

TEXT AND TUNE: Unknown ‖

You could say the author and composer of this spiritual as we know it today is both known and unknown. Some said they remember hearing slaves singing in the field about "walking beside the Lord." Others report a porter on a train singing it to himself where a composer overheard and wrote it down, adding some of his own lyrics. Songs with similar words were published in the 1800s, including one with a pseudonym for Fanny Crosby. A pastor named Rev. Elijah Cluke is credited for the current rendition that he arranged for African American musical conventions in the 1930s. In the decades since then it has been arranged and recorded by many singers and orchestras. Some of the more famous artists include Elvis Presley, Tennessee Ernie Ford, Mahalia Jackson, Willie Nelson, and most recently Harry Connick Jr. Hundreds of artists have recorded this song, but no composer has ever received royalties for the copyright. It is indeed a song of the people.

As you sing this hymn . . . you are expressing the cry of God's people throughout history. The best example of this is King David. Even though he preceded Jesus on earth, the songs, or psalms, that he wrote are heart expressions to God. Most are songs of praise, thanksgiving, and comfort, but many are laments, songs of sorrow. David, even though he was the king had many, many troubles. Charles Spurgeon states: "David no sooner escaped from one trial than he fell into another; no sooner emerged from one season of despondency and alarm, than he was again brought into the lowest depths, and all God's waves and billows rolled over him. It is probably from this cause that David's psalms are so universally the delight of experienced Christians."[96] (Read Psalm 73:26 printed over the music.)

The writer of this gospel song is weary and tired and alone. Like David, he cries out. Like David, we too want the comfort of knowing He is close when we are sad. Here is one of David's songs which begins with a plea, then moves to a declaration of his trust in God and His purpose in his life and ends with the ultimate hope of God's eternal presence. It follows the same narrative of the song of the unknown author here.

> Preserve me, O God, for in You I take refuge. I say to the LORD, "You are my Lord; I have no good apart from You.". . . .The LORD is my chosen portion and my cup; You hold my lot. The lines have fallen for me in pleasant places; indeed, I have a beautiful inheritance. . . . You make known to me the path of life; in Your presence there is fullness of joy; at Your right hand are pleasures forevermore. (Ps. 16:1–2, 5–6, 11)

Evidently, the slave or train porter had their values straight. "Just a Closer Walk with Thee" sounds much like the psalms of David. These authors are much alike—an unknown writer and the greatest king who ever lived. Both, in hardship and trouble, have cried out from their heart to God in lament; both have found that true satisfaction, joy, and peace are found only in a personal relationship with their Lord and Savior.

Just a Closer Walk with Thee

118

*My flesh and my heart may fail, but God is the strength of
my heart and my portion forever.*

PSALM 73:26

1. I am weak but Thou art strong; Je - sus keep me from all wrong;
2. *Through this world of toil and snares, if I fal - ter, Lord who cares?—*
3. When my fee - ble life is o'er, time for me will be no more;—

I'll be sat - is - fied as long— as I walk let me walk close to Thee.
Who with me my bur - den shares?— None but Thee, dear— Lord, none but Thee.
guide me gent - ly safe - ly o'er— to Thy King - dom shore, to Thy shore.

Refrain

Just a clo - ser walk with Thee, Grant it, Je - sus is my plea—

Dai - ly walk - ing close to Thee:— let it be, dear Lord, let it be.

TEXT AND TUNE: Unknown

CLOSER WALK

TEXT AND TUNE: Charles A. Tindley   ‖ b. July 7, 1851, Berlin, Maryland
d. July 26, 1933, Philadelphia, Pennsylvania

Charles Tindley's father was a slave; his mother was free. He grew up in the world of slavery. After the Civil War, Charles moved to Philadelphia, where he worked as a brick carrier until taking a job as janitor of Bainbridge Street Methodist Episcopal Church. He never attended school but taught himself to read and write. Seeking help from a Jewish rabbi, he learned Hebrew. By correspondence courses, Charles studied theology and learned Greek well enough to pass the Methodist ministry pastoral exam, second in a very large class! Although musically illiterate, he loved to sing and wrote gospel songs. He was called the "Grandfather of Gospel Songs"[97] because he had a significant influence on the songwriting of Thomas Dorsey, known as the "Father of Gospel Songs."

Tindley's first church was in Cape May, New Jersey. His family was so poor that one morning during a great snowstorm they sat down at the breakfast table with only a piece of bread. It was so stale they had to dip it in water to chew it. Tindley had his family get on their knees and thank God for their lives, for the snowstorm, and for the sun that would come out when the storm was over. As they sat at the barren table, they heard a great noise outside. A man with a sack of food plus a cartload of firewood came to the door and said, "Knowing you were the new parson here, and not knowing how you were making out in this storm, my wife and I thought you might need some food."[98] "Not once did he complain about the shortage of provisions, but thanked God for what they had," his son, E. T. Tindley writes.[99]

Charles Albert Tindley became one of Methodism's greatest preachers and was known as the "Prince of Colored Preachers."[100] He composed hundreds of gospel songs, created one of the first soup kitchens in his city, and led economic development for African Americans in Philadelphia through a savings and loan that helped his people achieve homeownership. Rev. Tindley eventually became the pastor of the church he once served as a janitor. During his pastorate it grew from 300 in attendance to over 12,500. After his death, the church was renamed Tindley Temple.

As you sing this hymn . . . you are singing what is called a *lament,* an expression of sadness. Forty-two of the 150 psalms, almost one third, are songs of lament. God wants us to express our feelings of pain, and we do not need to hide them from Him. Remember the stories of God's presence with His children in the Bible: the three Hebrew children in Nebuchadnezzar's fiery furnace, Paul and Silas in the Roman jail are two of them. Never be afraid to weep and sing about your difficulties or hardships and ask God to stand with you in them. Read this promise from the prophet Micah: "He shall stand and shepherd His flock in the strength of the LORD" (Mic. 5:4).

Stand by Me

He shall stand and shepherd His flock in the strength of the LORD,
in the majesty of the name of the LORD his God.

MICAH 5:4

1. When the storms of life are ra - ging, stand by me;
2. *In the midst of trib - u - la - tion, stand by me;*
3. In the midst of faults and fail - ures, stand by me;
4. *In the midst of per - se - cu - tion, stand by me;*
5. When I'm grow - ing old and fee - ble stand by me;

when the storms of life are ra - ging stand by me.
in the midst of tri - bu - la - tion stand by me.
in the midst of faults and fail - ures stand by me.
in the midst of per - se - cu - tion stand by me.
when I'm grow - ing old and fee - ble stand by me.

When the world is toss - ing me like a ship up - on the sea,
When the hosts of sin as - sail, and my strength be - gins to fail,
When I've done the best I can, and my friends mis - un - der - stand,
When my foes in war ar - ray un - der - take to stop my way,
When my life be - comes a burd'n and I'm near - ing chil - ly Jord'n,

Thou Who ru - lest wind and wa - ter, stand by me.
Thou Who nev - er lost a bat - tle stand by me.
Thou Who know - est all a - bout me stand by me.
Thou Who res - cued Paul and Si - las, stand by me.
Oh Thou Li - ly of the Val - ley, stand by me.

TEXT AND TUNE: Charles A. Tindley

STAND BY ME

Spiritual Give Me Jesus

TEXT AND TUNE: Unknown ‖

Spirituals were created extemporaneously and passed on orally, therefore, the original dates and composers are unknown. The first printed version of "Give Me Jesus" appeared in a Methodist hymnal in 1849. It is also in *Slave Songs of the United States,* New York, 1867 which authenticates it as a spiritual. Since then, numerous other stanzas have appeared such as "When I'm happy hear me sing," "When in sorrow hear me pray," "When I'm dying hear me cry," and "When in heaven we will sing." However, the four stanzas here are the most common.

Singing a song written by people who were horribly treated and deprived of ownership—even of their own selves—reminds us that possessions will never satisfy. Only Jesus can save and satisfy us, not possessions, status, relationships, or anything else the world offers.

One of the wonders of this spiritual is the beauty of the melody. It was not composed by an educated or trained musician, yet it was remembered for decades before it was ever printed. Today there are several beautiful choral arrangements that reflect its deep emotion. Also, recordings by Fernando Ortega and Jeremy Camp have found a large audience in recent years.

As you sing this hymn . . . notice this is a prayer to begin a day. Morning is a new beginning when we declare our values and establish our priorities. Jesus is the only one worth worshiping, and our prayer is for His presence and mercy. You may have heard your mother and father declare that Jesus is their priority. Pay attention! In times of fear or despair, pictured here as midnight, we cry out for Jesus. Even at the end of life, it is not too late to seek Jesus and His salvation.

This song reminds us of Matthew 16:26 (read verse above the music). What does it mean to gain the whole world—money, fame, pleasure, power, prestige? What is your soul? It is the part of you that is spiritual and eternal. It is what separates us from all other living creatures. It is the eternal part of us that Jesus came to save.

To lose your soul is to die without Christ's forgiveness and spend an eternity in the lake of fire or what the Bible calls hell. The New Century translation of the Bible says it this way: "It is worthless to have the whole world if they lose their souls. They could never pay enough to buy back their souls" (Matthew 16:26).

Do Christians often get their priorities upside down? Certainly. Unfortunately, if we have declared Jesus as our Lord and Savior, we may still seek the world's values. So each morning (or any time of day) we should declare Jesus as our priority by how we live. Memorize this refrain and let it be your heart's cry to God every day: "I want Jesus. I might have all this world, [but] give me Jesus!"

Give Me Jesus

For what will it profit a man if he gains the whole world and forfeits his soul?
Or what shall a man give in return for his soul?

MATTHEW 16:26

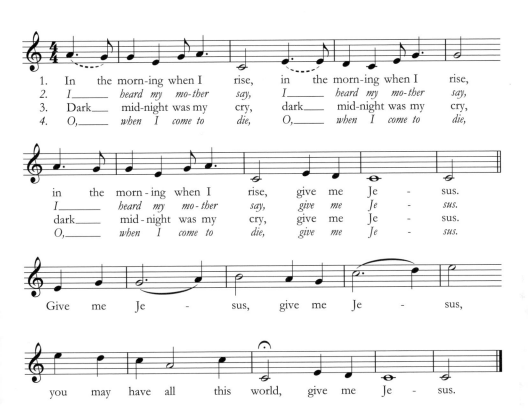

1. In the morn-ing when I rise, in the morn-ing when I rise,
2. I_____ heard my mo-ther say, I_____ heard my mo-ther say,
3. Dark_____ mid-night was my cry, dark_____ mid-night was my cry,
4. O,_____ when I come to die, O,_____ when I come to die,

in the morn-ing when I rise, give me Je - sus.
I_____ heard my mo-ther say, give me Je - sus.
dark_____ mid-night was my cry, give me Je - sus.
O,_____ when I come to die, give me Je - sus.

Give me Je - sus, give me Je - sus,

you may have all this world, give me Je - sus.

TEXT AND TUNE: Unknown

GIVE ME JESUS

About the Authors

David and Barbara Leeman founded Hosanna Hymnals to introduce classic songs of the church to a new generation. Barbara taught private piano and classroom music, serving twenty-three years at Providence Christian School of Texas. David served for over forty years as minister of music and worship at churches in California, Oregon, Illinois and Texas. Both are graduates of Biola University School of Music. Barbara earned teaching credentials from the University of Oregon and Dave a Master's degree in choral conducting from California State University in Fullerton. The Leemans have four grown children who love hymns and twelve grandchildren who are learning to love them!

Jonathan Leeman, editor of this collection, is Barbara and Dave's oldest child. He is editorial director at 9Marks, author of numerous books on the church, and teacher at several seminaries. Jonathan serves as an elder at Cheverly Baptist Church, Cheverly, Maryland.

Notes

1. Connie Foss More, *The Selected Writings of Zoltán Kodály* (London: Boosey & Hawkes, 1974), 122.

2. Ibid., 148.

3. Martin Luther, "Foreword to Georg Rhau's Symphoniae iucundae," 1538, quoted in *R. J. Grunewald* (blog), "Martin Luther's View on Music," https://www.rjgrune.com/blog/martin-luthers-view-on-music.

4. Donald S. Whitney, *Family Worship* (Wheaton: Crossway, 2016), 44.

5. Robert J. Morgan, *Then Sings My Soul* (Nashville: Thomas Nelson, 2003), 167.

6. Stuart Townend, "Preparing to Worship," October 1, 2012, https://www.stuarttownend.co.uk/preparing-to-worship/.

7. Keith Getty, personal conversation with author, 2013.

8. "Cecil Frances Alexander," EnglishVerse.com, https://englishverse.com/poets/alexander_cecil_frances.

9. Erik Routley, *Hymns and the Faith* (Grand Rapids: William B. Eerdmans, 1968), 106, 109.

10. "The Real Value of Negro Melodies" (interview with Antonín Dvořák), *New York Herald,* May 21, 1893, 28.

11. "Isaac Watts: Father of English Hymnody," Christian History, https://www.christianitytoday.com/history/people/poets/isaac-watts.html.

12. James Moffatt, *Handbook to the Church Hymnary* (Oxford: Oxford University Press, 1927), 318.

13. E. E. Ryden, *The Story of Christian Hymnody* (Philadelphia: Fortress, 1959), 40.

14. Ira David Sankey, *My Life and the Story of the Gospel Hymns* (New York: Harper & Brothers, 1906), 146–47.

15. Stuart Townend, "Tips for Writing a Successful Hymn," BBC Religion and Ethics, 2004. Archived at https://philipandjenny.com/2006/09/15/tips-for-writing-a-successful-hymn. Reproduced with the permission of Stuart Townend.

16. Ibid.

17. Stuart Townend, "How Deep the Father's Love for Us," https://www.stuarttownend.co.uk/song/how-deep-the-fathers-love-for-us/.

18. "Jeannette Threlfall," Hymnary.org, excerpts from John Julian, *Dictionary of Hymnology* (London: John Murray, 1907), https://hymnary.org/person/Threlfall_J.

19. "Jeannette Threlfall," Hymnary.org.

20. C. Michael Hawn, "History of Hymns: 'The King of Glory Comes,'" June 10, 2013,

Discipleship Ministries, The United Methodist Church, https://www.umcdiscipleship.org/resources/history-of-hymns-the-king-of-glory-comes.

21. Stuart Townend, "Come People of the Risen King," https://www.stuarttownend.co.uk/song/come-people-of-the-risen-king/.

22. "Hymn of Promise," Hymntime, http://www.hymntime.com/tch/htm/h/y/m/n/hymnprom.htm.

23. Ernest K. Emurian, *Famous Stories of Inspiring Hymns* (Grand Rapids: Baker, 1976), 152.

24. E. E. Ryden, *The Story of Christian Hymnody* (Philadelphia: Fortress, 1959), 323.

25. Erik Routley, *Hymns and the Faith* (Grand Rapids: William B. Eerdmans, 1968), 70.

26. Thomas Jackson, *The Life of the Rev. Charles Wesley, M. A.* (New York: G. Lane & P. P. Sandford, 1842), 787.

27. E. E. Ryden, *The Story of Christian Hymnody* (Philadelphia: Fortress, 1959), 295.

28. Kenneth W. Osbeck, *101 Hymn Stories* (Grand Rapids: Kregel, 1982), 24.

29. Theron Brown and Hezekiah Butterworth, *The Story of the Hymns and Tunes* (New York: American Tract Society, 1906), 28.

30. "Saward, Michael John," Praise!, https://www.praise.org.uk/hymnauthor/saward-michael-john.

31. "Isaac Watts: Father of English Hymnody," Christian History, https://www.christianitytoday.com/history/people/poets/isaac-watts.html.

32. Robert J. Morgan, *Then Sings My Soul* (Nashville: Thomas Nelson Publishers, 2003), 37.

33. Michael Van Patter, "First Hymn: God Works in a Mysterious Way," Hymns of the Weak (blog), August 30, 2010, https://hymnsoftheweak.wordpress.com/2010/08/30/first-hymn-god-works-in-a-mysterious-way.

34. Jane Stuart Smith and Betty Carlson, *Favorite Women Hymn Writers* (Wheaton, IL: Crossway, 1990), 21.

35. Robert J. Morgan, *Then Sings My Soul* (Nashville: Thomas Nelson, 2003), 255.

36. Ibid., 35.

37. Kenneth W. Osbeck, *101 Hymn Stories* (Grand Rapids: Kregel,1982), 14.

38. Ibid., 84.

39. Ibid., 85.

40. Robert J. Morgan, *Then Sings My Soul* (Nashville: Thomas Nelson, 2003), 169.

41. Ibid., 169.

42. Daniel Curry, "1876 A.D.: Ira Sankey Sings on Christmas Eve," *Deeds of God*, https://www.deedsofgod.com/index.php/39-1876-ad-ira-sankey-sings-on-christmas-eve-mainmenu-275.

43. Robert J. Morgan, *Then Sings My Soul* (Nashville: Thomas Nelson, 2003), 45.

44. Ibid., 45.

45. Ernest K. Emurian, *Famous Stories of Inspiring Hymns* (Grand Rapids: Baker, 1976), 19.

46. Kenneth W. Osbeck, *101 Hymn Stories* (Grand Rapids: Kregel, 2012), 40.

47. Steve Brown, "A Modern Day Hymn?" Blended Worship Resource, June 6, 2009, https://blendedworshipresource.wordpress.com/2009/06/06/a-modern-day-hymn/.

48. Phil Christensen and Shari MacDonald, *Our God Reigns* (Grand Rapids: Kregel, 2000), 93.

49. Ibid., 93.

50. Roy Jenkins, "The Welsh Revival," BBC, June 16, 2009, https://www.bbc.co.uk/religion/religions/christianity/history/welshrevival_1.shtml.

51. Robert J. Morgan, *Then Sings My Soul* (Nashville: Thomas Nelson, 2003), 111.

52. Ibid., 153.

53. Kenneth W. Osbeck, *101 Hymn Stories* (Grand Rapids: Kregel, 2012), 58.

54. Erik Routley, *Hymns and the Faith* (Grand Rapids: William B. Eerdmans, 1968), 237.

55. E. E. Ryden, *The Story of Christian Hymnody* (Philadelphia: Fortress, 1959), 421.

56. Erik Routley, *Hymns and the Faith* (Grand Rapids: William B. Eerdmans, 1968), 8.

57. "Henry Van Dyke Biography," The Famous People, https://www.thefamouspeople.com/profiles/henry-van-dyke-239.php.

58. William J. Reynolds, *Songs of Glory* (Grand Rapids: Zondervan, 1990), 161.

59. Erik Routley, *Hymns and Human Life* (Grand Rapids: William B. Eerdmans, 1959), 165.

60. "Michael Perry," Hope Publishing Company, https://www.hopepublishing.com/75.

61. "Background," Jubilate, https://www.jubilate.co.uk/page/background.

62. Kenneth W. Osbeck, *101 Hymn Stories* (Grand Rapids: Kregel, 2012), 181.

63. Erik Routley, *Hymns and the Faith* (Grand Rapids: William B. Eerdmans, 1968), 129.

64. All quotes in this section from "Clarkson, Edith Margaret, Biographical Statement," Buswell Library Special Collections / E. Margaret Clarkson Papers, https://archives.wheaton.edu/agents/people/2679.

65. Ibid.

66. Ibid.

67. Emil Naumann, *The History of Music* vol. 2 (Cambridge: Cambridge University Press, 2013), 879.

68. Jane Stuart Smith and Betty Carlson, *Favorite Women Hymn Writers* (Wheaton: Crossway, 1990), 32.

69. Ibid., 32.

70. Paul Westermeyer, *Profiles in 20th-Century Hymn Writing* (St. Louis: Concordia, 1995), 77.

71. Donald Hustad, ed., *The Worshiping Church, A Hymnal, Worship Leaders' Edition* (Wheaton, IL: Hope Publishing Company, 1991), 464.

72. E. E. Ryden, *The Story of Christian Hymnody* (Philadelphia: Fortress, 1959), 399.

73. Robert J. Morgan, *Then Sings My Soul* (Nashville: Thomas Nelson, 2003), 117.

74. "Horatio Bonar," Hymntime, http://www.hymntime.com/tch/bio/b/o/n/a/bonar_h.htm.

75. Keith Getty, "Speak O Lord: Song Story," https://store.gettymusic.com/us/song/speak-o-lord/.

76. Elsie Houghton, *Classic Christian Hymn-writers* (Fort Washington, PA: Christian Literature Crusade, 1982), 201.

77. Kenneth W. Osbeck, *101 Hymn Stories* (Grand Rapids: Kregel, 2012), 81.

78. E. E. Ryden, *The Story of Christian Hymnody* (Philadelphia: Fortress, 1959), 287.

79. C. Michael Hawn, "History of Hymns: 'We Gather Together,'" Discipleship Ministries, The United Methodist Church, November 14, 2013 , https://www.umcdiscipleship.org/resources/history-of-hymns-we-gather-together1.

80. Kenneth W. Osbeck, *101 Hymn Stories* (Grand Rapids: Kregel, 2012), 129.

81. E. E. Ryden, *The Story of Christian Hymnody* (Philadelphia: Fortress, 1959), 357.

82. Ibid., 266.

83. Jeff Mirus, "St. Augustine on Our Sins in the Enjoyment of the Mass," Catholic Culture, June 13, 2014, https://www.catholicculture.org/commentary/st-augustine-on-our-sins-in-enjoyment-mass.

84. Robert J. Morgan, *Then Sings My Soul* (Nashville: Thomas Nelson, 2003), 183.

85. E. E. Ryden, *The Story of Christian Hymnody* (Philadelphia: Fortress, 1959), 303.

86. "Telegram from Anna Spafford to Horatio Gates Spafford re being 'Saved alone' among her traveling party in the shipwreck of the Ville du Havre," Library of Congress, American Colony in Jerusalem Collection, https://www.loc.gov/resource/mamcol.011.

87. "Francis Ridley Havergal," Hymntime, http://www.hymntime.com/tch/bio/h/a/v/e/haver gal_fr.htm.

88. Kenneth W. Osbeck, *101 Hymn Stories* (Grand Rapids: Kregel, 1982), 240.

89. E. E. Ryden, *The Story of Christianity Hymnody* (Philadelphia: Fortress, 1959), 420.

90. "May the Mind of Christ My Savior," ReCollections, College-Related Publications, Wheaton College Archives, May 3, 2010, https://recollections.wheaton.edu/2010/05/may-the-mind-of-christ-my-savior/.

91. Bob Kauflin, "O Great God at Together for the Gospel," Worship Matters, May 20, 2010, https://worshipmatters.com/2010/05/20/o-great-god-at-together-for-the-gospel/.

92. Eileen Guenther, *In Their Own Words: Slave Life and the Power of Spirituals* (Saint Louis: MorningStar, 2016), 58.

93. Miles Mark Fisher, *Negro Slave Songs in the United States* (New York: The Citadel Press, 1953), 30.

94. Howard Thurman, *Deep River and the Negro Spiritual Speaks of Life and Death* (Richmond, IN: Friends United Press, 1975), 60.

95. Matthew Henry, *Matthew Henry's Commentary on the Whole Bible*, Vol. IV (New York: Fleming H. Revell Co.), 464.

96. Charles Spurgeon, *Morning and Evening* (Peabody, MA: Hendrickson, 1995), 466.

97. "Charles Albert Tindley (1851–1933), Grandfather of Gospel Music," Discipleship Ministries, The United Methodist Church, February 18, 2005, https://www.umcdiscipleship.org/resources/charles-albert-tindley-1851-1933-grandfather-of-gospel-music.

98. E. T. Tindley, *The Prince of Colored Preachers: The Remarkable Story of Charles Albert Tindley* (Wilmore, KY: First Fruits Press, 2016), 12.

99. Ibid., 12.

100. Ibid., 4.

Author, Composer, Source Index

Composers and Sources listed in italics.

Topical Index

Alphabetical Index

HosannaHymnals.com

Revealing our infinite God through great hymns and their stories.

Piano accompaniment books for

HOSANNA IN EXCELSIS &
OUR HYMNS, OUR HERITAGE

Recordings for
(USB flash drive)

HOSANNA IN EXCELSIS

All 43 hymns with two recordings each. One track with
voices and piano and one track with piano only for singing along.

OUR HYMNS, OUR HERITAGE

All 120 hymns, with piano only for singing along.

*Also on the website, bonus materials regarding hymns,
family singing, and congregational singing.*

HosannaHymnals.com

Immerse yourself in the legacy of music that celebrates the Christmas season.

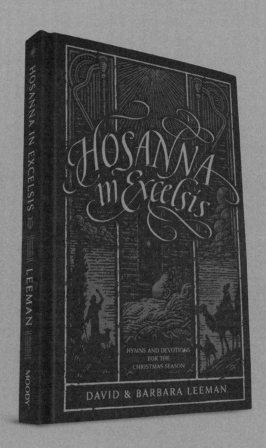